BADGELAND

MEMOIR OF A LABOUR PARTY YOUNG
SOCIALIST IN 1980S BRITAIN

STEVE RAYSON

BAVANT PRESS

For my children and grandchildren.

ACKNOWLEDGEMENTS

I want to start by thanking my wife, Christine, for her love and patience over the two years I spent writing this book.

I also need to thank my brother and sister, Andy and Paula, for their close reading, suggestions and support.

I am particularly grateful to Stephen Walsh for his invaluable advice and encouragement.

I want to thank my editor Sally Orson-Jones, my copyeditor and proofreader Louise Lubke Cuss, my cover designer Kate Chesterton, and Lizzie Richmond at Bath University Library for providing me with copies of *Spike* our student newspaper from 1980 to 1983.

Thanks also go to all those that took the time to read the draft manuscript and provide me with feedback, including Rob Ashton, Virginia Barder, Rachel Brastock, Peter Casebow, Donald Clark, Tim Crisp, Chris Cullen, Matt Dunkley, Ian Farringdon, Colin Franks, Dru Furneaux, Deborah Grubb, John Helmer, Alec Keith, Peter Kilmister, Helen King, Don Milligan, Neill McWilliams, Susan Moeller, Jan Morgan, Giles Palmer, Teresa Pole-Baker, Jennifer Sinclair, Phil & Carol Shoosmith, Denise Stokoe, Rebecca Surender, David Warren and Li Whybrow. I also received valuable feedback from John Harris, while we were working on our respective memoirs, before he sadly passed away in 2022. We miss you John.

Finally, I want to thank my parents for their love, patience and support while I was growing up.

PRAISE FOR BADGELAND

'Steve Rayson's depiction of British politics in the 70s and 80s is pitch perfect but this book is much more than that. It's a tender reflection on father/son relationships in working class communities and the fault line that can develop between them through a university education. The best memoir I've read in years.'

— ALAN JOHNSON, FORMER HEALTH
SECRETARY

"Steve Rayson recalls with warmth, insight and wry humour a time when for many of us everything seemed possible."

— LORD PAUL BOATENG

"Funny, charming, well observed and a joy to read."

— GILES PALMER

"Funny but poignant, brutally honest yet endearing."

— MARK FEARN

"One man's personal journey, ... delivered with a warmth and affection that has the reader yearning for the place and time that Rayson describes."

— CHARLIE DOWNES

CONTENTS

PROLOGUE

After the Battle of Culloden in 1746, someone wrote that they would never know how many people died, because "it is the victor who writes the history and counts the dead". In politics the winners shape the historical narrative. The best-selling memoirs are those of Thatcher, Obama and Blair, not Kinnock, McCain and Howard. Remember him? Publishers embrace the stories of the victors. The foot soldiers of defeated armies rarely get a hearing.

When my grandson was born in 2020, I decided it was time to write my story. My experience as a member of the Badgeland tribes of the 1980s. We wore the CND peace symbol and badges that read: 'Coal not Dole', 'Nuclear Power, No Thanks', 'Rock Against Racism', 'Jobs not Bombs', 'Tories Out', 'Free Nelson Mandela', 'Tony Benn for Deputy', and 'Keep GLC working for London'. Our chests demonstrated our opposition to poverty, nuclear weapons, fascists and apartheid. Like The Jam, Luke Skywalker and Tintin we were sure we had right on our side. In old photographs you can see us on marches against nuclear weapons, the closure of mines and mass unemployment. Our generation was going to create a better world.

But in the summer of 1987 everything changed.

This is my two pennies, as my dad would say.

~

A word of warning: Memory is an unreliable narrator.

Material recorded on a magnetic cassette tape, the main recording device when I joined the Greater London Council in 1983, is said to have a lifespan of thirty years. It is now forty years since I entered County Hall as a graduate trainee. I'm hoping my memory holds up better than the bootleg cassettes I recorded as a teenager. Tapes that frequently escaped their casing in large spools and which I tried to rewind using a pencil.

My brain appears to decide quite randomly on the memories that it stores away. Many of my life experiences are not deemed worthy of the storage capacity, and the 'record' button never gets switched on. Or at least that's how it seems to me. This is how I explain the black holes, the gaps in my personal timeline.

For example, I have no recollection of the application process for the GLC. There must have been a recruitment process but I have absolutely no memory of it. I assume I had an interview in the early summer of 1983 but I simply can't recall attending one. I do remember campaigning in the general election that year and knocking on the doors of council flats in Bath with George, a large shaggy bear of a man. A Hagrid with a thick Bristol accent who called everyone 'lover'. I also recall every time a door opened the first thing I heard was the sound of Spandau Ballet's *True*, the top selling record throughout May 1983. For weeks I continually hummed and sang along with Gary Kemp's ode to the Altered Images singer Clare Grogan.

This sums up the nature of my memory. I can't recall

anything, not a thing, zip, zilch, nada, about the recruitment process for my first job, but I can sing every lyric of *True*.

The limitations of my memory mean that the conversations and dialogue in this memoir are creative reconstructions or approximations, but I have tried to truthfully convey their core essence. I have used the common vernacular of the time and I apologise to those that may find the language offensive.

Many of the characters that appear are composites and names have been changed to protect the privacy of those who are still around.

I have included a glossary at the back of the book for those that may not recognise the references to characters, TV shows and songs of the 1970s and 1980s.

We all tell stories about ourselves. Those of us with the privilege of time and with more narcissistic tendencies write memoirs but we all develop a narrative about who we are. We tell our story to others but the primary audience is always ourselves; it helps us to make sense of our place in the world. It is a story that changes in the retelling as we move through life. The story we tell ourselves at seventeen is not the story we tell ourselves at twenty-five or sixty-five.

Finally, the story we share with others is never the whole story. Edith Wharton said a person's life is like a house of rooms and we only let people into some of the rooms. Even the story we tell ourselves is not the whole story. There are rooms where we keep the door firmly closed. So while this is an honest and faithful memoir, sometimes we only see what we want to see and only remember what we want to remember. My advice, as in life generally, is don't take this story, or indeed any story, at face value: 'question everything'.

PART I

SWINDON

1

VICTOR HUGO

I n Swindon I was lying on my bed listening to Bob Marley. The *New Musical Express* had a picture of Debbie Harry on the front cover and declared, 'The Revolution will be Peroxide'. Inside Joe Strummer of the Clash said his band was anti-racist and anti-fascist; and their song *English Civil War* was a protest against far right groups. As I browsed the *NME* I decided there were two types of young people. Revolutionaries, who wore badges, and Tories. I also realised that seventeen-year-old boys who didn't share bedrooms with their brother must fantasise about Debbie Harry all the time.

My badges demonstrated I was on the side of Joe Strummer against the racists and the fascists. During the school disco at fifteen I had sang along with the Sex Pistols about the Queen and her fascist regime. That was when my friend Kevin claimed he invented pogoing, which took the form of screaming and jumping into people. My generation was going to defeat the fascists. I wasn't really sure what fascists were at the time. But I knew they were right wing and we didn't like them, much like Oxford football fans.

The *NME* said over a hundred thousand people had

attended a Rock Against Racism concert in Hackney organised by the Anti-Nazi League. The headliners were The Clash, Tom Robinson, X-Ray Spex and the amazing Steel Pulse from Handsworth. Black and white bands playing together was Rock Against Racism's founding principle. It wasn't fair; why didn't they organise concerts like that in Swindon? In solidarity I pinned a red and yellow Anti-Nazi League badge to my jacket. I was sure people would admire my stand against the fascists, but it didn't always work out that way.

One Tuesday I was on the number 17 bus sat next to a lady with hair like wire wool. I could see her squinting and scrutinising my badge through her horn-rimmed glasses. I was expecting her to congratulate me on taking a stand against the racists but what she actually said was, "That is not a very nice thing to have on a badge."

"Sorry?" I said.

"Nazi. You shouldn't wear badges supporting the Nazis."

"No, it is an *anti*-Nazi badge. You see on the other side of the red arrow, the word anti." I pointed to the left-hand side of the badge.

She looked at me unconvinced and turned away to gaze out of the window. Old people were so stupid sometimes.

Despite these odd hiccups, in Badgeland we were proud to display our beliefs, and our political demands, on our chests. We were like twelfth century pilgrims who wore pewter badges to demonstrate their devout status.

Dad didn't say anything when he first saw my badges, but I noticed his brow furrow into a deep frown. He also said nothing when I joined the Labour Party Young Socialists. Maybe he was hoping I would give up my radical socialist ideas as I grew older. I suspect he agreed with Victor Hugo who was reported to have said:

"If you're not a socialist before you're twenty-five, you have no heart. If you are a socialist after twenty-five, you have no head."

Maybe twenty-five was the age of reason. The age when radicals put away their posters, took off their badges, and started calling for tougher sentences for criminals. Or maybe it was when they turned thirty and became old people. It was never going to happen to me. I was determined to fight against everything that was right wing, including Thatcher, fascists, the royal family, second homes, Barclays bank, BMWs, public schools, the National Trust and posh restaurants. Other people might swap their socialist dreams for a Ford Escort, two kids and a council house but not me. In the bedroom mirror I admired the badges on my chest and decided I was going to be a lifelong radical.

Later I would learn that politics isn't all it seems at seventeen.

2

SWINDON TOWN, RED AND WHITE ARMY

The gates of Penhill Secondary School were just ten paces from the top of our drive. We were so close my friend Kevin and I would use fishing catapults to fire tomatoes from my dad's greenhouse into the playground, where the girls were playing netball after school. Afterwards we would race each other down Penhill Drive, pedalling furiously on our bikes to be the first to Kevin's house, which sat opposite St Peter's, the 1950s brick-built council estate church.

Penhill was one of Swindon's four Ps. The others were Pinehurst, Park North and Park South. These days the P estates feature frequently in the headlines of the *Advertiser*, the town's local paper, but not in a good way.

'People living in Pinehurst and Penhill are afraid to leave their houses – even in daylight.'

'Police crackdown on gang violence in Penhill and Pinehurst after series of stabbings this summer.'

It wasn't that bad when we were growing up. There was

only one stabbing I can remember. Most crime was minor and habitual. Stuff 'fell off the back of a lorry', materials were hidden under overalls and occasionally someone would ask my dad to store things in our loft for a while, but we weren't afraid to walk the streets at night.

Today if you ask people about the places they would like to visit in the United Kingdom, they will say Oxford, Cornwall, Edinburgh or the Lake District. I will bet my favourite 'Free Nelson Mandela' badge that they don't say Swindon. The author Mark Haddon didn't help the town's image by referring to it as the 'arsehole of the world' in his best-selling book, *The Curious Incident of the Dog in the Night-time*. Haddon might have been born in the same year as me but he was not a Swindon boy. Those of us who grew up in the town in the 1970s loved the place. We had the ABC Cinema, the Oasis, the Brunel Centre, and most importantly Swindon Town Football Club.

The Oasis wasn't like the boring swimming pools in other towns. It had a glazed dome through which you could see the sky. It was huge. There were tropical plants, a tiled yellow beach and a water slide. Inside the air was heavy with chlorine and the humidity glistened on your skin. Boys from the P estates would stroll around showing off their abs and biceps. They wanted to look like Rocky and took turns doing his one-handed press-ups. When we heard the call of Tarzan we all ran into the water and an amazing machine caused waves to rise up from the back of the pool. Over the loudspeakers they played *Woah, we are going to Barbados* and hundreds of us sang along. I would sit on the tiled yellow beach and let the waves wash over me. I couldn't imagine anywhere else I would rather be.

According to our history teacher Swindon got its name from the Saxons who kept pigs on the hill. It was recorded in the

Domesday Book as Swin Dun, or swine hill. In 1976 there were a hundred and thirty thousand of us living in 'pig hill' and the population was expanding rapidly. The *Advertiser* said we were the fastest growing town in Europe. We could shag for Britain in Swindon. My younger brother Andy and I were peak baby boomers. Our schools were full of portacabins that housed the vast numbers of children born in the early 1960s.

The Brunel indoor shopping centre opened in 1978. It was 'space age' according to a BBC West reporter, with an eighty-three metre high glass and steel tower that dominated the Swindon skyline. It was sleek and sophisticated. One architect said it could have been designed by Frank Hampson, the illustrator who created *Dan Dare, Pilot of the Future*. A year after its completion, just before my seventeenth birthday, someone committed suicide by jumping from the tower and crashing through the roof of the glass covered courtyard below.

In Swindon we were innovative and ahead of the times. For example, we invented modern roundabouts. The town's famous 'magic roundabout', named after the children's TV programme, allowed traffic to flow both clockwise and anti-clockwise, and it scared the hell out of visitors.

It was installed in 1972, outside the County Ground, the home of the football club. In the fifties the team had been nicknamed 'the railwaymen' after the town's large railway works. We may not have been Liverpool or Manchester United but Swindon boys were red and white to our bones.

At the County Ground inter-estate rivalries were set aside as boys from the P estates assembled to 'defend' the town from visiting fans. They called themselves the Swindon Town Aggro Boys and stood at the back of the Town End, which was 'our manor'. Kevin and I stood at the front of the stand, away from the STAB boys, but we joined in with their chants. "You're going home in a fucking ambulance."

It was common not only to taunt the opposition fans but to

also throw things at their players. In March 1978, four days before my sixteenth birthday, the Wrexham goalkeeper was hit by a golf ball, multiple stones and a dart, which stuck in his nose. In some ways you had to admire the throwing accuracy of the Swindon fans. Kevin, inspired by Bruce Lee films, made ninja throwing stars out of the tops of baked bean cans to throw at the opposition fans. They were a bit flimsy but you didn't want to have one thrown at you.

For those that don't attend football matches it is probably difficult to appreciate the joy of tribal banter and communal singing. You could swear and shout as loudly as you wanted and no one seemed to mind. Our favourite chants included "The referee's a wanker." We also noted that the ref was probably blind from all that wanking.

Our own players got as much stick as the opposition. Kevin, who was the spitting image of Dennis the Menace with his black curly hair, would shout, "Run faster you fat bastard, my gran could have scored that." However, if the opposition fans had a go at our fat bastard we would get behind him and sing his name. To warm ourselves up on cold days we sang songs that required clapping or the stamping of feet. There was a visceral sense of belonging as we chanted, "Swindon Town, red and white army." The taunts to the opposition fans ranged from, "Are you Oxford in disguise?" to the STAB boys' more direct, "You're going to get your fucking heads kicked in." Kicking people's heads in was a thing in the seventies.

~

Most of the time we wore daps but not when we went to the football. In other parts of the UK rubber-soled shoes were called plimsolls or pumps but in Swindon they were daps. People said the name came from 'Dunlop Athletic Plimsolls' but who knows? What I did know is that you didn't want to get 'dapped' in the shower. Getting 'dapped' was being hit hard with the sole of a dap on your wet backside which stung like crazy and left a red mark as you got dressed. It wasn't just the other boys you had to watch out for, the games teachers took great pleasure in smacking your arse as you made your way to or from the shower.

You wore your Dr Martens to football matches, a stiff leather boot with yellow stitching around the sole that came in macho colours like oxblood. According to Kevin the best boots were steel capped, as they were much more useful for fighting. Elton John got it wrong; it was Saturday afternoons not Saturday nights that were alright for fighting. Okay, maybe there were fights in the evenings as well, I was just less aware of them. To be honest daps were probably more appropriate for football matches as you could run away faster but protocol demanded that you look 'hard' in your boots. Anyone turning up in daps was just asking for a kicking.

In October 1977, there were nearly six thousand of us watching Swindon draw at home to Port Vale. In the Town End we cheered a rare goal from Stevie Aizlewood. In Blackpool that same week Margaret Thatcher was wearing a lime green dress and applauding another teenager, the sixteen-year-old William Hague, who spoke at the Tory Party Conference. What a weird kid; he looked sixty-five. He wore a strange jacket with large lapels like butterfly wings. I couldn't see but I was fairly sure he wasn't wearing Dr Martens.

Kevin tore away the leather from the front of his boots to reveal the steel caps. Evidently this was a marker of how 'hard' you were. On the way to the football he also used to steal toilet rolls to throw on the pitch. No, I am not sure why either, it was just something he did. Like how he made us hold our collars after seeing an ambulance until we saw a four legged animal. I wasn't brave enough to participate in the stealing but I remember a sense of pride when a toilet roll he threw was visible on *Match of the Day*. It was lying on the back of the net when Swindon scored. It was the talk of the school playground – "Did you see Kevin's toilet roll on TV?" I am not sure it was what Andy Warhol meant by fifteen minutes of fame but it was fame nonetheless.

I was never 'hard' like Kevin but at the County Ground I stood in solidarity with my tribe, my working-class community. Football was our game, the posh kids could keep their golf, tennis, rowing and rugby union. This was our sport and our home. In the Town End we stood together against the world, though we hated Oxford, our local rivals, more than anyone else. On Saturday afternoons Kevin and I would stand shoulder to shoulder with the boys from the P estates, point our arms to the sky and chant, "Swindon till I die."

3

ONE WORKING-CLASS BOY IN A THOUSAND

Kevin was my adviser on fishing and all things 'hard'. It was Kevin who taught me how to catch tench at the local gravel pits, though I never took his advice on warming up maggots. He swore that on frosty mornings you could get them to wriggle more by putting them in your mouth. It was with Kevin that I raced out of Woolworths after he had pinched sweets from the Pick and Mix. Kevin was also responsible for my suspension from school, just six weeks before my 'O' level exams.

It was a sunny day and a group of us were sat in the courtyard, in the centre of which was a sunken pond. The fish were basking in the sunshine having remarkably survived multiple attempts on their lives, including Kevin's misguided experiment in spear fishing with his mum's knitting needles. The windows of the courtyard had just been cleaned by the caretaker and there was a wooden ladder propped up against the wall. Our uniforms had the dishevelled look of summer term, sleeves rolled up, top buttons undone and our ties hanging loose. We were sitting on two wooden benches, all except Kevin. He wasn't one for sitting. He was stood above us, one foot on the arm of each bench.

As we sat in the sun Bob, the economics teacher, walked past. I can't recall his surname; everyone knew him as Bob. He wasn't like the other teachers; he was less strict, less formal. Suddenly Kevin jumped down and shouted, "Let's tie Bob to the ladder!" Before I knew what was happening Bob was bundled to the floor by half a dozen boys and put on the ladder.

Despite his protestations Bob's arms were held above his head and tied to the ladder with shoelaces. I am still not sure where they came from. Suddenly he was being carried to and suspended over the fish pond, the ladder acting like a bridge from one side of the paving slabs to the other. Within minutes the courtyard was full of dozens of students, all gawping at Bob lying over the water like an exhibit at the zoo. Then a frantic Miss Skedge arrived and screamed at the students to untie her fellow teacher. I slipped away in the melee.

At the next morning's assembly the headmaster spoke about a grave incident and asked those boys responsible to go to his office immediately afterwards. Kevin nodded at me. I am still not sure why I went with him to stand outside the office; my role was minor. When Kevin was struggling to tie Bob down he had shouted at me to help and, I admit, I briefly held Bob's arm. But as I told the headmaster, I didn't tie him up or place him over the pond. He was not interested in such fine distinctions. I was suspended along with the others for two weeks which didn't help my 'O' level exam preparation.

To be fair I place most of the blame for my mediocre 'O' level results on National Health glasses rather than my suspension. I was short-sighted and couldn't see what teachers wrote on the blackboard in class. My mum took me for some tests and, after proving I couldn't read even the largest letters on a revolving eye chart, I was given a choice of NHS glasses. They all had clear frames and circular, plastic-coated metal arms that hooked around your ears to ensure they stayed on during games.

I chose the 'ice blue' frames which made me look a little like Brains from *Thunderbirds* but they rarely made it out of my satchel at school. Wearing glasses was not cool. Rocky and Bruce Lee didn't wear glasses. If you wore NHS glasses you might as well have stamped 'poor as well as blind' on your forehead. To the boys from Penhill wearing glasses was seen as an invitation to 'bundle' you. This involved five or six boys jumping on you, punching your arms and trying to give you a dead leg by kneeing you in the thigh. Spectacle-wearing boys were called 'specky four-eyes', 'weaklings' and 'spastics'.

There was no way I was going to wear my glasses in school, despite the obvious downside to being blind at ten paces. To compensate for my lack of vision I tried to move forward in the classroom but the front desks were always taken by girls. The blackboard remained a blurry mystery to me.

I admit I was distracted from my studies by football, fishing and girls. I was fairly much like Swindon when it came to girls, in a lower league but with potential to cause the odd upset. I was particularly absorbed by a freckled American girl called Tracey, who put her tongue in my mouth at the Brunel Rooms under-eighteens night.

It also didn't help that our exams coincided with the start of the fishing season. I spent the day before my history exam with Kevin and Glynn catching chub and grayling on the river Thames at Hannington. The combination of my suspension, my poor eyesight, girls, football and fishing – where I did wear my glasses – fairly much did for my 'O' level results.

Maybe 'O' levels didn't really matter so much. The school assumed most of us boys would join our fathers in the local factories and organised a work experience day for us in the summer term. Kevin and I spent a day in the Pressed Steel Fisher factory where our dads worked. I wasn't sure what to expect; I hadn't been in a factory before. The press shop where my dad worked was like a huge aircraft hangar. The air smelt like the iron shavings we created when drilling in our metalwork class.

Once you stepped inside there was no colour, just shades of darkness. The pressing machines were like a row of black robots two to three storeys high. You had to shout to be heard over the constant noise, and even shouting was useless when the presses slammed down and thumped out the roof of a Morris Marina. When the presses stopped for the tea break the noise still echoed in my ears. The men in their dark overalls wore no ear protection and suffered severe hearing loss. Despite warnings about the risks, the company refused to provide protective equipment throughout the 1970s. Hundreds of men, who could constantly hear the presses pulsating in their heads, were given pitiful levels of compensation.

Other factory jobs were similarly hazardous, resulting in lower life expectancy and higher sickness. It was in the town's railway carriage works that my dad was exposed to asbestos and later developed mesothelioma, cancer of the lung. It didn't become apparent until years later. My dad was originally a chippy by trade and worked as a coach trimmer. Asbestos was used extensively in the construction of the carriages as lagging, insulation and for fireproofing upholstery. Blue asbestos was also sprayed onto the carriage walls. There was limited ventilation and no protective masks, despite warnings for decades that mesothelioma was linked to asbestos dust exposure. The bosses didn't care about the health of working-class people.

In their lunch breaks my dad and his mates moulded blue asbestos into footballs and played five-a-side. The fibres he inhaled lodged in the lining of his lungs and developed over the decades into a malignant tumour. It was only after three of his former workmates died from asbestosis that he decided to get tested. He never really recovered from the diagnosis. The doctor said matter-of-factly there was no cure and it was not possible to reverse the damage to the lungs. The insurers beat down his compensation claim on the grounds he was lucky: his tumour was on the outside of the lung so he would live longer than the others.

The second half of the work experience day was a tour of the factory offices organised by one of our teachers. I left my dad and his mates to eat their sandwiches in a dark windowless room. They joked that now I would see how the other half lived. I was collected up with the other students and we were escorted to the office block. We had our lunch in the canteen, a large and sunny open room with plate glass windows that overlooked the car park. I was struck by how light and clean it was. The air was fresh and perfumed by vases of white flowers.

After lunch we were shown around the offices. They told us about the different jobs such as design, technical drawing, accountancy and logistics. The men wore suits and ties rather than dirty overalls. There were also women in the offices. The older women wore pleated skirts and cream blouses while the younger ones wore pinafore dresses and roll neck sweaters. The office staff didn't appear to mix with those on the factory floor. They had separate entrances. My dad and his mates cycled to the small northern gate while the office staff came through the main car park entrance to the south. That evening Dad quizzed me about the offices; were they true, the things he had heard? To him and his mates the offices were a mysterious world far away from the factory floor.

The morning break in the press shop had been full of laughter as the men asked Terry if he was still fucking the bird in accounts. "How is old spanner lips?" my dad asked. From the confused looks I wasn't the only one who didn't get the reference. The men looked expectantly at Dad, who sat back, savouring the moment as he waited to deliver the punchline. "Well," he said, "I heard she always has a tool in her mouth." The men fell about and slapped their thighs. One of the men held up a photo of a bare-chested girl in the *Sun* and said, "I wish my missus had tits like that." To which my dad responded, "I bet you have to get on your hands and knees to find them these days." There was more raucous laughter. I shifted in my chair and hoped I didn't look as awkward as I felt.

I wasn't sure what I wanted to do when I left school but after my work experience day I knew I didn't want to work on the presses. I also didn't want to work in a factory. I was not like my dad or Kevin. They were at ease in the company of men and male banter. Kevin loved the work experience day. He couldn't wait to leave school to join his dad in the factory and down pints with the men in the club. Maybe I was just weird. I was uncomfortable with groups of working-class men discussing tits. It wasn't that I disapproved or looked down on them. At least that is what I told myself. That night I didn't tell Dad. I didn't want him to be disappointed. Instead I told him how much I had enjoyed seeing him, which was true.

According to my teacher, to get a job working in the offices rather than the factory floor I should stay on at school to do 'A' levels. I thought again about the press shop, I could still hear the thunderous noise in my ears. I was worried Dad would be disappointed but I wanted to stay on at school and become an office worker. George Orwell claimed, "There is not one working-class boy in a thousand who does not pine for the day when he will leave school." I must have been the one in a thousand.

When I finally summoned up the courage to tell my dad he supported me. He even said it was a good decision. I think he knew I wasn't like him. I think he'd known for many years. I recalled the disquieted look on his face when he tried to teach me how to make dovetail joints in the garage. I never had the practical skills that he and my brother possessed. They could install central heating and build extensions, things I would always have to pay someone to do for me. I was relieved by Dad's response and applied to the school to stay on to do 'A' levels.

My school had been one of those forced by Shirley Williams to become a comprehensive, which meant it was open to all local kids regardless of ability. It had previously been a selective grammar school and, given a choice, it would rather not take kids like me. I suspect the school was surprised by my application. The kids who stayed on to do 'A' levels were generally from the Cotswold villages north of Swindon. They came to our school on a bus with their musical instruments, and were in the top classes. At lunchtimes they studied Latin, while Kevin and I were kissing girls in the alley and fumbling under school sweaters.

The school rejected my application to stay on and refused me a place. The headmaster said I was not suited to 'A' levels and would struggle to keep up. Maybe he had a point about my grade 'D' in history; it wasn't the best indication of my suitability to study the subject at 'A' level, but I think he was more influenced by my two-week suspension. He didn't look favourably on boys who tied teachers to ladders and suspended them over the school fish pond.

When Dad found out the school had refused my application to do 'A' levels he was furious. I was surprised by his reaction; I could never recall him taking an interest in my studies. I didn't think he even knew what 'A' levels were. I had never seen him so angry and determined. He kept clenching and unclenching his fist. He was absolutely adamant that I should have the opportunity to stay on at school and made an appointment to see the headmaster. He put on the suit he wore for weddings and funerals, and stomped to the school with a determined stride.

I later discovered his emotional response wasn't just about wanting the best for me, this was about something much deeper. Despite his family's poverty Dad had passed the eleven plus but was refused a place at his local grammar school after an interview. He was convinced it was because he was poor, had ragged clothes and wasn't the right social fit. Dad wanted to put right this wrong in his life. He was determined that I would not suffer the same injustice he felt he had suffered. I don't know what he said to the headmaster but the school relented and I was allowed to stay on. Life generally moves along as a series of small incremental decisions but there are those rare times when something fundamental changes the path you are on. This was one of those days.

4

DAD AND THE CLUB

I believe Dad's determination to fight for me to stay on at school was linked to what happened shortly after his fifth birthday on the night of Saturday, 24 November 1945.

That evening my dad's father Ernest Rayson, a farm labourer, was cycling on the road from Swindon to Marlborough. The sun had set at four in the afternoon and the sky was dark as he left the Plough on the Hill and turned right onto the unlit country road. It was less than half a mile to his house in the village of Badbury. Two miles behind him a US army truck was being driven somewhat erratically as American soldiers made their way back to their base at Draycot.

Ernest had celebrated his thirty-fifth birthday the previous Saturday with his wife, Elsie, and their three children: Bill, Jean and my dad Cliff. Their village was near the top of a chalk hill, one of a series that made up an ancient path called the Ridgeway. As he cycled along the road he could see the top of the path illuminated by a waning gibbous moon. Dark fields fell away to his left. He heard the truck as it raced along the road behind him. The lights were bright on his back and his shadow stretched out forever on the road ahead of him. The driver, possibly distracted by his mates chatting about the Swindon women they had charmed, or his awareness dimmed by pints of Badger's beer, did not see Ernest until it was too late. His body was carried over a hundred feet up the road. He was dead by the time the truck came to a stop, and his shadow had disappeared.

The accident plunged the family into immediate poverty and Elsie worried about keeping the family together. The children of widows were frequently fostered, or placed into institutional homes, when their mothers could no longer afford to house, clothe and feed them. After initially denying responsibility for the accident, the Americans agreed to pay £200 compensation to Elsie, and to each of the children on their twenty-first birthdays. The money enabled the family to stay together but it did not compensate for the loss of Ernest, and life was tough for my dad. Once when my brother and I were complaining he came into our bedroom, sat on the end of my bed, and told us a story about him as a child sitting on the pavement crying with hunger. We stopped complaining and he never mentioned it again.

Early experiences influence our perspectives on life and risk. The experiences of losing his father and his job meant that Dad constantly sought security. Money that could have paid for holidays, or an Action Man, was placed inside the savings book and taken to the building society. He valued things based on their practicality. Shoes were shoes; as long as they were functional, why would you pay more than you had to? He couldn't begin to understand why someone would buy a painting or a work of art. The only frames that hung on our walls were family photographs. We didn't do foreign holidays, unless you counted the trip we once made to Barry Island in Wales. Dad was determined to build a rainy day fund for that moment when life would try to take everything away from him.

He didn't know when that day would be, but he knew it would come.

~

In October 1961, on his twenty-first birthday, Dad received the £200 compensation from the American military for his father's death. He used the money as a deposit to buy our house and we moved in when I was four months old, in July 1962. Mum was nervous about buying the house. She was concerned they couldn't afford the mortgage on Dad's wages as a railway apprentice but he reassured her they would be okay. He only had a few more months to go before he completed his apprenticeship. Once he became a fully qualified coach fitter his earnings would almost double to £14 a week. So they would be alright.

Things didn't turn out as planned. In the middle of 1962, British Rail decided to stop building new trains in Swindon. The workshops would continue to repair carriages but the work was scaled down. When Dad completed his five-year apprenticeship, three months after moving into our house, the railway works no longer had jobs for newly qualified men and they made him redundant.

For working-class people life is always insecure. Those without wealth, who live from pay cheque to pay cheque, are only an hour away from poverty. Just one accident, illness or redundancy notice can change their lives in an instant. Insecurity floats over the streets of working-class communities like the grim reaper looking for the next victim. I think it is why many working-class people are so good at living in the moment, it might be their last.

The Upper Stratton Workman's Reform Club came to my dad's rescue. He joined in the summer of 1962. The club's name was written in black letters on a white sign that hung above the door. The public bar was at the front of the building. At the back, through a set of foldaway doors, was the skittle alley. The skittles were large wooden blocks shaped like many of the men, widest at the waist with their beer bellies. It was a men's only club in the 1960s and women were barred from the public bar. They were allowed in the skittle alley, but they had to reach it by going up the stairs, through the snooker room, and down the back stairs, rather than walking through the bar where they might disturb the men. On Saturday nights the foldaway doors between the public bar and the skittle alley were opened creating one large room for the bingo. The women though were required to stay in the skittles half of the room.

It was through the men in the club that Dad found a job at the Pressed Steel Fisher factory. It meant my parents could pay the mortgage and keep the house. Others were less fortunate. Terry, who shambled into the club each lunchtime, and sat on his own at the bar, had lost his house, his wife and his children after he was made redundant.

Dad looked like David McCallum, who played Illya Kuryakin in *The Man from U.N.C.L.E.* on TV. When I was young I imagined him as a secret agent helping Napoleon Solo to save the world. I wasn't sure who my mum looked like. There was a black and white photograph of her when she was younger. She had won a baking competition in Malmesbury and was holding up her prize cake. She looked like one of those smiling women in the pictures of the VE celebrations after the war. While my dad was relaxed, my mum was the opposite. She was always on the move and hoovering under your feet as you sat on the sofa. There was no greater sin than leaving crumbs on the carpet.

Both my parents came from large families. My mum had nine siblings. Her mother, my grandmother, was the eldest of thirteen and my dad's mother, my nan, was the youngest of thirteen. They were born on the same date and died on the same date. Mum often reflected on the symmetry. I had more relatives than I could count scattered across Gloucestershire, Somerset and Wiltshire.

On Friday nights Andy and I would wait for Dad to return from the club and jump on him from the sofa. He would jab playfully at our bodies saying, "Mind your backs, your belly's in danger." Mum didn't join in with the play fighting and would caution us to be careful as we rolled from the sofa to the stiff swirly carpet on the floor. Dad would hold us down and sandpaper our faces with his stubble as we yelled and struggled to free ourselves. He hugged us in a protective aroma of tobacco and alcohol. Afterwards he would chivvy us to our bedrooms: "Come on, up the apples and pears."

My sister Paula, was born in the front bedroom. The one with the bay window and net curtains overlooking Penhill Secondary School. While Mum was giving birth, Andy and I were lying in our beds, throwing rolled-up socks at each other. We should have been sleeping but there was a fair bit of noise and commotion from our parents' bedroom next door. Dad came in to see us with a smile as wide as the Severn Bridge. He said we had a baby sister. A sister, we were not really sure what that meant for us. We were more excited to see if our plastic soldiers would melt over a candle.

On Saturdays Dad and his mates played football together for Highworth Town in the Wiltshire Combination League. He often took us to watch and we would hang around in Ralgex-infused changing rooms listening to the banter of naked men. They all had rhyming names: Dougy, Ringy, Micky, Kenny, Tubby and my dad, Cliffy. Dad played as an attacking winger; he was small but quick. "He'd give Alan Wells a run for his money", according to the lads in the changing room. Dad claimed he was five foot seven, "same as George Best", but this was always disputed by my mum. "You're not five seven. You're the same height as me, five foot five. You look at our wedding photo." He would always smile back at her and say, "You just got the maggot."

～

Dad loved football. In March 1969, he had travelled to Wembley with his mates to watch Swindon play Arsenal in the League Cup final. He said I was too young to go, even though I was about to turn seven. On the doorstep before leaving he gave us a big hug and said, "See you later, alligator." My younger brother Andy and I replied, "In a while crocodile." I thought our clever dad had made the saying up; it was like our family's secret code. I hadn't heard of Bill Haley and the Comets.

Dad was realistic about Swindon's chances. We were a Third Division team; it was fantastic we had got to the final but Arsenal were a powerful outfit. They had famous international players like Frank McLintock, Bobby Gould and Bob Wilson. We had one: Rod Thomas, a fullback who had played three times for Wales. To everyone's shock and surprise Swindon won. Our captain Stan Harland walked up the famous Wembley steps in a daze of disbelief to collect the cup from Princess Margaret. It was like a blue moon rising on the Twelfth of Never. In the fifty plus years since, no Third Division team has won the League Cup.

I am not sure when Dad got back from London but his celebrations meant we never saw him until the Sunday. We were playing on the floor in the lounge with our armies of moulded plastic soldiers when he came in grinning like a demented Ken Dodd. He gave us each a Grenadier guardsman figure that he had brought back from London. They came in clear plastic tubes and were really for American tourists. They were a bit fragile for boys who tied makeshift parachutes to their backs and launched them from the bedroom window to the concrete floor below.

That afternoon we huddled on the sofa to watch a replay of the game on our black and white TV. Andy and I sat on either side of Dad, and he hugged us tightly as the players walked out of the tunnel. Wembley was like a Wiltshire farmer's field, more suited to mud wrestling than football. The crowd was huge, almost a hundred thousand people. Swindon were leading 1-0 when Arsenal equalised just four minutes from time. My dad was giving us a running commentary: "We thought it was all over now."

Then in extra time Don Rogers, our star striker, poked in the ball from three yards, and we were ahead again. With just minutes remaining Rogers ran sixty yards towards the opposition goal. Dad dropped from the sofa to his knees shouting, "Go on!" Rogers rounded the Arsenal keeper, Bob Wilson, to make it 3-1 to Swindon. We all embraced and ran around the room cheering, accidentally knocking over the dried bullrushes in the copper coloured vase on the hearth. Mum told us to calm down. It was as good as being in the stadium the day before. We were giant killers, a Third Division team that had beaten the mighty Arsenal of the First Division. We were Swindon, the scrappy underdogs.

After a few years Dad became more involved with the club. On Saturday nights he started calling the bingo and made up his own rhyming calls: "Bugger me, it's number three." Later he became a club committee member which required attending Monday evening meetings and taking his turn to be on duty. On these nights he helped collect up glasses, sorted any trouble and encouraged men to drink up after last orders at ten-thirty. Ernie, who resembled Andy Capp from the *Daily Mirror*

cartoon with his flat cap, frequently fell asleep over his pint and had to be woken at closing time. The staff would shout across the bar to him, "Hey Ernie, time to get your milk cart." The ringing of the bell and shouts of last orders would often fail to rouse him, and it was the responsibility of the duty committee member to physically wake him up to go home.

One Tuesday evening the shouting failed to rouse Ernie so my dad walked over and shook him gently by the shoulder. "Come on, Ernie. Drink up, time to go." He didn't respond. "Come on Ernie, you can't stay here," said Dad, shaking him more vigorously. Ernie slumped slowly onto his right side as if he wanted to lie down and sleep on the leather bench. He had passed away at some point during the evening. Dad told us the story with a smile. "The worst thing was he didn't even finish his pint, such a waste. Still, not a bad way to go." If he could, my dad would have chosen to die like Ernie, but with an empty glass on the table in front of him.

5

SIXTH FORM SOCIALIST

In the sixth form my friendship group changed. Kevin, whose toilet roll had made him famous, left school to work with his dad. My friend Glynn also left to work at the Plessey factory making radio components. He was obsessed by technology and would spend hours in his bedroom playing with a small computer device that plugged into his portable TV. It was his name that topped the scoreboard of Space Invaders machines across the town.

In the absence of Kevin and Glynn, I became friends with Tessa, who sat next to me in our economics class. Almost immediately it became clear that statistics were not her strong point. She always got top marks in English but if you put a table of numbers in front of her she would panic. We worked well together; she told me what was written on the board and I worked out the answers for us. While all the other girls wore blue V-neck sweaters and white blouses, Tessa wore a grey turtleneck jumper. She was Anglo-Indian, and the only non-white face in our year. When working together, she would put her hand on my arm and occasionally lean her shoulder against mine to see what I had written. She seemed older and more worldly than everyone else I knew. Glynn told me in hushed tones that she was a troublemaker and a 'socialist'. I wasn't sure what that meant but I liked her.

One Friday lunchtime we were playing cards in the sixth form common room when someone threw their cards across the table and called another student a cheating Arab. Tessa challenged them. "Why do you have to use the word Arab?" The other students didn't understand; why couldn't they call someone a cheating Arab? John told Tessa to fucking lighten up, couldn't she take a joke? Tessa shouted back: "You're just a fucking racist." John threw the rest of the cards on the floor, mumbled something inaudible and slammed the door as he left.

That night I felt bad that I hadn't intervened to support Tessa. I tried to justify it in my head. My friends weren't racist; it was just a phrase they used. But no matter how much I tried to persuade myself, something nagged at me that it was wrong. It was like when you try to convince yourself you don't feel sick despite the heaving and rolling sensations in your stomach.

The more I spent time with Tessa the more I became aware of the casual sexism, homophobia and racism of the language around me. I hadn't really thought about these things before. The Irish jokes my dad told, the police vans called paddy wagons, and the cheating Arabs. The ponces, Pakis and poofs. When I raised it with Glynn he insisted that 'Paki' wasn't racist, it was just like when people called him Taff but I was uncomfortable. Maybe I was also a socialist like Tessa?

I was at Kevin's house in Penhill when I next heard the word socialist. His home was dark, dirty and disordered. It smelt of spices and tobacco. In the summer the sun struggled to illuminate shafts of dust in the thick opaque air. His dad always had grimy skin as if he had just emerged from a coal mine or from under his truck. He would push his nicotine-stained fingers through his thick curly black hair. He was like the love child of Medusa and David Essex. His wife was slight, dark skinned, and had long black hair that reached almost to her waist. She reminded me of Morticia from the *Addams Family*.

Smoke from their rolled cigarettes swirled around the small rooms and clung to me each time I visited. For days afterwards the acrid fumes would linger in my clothing. It wasn't the rich, sweet smell of the Panatela cigars my dad smoked at Christmas; it was thinner, more acidic.

Kevin's father loved chess. We would play for hours with the board balanced on a footstool between us. He would sit on the battered sofa holding a cigarette high in his hand as he contemplated his next move. I was impressed at his ability to roll cigarettes on his knee and lick the papers while never taking his eyes off the game.

I would sit on the floor, occasionally raising myself up on my knees to get a better view of the board. I would always lose but I relished the challenge. He would coach me, pointing out the importance of controlling the central squares, of developing your pieces and of positional play rather than my mad dash across the board to attack his king.

One day Kevin's father was arguing with Kevin's older brother about politics. I don't recall the exact conversation but I do remember him saying, "You can't call yourself a socialist if you haven't read *The Ragged Trousered Philanthropists*." It was clear from the conversation, from the way he spoke, that it was more than a book. It was something sacred, more akin to the Bible, something revelatory.

I didn't know the book; my parents didn't read books. I remember my teacher's disbelieving shake of the head at junior school when I said we didn't have any books at home. "Not even the Bible?" she asked, her eyebrows raised. I decided not to say that the Gideons once gave me a purple-bound copy of the New Testament but my mum gave it to a jumble sale during one of her clear outs. I didn't mind the loss of the Bible; I was more upset later when she gave away my Beatles yellow submarine and my Captain Scarlet Spectrum Pursuit Vehicle because she thought I had "grown out of them".

A few weeks after the conversation with my teacher I was unexpectedly called to the stage at the school prize giving. I was given a hardback copy of *Mr Midshipman Hornblower*. Inside the front cover was a sticker which said I had won a 'progress prize'. I think it was like the UEFA cup, a second-tier competition for those that didn't win in the main event. I proudly took the book home to show my mum.

When I was at secondary school my parents purchased the Children's Encyclopaedia Britannica from a man who sold them door to door, like the man from Pearl Insurance who regularly collected our premiums. The new shiny embossed volumes were added to the side cabinet underneath the Babycham glasses.

After listening to Kevin's dad I looked up Socialism in volume 16 of the Encyclopaedia. According to Britannica, socialism was a belief that the social interests of the community as a whole should come before any individual interests. It said socialists believed that education should be free and that industries should be owned by the nation rather than private individuals. I agreed, they should definitely not be owned by bosses that didn't care about the workers.

On my next trip to Beechcroft Road library I enquired about Tressell's book. I wanted to learn more about socialism and be able to discuss it with Tessa. She was not like the girls we kissed in the alley. She was serious, intellectual and mature. Her boyfriend, Phil, was much older than us and talked knowledgeably about politics. He looked like Mick Jagger, whereas I resembled Jilted John on *Top of the Pops* wearing a 'Gordon is a Moron' badge.

To my surprise the library assistant not only knew *The Ragged Trousered Philanthropists*, she also knew where it was located. She took me over to one of the bookshelves and handed me a thick paperback which had clearly been read many times. The title of the book had faded on the spine and the back cover had been sellotaped to mend a tear. I took the book home with a sense of anticipation though I was a little daunted by its size. I had been hoping for something more like the *ABC Book of Birds*.

The introduction by Alan Sillitoe said the book, published in 1914, was a working-class novel which exposed the real nature of class conflict. I wasn't sure what he meant but as I read everything became clear. It was really very simple. The more the business owner in the book, Mr Hunter, drove down the wages of the painters and decorators that he employed the greater was his profit. It was a zero sum game, the more he paid the workers the less he received so he continually found ways to maximise his share.

According to Sillitoe the 1942 Beveridge Report, which made the case for government intervention in the areas of housing, education and health, was based on Tressell's socialist ideas set out in *The Ragged Trousered Philanthropists*. He also argued the book had helped Labour win the 1945 election. A victory that enabled Beveridge's proposals to be put into practice and led to the creation of the modern welfare state. After reading Tressell I understood my place in the world. I was working class and a socialist.

In the autumn of 1978, I bought some hard contact lenses

with my Saturday job money. It felt like I had grit in my eyes but it was worth it. Walking down the street I would stop and marvel at the sharp lines of tree branches against the sky. Even with my *Joe 90* glasses the world had never been as crisp and clear.

In our economics lessons Tessa and I were taught about supply and demand by Bob, who had either forgiven me for the ladder incident, or didn't know I was involved. Bob reminded me of the comedian Jasper Carrot. He was the most approachable and informal of our teachers. His tie always hung loosely below the unfastened top button of his shirt, like it was objecting to being there.

One Tuesday morning Tessa put her hand up and asked if the constant tension between supply and demand also applied to the conflict between owners and workers. Bob smiled and said it did. He took his chalk and drew a new graph on the blackboard – scratching rapidly he labelled the vertical scale 'Wages' and the horizontal scale 'Quantity of Labour'. With my new lenses I could clearly see the intersection of the two lines he drew on the board. He explained how the supply and demand for labour affected wages. He also said that the average wage in the UK was £98 a week for men and £60 for women.

"Fucking outrageous," hissed Tessa under her breath but clearly audibly.

I asked Bob a question based on my reading of *The Ragged Trousered Philanthropists*.

"Does capitalism mean that companies are always looking to drive down wages to increase profit?"

When I said the word 'capitalism' other students stared at me. David, a tall, thick-set, blond haired boy, who captained the rugby team, sat back in his chair, raised his eyes to the ceiling and muttered, "Bloody socialists". Despite the disdainful looks of the other students Bob said it was a good question. He explained that the economist Karl Marx had written about this tension. David said something inaudible at the mention of Marx and received one of Tessa's death stares. Without putting her hand up, or waiting for Bob to finish, she interrupted him.

"Marx also said it is not enough to understand the conflict between owners and workers," said Tessa. "You have to choose sides. It's like the trade union song says, you have to decide which side you are on."

David leaned back and gave a theatrical yawn, placing his hand over his mouth. He had chosen his side.

Sat in the sixth form common room afterwards Tessa told me the song *Which Side Are You On?* was written by a women called Florence Reece. She said it was about J. H. Blair, a sheriff in Harlan County who had evicted trade union organisers from their company homes during the depression in America. Blair had raided and ransacked Reece's house in search of her union leader husband. The raid had inspired Reece to write the song. Tessa told me you couldn't be neutral. You were either on the side of the union or you were a thug for J. H. Blair. I understood. I had seen *Star Wars*. I also knew from Tressell that there were two sides: the idle business owners, who lived off the labour of others, and the exploited workers. It was like football – you had to stand with your tribe.

Tessa told me we also had to act. Again I understood. I had watched *Flashing Blade*, a swashbuckling TV series. The inspirational theme song said you had to fight for the things you believed in, for what was right. Tessa said she had joined the Labour Party Young Socialists and spoke passionately about changing the world.

When I got home after school I looked up the Labour Party in volume ten of the Children's Britannica. It said the British Labour Party wanted to bring about socialism and had been established by James Keir Hardie. It confirmed what Sillitoe had written, namely that the 1945 Labour government, inspired by Tressell, created the National Health Service, where I had my appendix removed. They ensured workers got proper sickness benefits, pensions and payments if they were unemployed. They also nationalised the coal mines, railways, gas, electricity, steel works and iron works. The party's history in my 1973 edition of Children's Britannica finished in 1970 when Harold Wilson was the Labour prime minister.

After tea Dad was sat in his usual chair by the fireplace reading the *Advertiser*, while we watched children's TV. I was getting too old for the programmes, like John Noakes who retired from *Blue Peter* that summer. Dad was always reluctant to discuss politics but I wanted to know if he supported the Labour Party. Maybe like other teenagers, torn between simultaneously rebelling and conforming, I needed to know if he would approve of my decision. I knew he would never say anything but that was worse somehow. His face could signal disapproval and disappointment in a way that was more devastating than any words.

"Dad, do you vote Labour or Liberal?" I asked. I was sure he would never vote for the Conservatives and the dark side. He lowered the paper, tilted his head and stared at me, unsure whether to reply. I waited. "Labour," he finally said and lifted the paper to resume reading. This was how it was with Dad when you discussed politics; he just gave you one-word answers or avoided the conversation entirely. I was happy he voted Labour but I wanted to know why.

"Why do you vote Labour?"

"Your dad is trying to read," said my mum, as if anticipating an argument she would rather avoid.

"I only want to know why he votes Labour."

Dad looked pained and lowered his newspaper reluctantly. "Because it is the working man's party. Now can I get back to the paper?"

"Sure, thanks."

I wasn't going to get any more out of him but he had

confirmed that the Labour Party was our party, the party of the workers. The next day I told Tessa I wanted to join the Labour Party Young Socialists (LPYS). It was the autumn of 1978, I was sixteen and I chose the side of the workers. The side of Tressell, The Clash and Tessa.

6

THE LABOUR PARTY YOUNG
SOCIALISTS

I was as excited at joining the LPYS as teenage girls were about becoming members of the Bay City Rollers fan club. My membership card was in a small red plastic wallet that smelt like bubblegum. On the front cover was a raised fist under the words, 'Youth Get Organised' and underneath it said, 'Socialism – The Hope and Future for Youth'. It was at an LPYS meeting that I met Trotsky.

At my first meeting I sat next to Tessa and an older fair haired guy in a camouflage jacket. He confided to me that he was an anti-vivisectionist activist and supported the Bicester Two. I nodded knowingly. I didn't have a clue what he was talking about. Whatever anti-vivisectionists were I had never heard them discussed by my dad or his mates. Dad had taught me about betting odds when he went to the bookies to place our bets for the Grand National, he had showed me how to do a mortise joint in the garage and how to bowl off spin in the drive with a tennis ball, but I was fairly sure I had never heard the word anti-vivisectionist cross his lips. I followed the advice of Mark Twain, not that I had heard of him at the time, but I knew it was better to nod and look ignorant rather than open my mouth and remove all possible doubt.

When I got home I looked up anti-vivisection in the Children's Britannica but I couldn't find it either in the A's which ended at antiseptic or in the V's which went from vitamin, from the Latin word for life according to the encyclopaedia, to Vladivostok, which means 'ruler of the East', but there was nothing on vivisection. I later discovered the Bicester Two were imprisoned for raiding an Oxford laboratory that conducted experiments on animals and subsequently formed the Animal Liberation Front after their release.

Tessa and her boyfriend knew much more than I did. When we visited Phil's house his parents talked to us about politics. Their house had Persian rugs on the floor and more books than our local library. Phil said his parents were always arguing about Labour Party policies. In my house we argued about the best Don Rogers goal. For the record it was his 1973 goal for Palace against Stoke City. He ran from inside his own half, ghosted past three or four defenders on a pitch that resembled a peat bog and chipped the ball over the keeper. Even Maradona couldn't have done that. My dad said it was one of the best goals ever and he was right, it won that season's Golden Goal.

The more I mixed with Tessa, Phil and the people from the Labour Party the more I was conscious of my lack of knowledge. I kept discovering new words. In my classes the teachers also used words in ways I didn't understand. They may as well have been speaking Latin, which they also did sometimes. I appeared to be the only person who didn't understand. The other students would say things like, "Ah yes, cornucopia from the Latin copia which means plenty." How the hell did they know this stuff? My dad had taught me that Latin football players from Italy and South America were dirty players and cheats. He would make this point often during

World Cup games and shout at the TV, "That was a dive, you cheating sod."

I was determined to expand my knowledge and spent many hours in the library trying to fill the black holes in my education. I became a sponge for new information. I was like a baby, wide-eyed and absorbing everything. I was inquisitive about the world and asking questions constantly. With my Saturday job money I bought myself a dictionary. It was a gold embossed red faux leather hardback which I still have on my bookshelf, along with the Children's Britannica encyclopaedias. With its thirteen hundred pages the dictionary remains the best thing I have ever purchased. It has an entry for antivivisectionism and a page on the Greek alphabet.

I read constantly to try to catch up, including Jane Austen novels for my English 'A' level course, but when I talked to my classmates they appeared to have read an entirely different book. I read the books hastily, skimming through them to find out what happened in the story. Surely that was the point. It was like Agatha Christie: you wanted to know who did it. They talked about characterisation, conflict, themes, style, symbolism and unreliable narrators. Tessa told me you had to read "between the lines" but there was nothing but blank white spaces between the lines of my books.

Tessa and Phil discussed books in the context of society and politics. They saw things that never occurred me. In our English class we discussed *A Passage to India* and Tessa was quick to point out the stereotypes and problematic elements of the book. I recall clearly a passage that she highlighted: 'Like most Orientals, Aziz overrated hospitality, mistaking it for intimacy'.[1] I hadn't really thought about it before.

Tessa also introduced me to Bob Marley's protest songs. I had previously enjoyed *I Shot the Sheriff* and *Jammin* but Tessa played songs like *Get Up, Stand Up*, which encouraged people to fight for their rights, and *Them Belly Full, But We Hungry*, which might have been written by Robert Tressell. Tessa became my adviser on all things political. One lunchtime in the common room she told me the police Special Patrol Group were "fucking bastards" who had killed Blair Peach in Southall. I nodded knowingly.

~

At the start of 1979 I purchased a copy of the *Big Red Diary* from Pluto Press. The cover logo said, 'Better Active Today Than Radioactive Tomorrow'. The diary had brief descriptions of socialist events from history as you moved through the months. I eagerly entered the details of my upcoming LPYS meetings into the diary. The meetings were held near the Town Hall in Old Town. A couple called Jim and Alice ran the meetings. When you arrived there was a table positioned by the door, like a check-in desk, on which they laid out copies of the *Militant* newspaper, along with booklets and leaflets. If I arrived early I would help set out chairs in a circle in the middle of the room. Optimistically I would put out dozens of chairs but generally only eight or so people came along, their footsteps echoing on the polished parquet flooring as they arrived.

Jim and Alice were both very earnest and called everyone comrade. As we sat on the red plastic chairs I listened intently to discussions that were completely alien to me. I took my *Big Red Diary* so they would know I was a socialist but I was conscious it was only a matter of time before they discovered I was really an imposter. They talked about South American dictators, apartheid, the Middle-East, 1956 Hungary, 1968 Czechoslovakia, the occupation of the six counties of Northern Ireland, and Stalinism. I kept my head down and wrote copious notes in my diary.

The meetings were run like seminars with short presentations followed by discussions based around articles from the *Militant*. I learnt to read the paper front to back prior to the meetings so that I was prepared. At the end of the meeting there was a discussion about upcoming events and people were encouraged to buy pamphlets on topics from Bolshevism to Ireland. At this time the caretaker would arrive saying, "Don't you lot have homes to go to."

Jim and Alice were like young missionaries dedicated to building support for the Militant group in the Labour Party youth section. They believed that the education of young people was the main task of radical Marxists. The Labour leader Jim Callaghan complained that such tutoring was being allowed to fall into the hands of the Militant group: "They do more education than anybody else."[2] I was their ideal target audience: young, passionate, angry about inequality and eager to learn. I also found my Militant education incredibly helpful for my 'A' levels, particularly history where we were studying Modern Dictatorships in Europe. I think our teacher was surprised by the essays I wrote on Stalinism and the Russian revolution, and the extensive range of references in my bibliography.

Occasionally we were joined by a comrade from Bristol that we called Trotsky, as he had a short beard, round John Lennon glasses and wore a mariner's peaked cap. Trotsky was like the regional sales manager for Militant. He came to check the meetings were running okay and bought bags full of newspapers, booklets and badges. At one meeting he gave me a Militant branded 'Tories Out' badge which I proudly pinned to my jacket. Trotsky also selected pamphlets for me to read by senior comrades, whose names appeared in the *Militant* newspaper.

∽

In the bedroom I would lie on the pink candlewick bedspread and read the Militant pamphlets. They were like mini dissertations and difficult to read but shaped my developing political ideology. Okay, it was a weird ideology formed by an esoteric mix of the *Flashing Blade*, Tessa, The Clash, Paul Weller, *The Ragged Trousered Philanthropists* and Militant pamphlets. Increasingly it was also shaped by comrades with Liverpool accents in our LPYS meetings. My ideology, such as it was, divided the world into two competing groups. You were either on the good side, the side of the workers and socialism, or the evil side, the side of the rich and the bosses. Tessa was right, you couldn't be neutral; being neutral was effectively perpetuating the existing system and taking the side of the rich. I was clear. You either wanted to change the system or you were an apologist for millionaire capitalists.

My increasingly political views did not make me great boyfriend material. It probably didn't help when I said Valentine's Day was just something made up by capitalists. Surprisingly, I rarely fell out with my girlfriends about politics, it was their parents I argued with. I was not subtle; I would raise controversial topics and ask them why they had chosen the dark side. Was it right that they had a nice car while other people were homeless? Was it okay that they ate out at a Wimpy while children were starving in Africa? At the time a Wimpy was the poshest restaurant I was aware of. I found it difficult to discuss politics without raising my voice and becoming angry. My girlfriends' parents were sceptical that a long haired socialist, who wore Militant badges, was the ideal partner for their daughters. They were probably right.

The back page of the Militant pamphlets was headed World Books. It promoted a series of works by Trotsky, Lenin and Engels about scientific socialism, the state, the capitalist crisis and something called the permanent revolution. At the bottom of the list of recommended books was *The Ragged Trousered*

Philanthropists. It stood out like a beacon of light. Other than Kevin's father I had never seen or heard anyone else talk about the book. My respect for Militant increased. They understood. Anyone who read and recommended Tressell understood. They were clearly my type of people.

Immediately above *The Ragged Trousered Philanthropists* on the World Books list was *Homage to Catalonia* by George Orwell. On my next trip to the Beechcroft Road library I searched for the book but the only Orwell book they had was *The Road to Wigan Pier.* I took it to the desk where the librarian removed the card from the book's pocket and replaced it with a due date card which she stamped.

It turned out *The Road to Wigan Pier* was exactly what I was looking for. Part one of the book was interesting but mainly made me feel happy I didn't live in a northern industrial town. According to Orwell the working-class people there smelt, had no teeth and terrible diets. I wasn't sure it was right to say such things but I knew what he meant about the smell. There were some flats on the Penhill estate where the stench hit you as soon as the doors were opened.

Orwell said all the people in Sheffield were troglodytes. I didn't know what that meant and had to look it up in my dictionary, which said troglodytes were cave dwellers or anthropoid apes. I still didn't understand. I looked up Sheffield in my Children's Britannica which said it was the largest town in the West Riding area of Yorkshire, that it made steel and that Mary Queen of Scots was imprisoned there in 1569. There was no mention of caves.

Part two of Orwell's book was a revelation. He said, "Socialism is such elementary common sense that I am sometimes amazed that it has not established itself already."[3] That was exactly how I felt; it seemed so obvious. I couldn't understand why we were not living in a socialist society.

7

1979 GENERAL ELECTION

My decision to get involved in politics was bewildering to my parents. They had started work at fifteen and did not read books about socialism or attend political meetings. They viewed all politicians with suspicion. The only time politics was discussed was when Dad's mates from the club came over to try his home brew. I was disappointed to discover they were not as enthusiastic about the Labour government as I was.

"It cost me six quid to fill the car up," said Tony. "It's getting bloody ridiculous. Petrol will be over a pound a gallon soon."

"It's not just petrol, our missus has been complaining about the housekeeping money," said Bob. "Says food and leccy prices are three times higher than what they were a few years back."

According to the newsreader, Reginald Bosanquet, inflation was out of control at the start of 1979 and there were widespread strikes about pay. Richard Baker, on the BBC News, said public sector strikes were leaving rubbish in the streets and bodies were not being buried in Liverpool due to a strike by gravediggers. My dad was frustrated when petrol stations were closed due to a lorry drivers' strike, which only ended when the drivers were offered a 20 percent wage increase.

"The Birmingham and Cowley workers have voted to down tools until they get a basic wage of ninety pounds a week," said Tony, "and we are going to join them."

"Ninety quid, that's a bit of a jump ain't it," said Bob.

"It's only seventeen percent, same as the workers in Ford got last month, and less than the lorry drivers got," said Tony. "Callaghan can bugger off with his five percent limit."

My dad nodded but said nothing as he passed round glasses of cloudy beer. My bother Andy held out a small glass decorated with red and blue flowers. Dad filled it with beer and winked at him. I didn't take a glass. I was suspicious of the clear plastic tubes and the aroma of rotten apples.

I wanted to intervene in the men's discussion to say that Tony Benn opposed the incomes policy and that it was the right-wing Dennis Healey who had agreed with the International Monetary Fund to use wage restraint to control inflation. But by the time I had formulated the right words in my head, the moment had gone. It was something that happened often.

"And where's Callaghan?" said Tony. He didn't need time to compose his words. "On bloody holiday in Barbados. Can you believe it? The bloke is completely out of touch."

I had seen the pictures of Callaghan in his baggy swimming shorts in my dad's *Daily Mirror*. I wasn't sure how you defended a Labour prime minister swimming in the Caribbean during one of the coldest winters on record, and when striking workers were huddled around braziers on picket lines. Politics was complicated.

~

I turned seventeen in March 1979, when the Labour Party lost a motion of confidence by a single vote in the House of Commons. They had clung to power for a year with the support of the Ulster Unionists. No longer. Thatcher had prevailed with the support of the treacherous Scottish National Party. An election was called for 5 May. Jim Callaghan was right, the SNP in backing Thatcher's 'no confidence' motion were turkeys voting for Christmas, and would lose their heads. They were just 'tartan Tories'. I hoped they would all lose their seats.

There was no way Thatcher was going to win. I was going to make sure of it and, despite not being old enough to vote, I pinned a red 'I am voting Labour' badge to my denim jacket. It wasn't fair that I couldn't vote. My future was going to be determined by old people who would probably be dead soon.

On the TV Margaret Thatcher appeared in a party political broadcast for the Conservatives, she appeared to be wearing a huge white ribbon tied in a bow around her neck. She looked deeply into the camera as if she was staring directly at me. She leaned forward and clasped her hands in front of her, as if in prayer. She spoke slowly, like the nurse who reassured me in the Princess Margaret Hospital before they removed my appendix. She said, "May this land of ours, which we love so much, find dignity and greatness and peace again." Then she smiled and tilted her head, like a praying mantis about to rip the head off its unsuspecting mate. She was tempting the British public to their deaths but I wasn't fooled. Thatcher and I had crossed paths before.

In 1971, I turned nine and became a proud 'milk monitor'. I helped with the task of distributing to my class one-third pint bottles of milk sealed with foil caps. This was a task generally reserved for girls; I think they were seen as being more responsible. This was probably a good call given my experience of nine-year-old boys, who ran around pretending to shoot people and who threw anything to hand as pretend grenades, mimicking explosions with large whooshes of their arms. I say pretending to shoot people but generally they pretended to shoot Germans as they acted out scenes from *Commando* magazine, shouting, "Achtung" and "Schweinhund". Despite being a boy, I took my duties as milk monitor seriously. I pushed straws through the foil caps, handed out the bottles and collected in the empties.

Health and safety rules these days would probably prohibit nine-year-old children being given glass bottles to run around with during their playtime. I suspect there would also be choices of soy, oat or rice milk. Choices were not something I recall at junior school. Dinners were placed in front of you at lunchtime and you fought for your share. There were no rules of war when it came to food. The dinner ladies that put large bowls of custard or rice pudding in the centre of our tables to share were making a big mistake. I am not sure how, but Kevin had already learned that snorting heavily and noisily before spitting into the bowl decreased the appetite of sensitive children and left more for him.

I had little time to enjoy my new 'milk monitor' responsibilities. Margaret Thatcher, then education secretary, removed free school milk for children over seven. For a few weeks we ran around in the playground shouting, "Thatcher, Thatcher, Milk Snatcher." I admit to being a bit confused about who Thatcher was at the time. There was a rumour that the Milk Snatcher was actually the wife of the Child Catcher in *Chitty Chitty Bang Bang*. This seemed entirely plausible. She was clearly evil, hated children and had taken away my 'milk monitor' job.

~

Immediately the election was called I volunteered to distribute Labour Party election leaflets. I wanted to ensure our local MP, David Stoddart, was re-elected. I didn't agree with him on many things, not least his desire to ban *The Sweeney*, but he was far better than any Conservative. I filled my school satchel with Labour leaflets and headed out to the Penhill estate.

In the park was a group of young lads wearing red and white Swindon Town scarves over their T-shirts and leather jackets, as they mimicked the style of the Fonz in *Happy Days* and Danny Zuko in *Grease*. They flew high on the swings singing *We Will Rock You* and threatening to put you back into your place. Once someone stole the chains and the seats from the swings; I am not sure they had much value but if something wasn't locked down, and even if it was, people stole it. The absence of the chains gave the boys the opportunity to demonstrate they were men by doing chin-ups on the top bar of the swing. On other days they would do wheelies on their bikes or race around the dirt tracks emulating Swindon Speedway's Barry Briggs. Their capped sleeves showed off the biceps they had been building in cold gyms with rusted weights listening to Thin Lizzy's *The Boys Are Back In Town*. They particularly liked songs about fighting and blood flowing. I am not sure how but when I passed the park my Labour badges mysteriously came loose and I had to put them in my pocket.

After a few days of leafleting I asked the local Labour Party members if I could help with canvassing and much to my surprise they agreed. I took my notebook from the radiogram and sat at the dining table to prepare my arguments. I drew a line down the centre of the page. In the left-hand column I wrote down all the reasons for voting Labour. I wrote words such as fairness and social justice. In the right-hand column I listed the reasons why voting Tory would be a disaster including cutting income tax for the rich, privatisation and anti-trade union legislation. As I sat back and reviewed my list of arguments I was confident we would win the election.

I joined the Labour canvassers outside Dewhurst the Butchers, equipped with a clipboard, multiple Bic biros, a satchel of leaflets and my own personal notes on why Thatcher was evil. Frank who organised the canvassing wore the ugly wide brown shoes designed for old people. I paced up and down as he provided us with a list of voter addresses to call on. I was eager to evangelise the Labour cause but much to my disappointment he told me I should not get into long conversations with Tory voters. I didn't understand. How was I going to persuade them to vote Labour? Canvassing, he told me, wasn't really about persuading voters, it was about gauging support, understanding the issues that concerned them and identifying those people that would vote for us. I nodded to acknowledge I understood but it wasn't enough to reassure him. Maybe it was the Mormonic glint in my eye. He said it would probably be better if I started by accompanying him to see how things worked. I knocked on the doors while he led the discussions and afterwards he showed me how to mark up the canvass returns.

Door knocking is not for the faint hearted. I was never that worried about having the door shut in my face or receiving abuse. It was the dogs that petrified me. As a newspaper boy I had come across houses where dogs threw themselves loudly against the other side of the door as you approached, and ripped the paper from your hand through the letterbox. Once I was only just inside the gate when I came face to face with an Alsatian. I turned to make my escape but I was no Usain Bolt and within seconds the dog's teeth were buried in my backside. I recall the embarrassment of being sat in A&E with blood pooling under me on the plastic chair. The owner said it was all my fault, I shouldn't have turned my back on the dog. Did he really think the homicidal wolf would have been dissuaded if I had offered it my groin rather than my backside? They were like that, the psycho dog owners on the Penhill estate.

As we walked the streets Frank said he was confident we were going to win. He told me Swindon had voted Labour in every general election since 1945. I had faith in the people of the town; they were honest working-class people, most of the time.

During the election I started watching news and political programmes obsessively, including ITV's *Weekend World* with Brian Walden and BBC's *Panorama* on Monday evenings. I was particularly intrigued by the swingometer used by Bob McKenzie on the BBC's *Tonight* programme. It was like the bottom half of a huge clock, shaded red on the left and blue on the right. I leaned forward to get a better look but I couldn't make out the numbers on the bottom. We really needed a bigger TV. Even dad's mate Bob had commented on the small size of our TV. "Nothing wrong with fourteen inches," my dad had replied with a grin. McKenzie said the polls gave Thatcher a ten point lead. He swung the white pointer to the right and forecast a Conservative victory. He was wrong. Our canvassing returns showed that the overwhelming majority of people on the Penhill estate were voting Labour. He obviously knew nothing about politics.

8

THE THURSDAY NIGHT CLUB

Which of these people is more likely to know what it's like to do the family shopping?

1. James Callaghan
2. Your husband
3. Margaret Thatcher

The advert appeared in my mum's *Woman's Weekly* magazine. It was part of the Conservative strategy to target housewives. Thatcher also appeared on the Jimmy Young Show on BBC Radio Two. My mum listened to the show when she cleaned the house. She would lift her brass ornaments, including the shepherd girl who had a bell under her skirt, and polish the wooden shelves while listening to the show's music, consumer affairs, recipes and interviews. It wasn't a political show but it was influential. At its peak it attracted nine million listeners. Thatcher appeared on the show many times and it was here that she crafted her narrative. Her story was simple, the Britain of Churchill had once been great, it had bestrode the world like a Colossus until socialists and the trade unions had dragged the country down, we were now the sick man of Europe. Her mission was to make Britain great again. It was a simple story of the past, the present and of an imagined future.

The Conservatives sought to make out Thatcher was just like any other housewife and she constantly talked in terms of household finances. "If the government won't economise every family in the country has to, instead." It was all economic gobbledygook.

Surely no one was stupid enough to buy the story of 'our Maggie', the housewife's friend. I told anyone that would listen to me, which was not many, that Thatcher was no ordinary housewife. She had married a wealthy businessman in 1951, who had financed her legal training. In the sixties they bought a three-storey house in Chelsea and a large country house in Kent. I couldn't believe that she owned two houses. Who the hell needed two houses?

At the dinner table my parents had to listen to me rant about her owning two homes. Dad ignored my escalating expressions of outrage. He left the table and Mum served us Arctic Roll, a jam sponge roll filled with ice cream, which only just fitted in the top freezer compartment of the fridge. I continued my tirade against people owning multiple houses but no one was listening.

The BBC's Michael Cockerell called Thatcher's 1979 election campaign "the most professionally organised ever" and one which was "made for the media". The Conservatives engaged an advertising company Saatchi and Saatchi. They created a poster of a queue of people at an unemployment office with the headline 'Labour isn't working'. Except the people in the poster were not unemployed but young Conservatives from Hendon, who wore shoes rather than Doc Martens or daps.

Thatcher also employed a television adviser called Gordon Reece. In his focus groups he found voters thought Thatcher sounded shrill, domineering and uncaring. They were right. We hated her voice. As a consequence Reece arranged for a National Theatre voice coach to teach her how to lower her pitch. Her voice became lower and more intimate. It also became slower and more patronising. I agreed with Keith Waterhouse who said, "I cannot bring myself to vote for a woman who has been voice trained to speak to me as if my dog just died."

Thatcher decided not to participate in a head-to-head TV debate with Callaghan. She was a coward; she was running scared. Instead she appeared at stage-managed events in front of adoring fans where Lulu serenaded her with a version of *Hello, Maggie*. Mum never really understood why I objected every time she put on a Lulu record.

Thatcher's campaign made a passionate case for individual freedoms. In her manifesto she argued, "The balance of our society has been increasingly tilted in favour of the State at the expense of individual freedom." Her campaign made no sense to me. She was no freedom fighter. That didn't stop her making a speech on 29 April, that castigated the Labour Party for eroding individual freedom. She said, "Freedom is the most precious thing of all ... government takes it away by stealth ... we will fight for these things, and fight, and fight, and fight again." Maybe she had watched *Flashing Blade*.

Thatcher promoted a pernicious set of myths about merit and social mobility. She argued it didn't matter where you were born, what your gender was or your race. If you worked hard, you would progress and move up the social ladder. Of course it was true for some, a precious few but not for the vast majority of people and it wasn't exactly a fair fight. Those of us from Swindon knew that we did not start life on an equal footing. Thatcher with her sculpted hair, her power suits and her pearls was not of our world. In Swindon a pearl necklace was slang for something quite different to the present Denis gave Margaret when her twins were born in 1953.

The idea of social mobility horrified the posh folk that lived in the Cotswold villages around Lechlade. They didn't want their Quentin or Charlotte to slide down the social ladder. They used their sharp elbows to ensure their family maintained its social status, and made sure their kids had a head start by attending private schools where they learnt Latin and the violin. In our sixth form, Charlotte, who had been privately educated, came to our school to do her 'A' levels. She spoke with a clarity and crispness about subjects which I knew nothing about. She had a cat with a weird name. Her mother, who was tall, thin and angular, said the cat was called Wesley Barrell, after a company that made bespoke British furniture. I didn't know what bespoke meant but I nodded knowingly.

From the way Charlotte's mother looked at my 'I'm voting Labour' badge it was clear that she didn't approve. She was also not impressed when I said private schools should be abolished. She argued, like Thatcher, that it was about freedom of choice, that she should be free to choose to send Charlotte to private school, neglecting the fact other people do not have such choices. To her the most evil thing in the world was the inheritance tax introduced by the Labour government in 1975. It was outrageous that they couldn't pass on their wealth to their children without paying tax. Like Thatcher she used meritocracy to justify inequality. They had earned their money unlike those at the bottom of the social ladder who hadn't worked hard enough. People made their own choices, whether that was working in the city or working down a mine. According to Charlotte's mother if someone was poor that was because they had chosen, by accident or design, to be poor.

In her last TV election broadcast Thatcher said, "Somewhere ahead lies greatness for our country again." It was a message she repeated over and over. She was like a Dalek from *Doctor Who*: 'Make Britain great again, make Britain great again, exterminate, exterminate.'

My parents agreed that Tessa could stay at our house on the night before the election because we had to be up early. It was our job to post leaflets before people left for work encouraging our supporters to turn out and vote. I found it hard to sleep. I wasn't sure if it was the anticipation of the election or knowing Tessa was sleeping in my sister's room.

After we had delivered our first batch of leaflets Tessa and I returned to the committee room where our campaign team checked the returns from polling stations and ticked off the people who had promised to support us when we were canvassing. The team told us they were preparing a 'get out the vote' operation. We were not asked to take part but it simply meant calling on those that hadn't voted and encouraging them to vote, even offering them a lift if necessary.

In the afternoon Tessa and I visited a polling station to collect returns from our supporters who sat outside, diligently writing down numbers from polling cards. At one polling station our recorder was a small lady wearing a headscarf. She was chatting happily to a Tory wearing a big blue rosette and sharing numbers with him. I gave her my death stare. Didn't she know it was wrong to talk to people from the Tory Party? When we returned we were left kicking our heels and by early evening we were pacing aimlessly. Finally we were told we could go home as there was little else for us to do.

1979 was the first time I stayed up to watch a general election unfold. It was my induction to the Thursday Night Club. Most people are not enthusiastic about elections, it is not just Brenda from Bristol. However, for a small group of us a general election is more exciting than all our childhood Christmases combined. We become more energised than a Labrador puppy spinning in circles waiting to be fed. We constantly monitor and evaluate every event during the campaign. It may look as if we are walking the dog or putting out the recycling but the reality is our brains are doing political calculations. We are weighing up the impact of the latest interview or opinion poll. We bore everyone with constant discussions about margins of error and historical voting patterns. Our partners, those that haven't left us or stopped listening, become resigned to discussions about political minutiae.

For people like us the space between elections is equivalent to the summer break for an obsessive football or *Strictly Come Dancing* fan. We fill our time researching data, reading policy papers, assessing party conference speeches and debating campaign strategies. Our Christmas wish lists are full of political biographies. In the absence of UK elections we turn to other people's elections. We become experts on the US electoral college or the two-stage French presidential elections. We also love referendums but nothing can quite match the buzz of a general election.

We are the Thursday Night Club. We stock up on coffee, beer, biscuits and chocolate before we settle down to watch the general election results come through. We clear our diaries and frequently book leave for the day after an election. These nights are our equivalent of a Northern Soul all-nighter. We know we will be exhausted the next day.

We never need to be asked if we stayed up for Portillo. In 1997 we watched live as Stephen Twigg's grin spread across his face. In 2019 we were still awake at 3.45 a.m. when Jo Swinson lost her seat. In 2016 we were still awake at 4.40 a.m. when David Dimbleby announced the result of the EU referendum: "The British people have spoken and the answer is ... we're out."

We don't just remember the big election shocks such as Theresa May failing to get a majority in 2017 or John Major succeeding against the odds in 1992. It is the small things, the details we remember that mark us out as a club member. For example, we know that the person John Prescott punched in 2001 had a mullet or 'Bundesliga hair' as it is known in Denmark. That David Cameron didn't simply forget which football team he supported but claimed to support West Ham rather than Aston Villa. That the pensioner Gordon Brown called a bigoted woman was Gillian Duffy, and that Neil Kinnock fell into the sea at Brighton not Blackpool or Bournemouth.

I sat down to watch the results full of Christmas Eve anticipation as the clock ticked towards ten o'clock. The present I wanted more than anything was a Labour victory. On the hour came the dramatic introductory theme music taken from Rick Wakeman's concept album *The Myths and Legends of King Arthur* which the BBC used for their election night programmes. It became known to those of us in the Thursday Night Club simply as Arthur. The faces of the three main party leaders appeared on bright red, blue and orange backgrounds. An electric green Big Ben emerged from a black hole, rosettes span around in circles and Wakeman went mad on his synthesiser. It reminded me of the *Doctor Who* theme tune which had sent me rushing behind the sofa in earlier years. As the music faded the screen displayed the words, 'Decision 79'. This was it.

On the TV David Dimbleby wore a garish pink tie as he presented the BBC election coverage. Maybe a red or blue tie would be taken as support for one of the main political parties. I was still thinking about his pink tie when he introduced the predicted result. The Conservatives were forecast to win but not decisively. My parents appeared indifferent to the news and said they were going up to bed. They left me to watch the results alone. My brother and sister were already in bed. My mum made me promise not to stay up too late as she closed the lounge door.

I sat enthralled in front of the TV. I was encouraged by the swingometer. According to the presenter the Conservatives needed a 4.5 percent swing to get a majority. The polls predicted a swing of 4.7 percent. That was close and within the margin of error. I prayed that Thatcher would not win. I was jumpy, my knees were bouncing and I started eating digestive biscuits at a rather frantic pace while I waited.

My optimism increased when the BBC reported on a poll conducted in Derby North. According to the reporter the seat was the forty-third on a list of marginal seats that Thatcher needed to win to have a majority and become prime minister. The poll predicted a small swing to Labour, which meant Thatcher was not going to get the seats she needed. We were going to defeat the dark side. I loved the BBC for its poll and I loved Derby North for its good sense. I treated myself to another digestive.

Two minutes later the BBC corrected the poll saying it actually showed a 2 percent swing to the Conservatives. For God's sake, the BBC was useless. How could they get something so simple so wrong? What were the people of Derby North thinking? As if to answer my question the BBC asked a panel of four undecided voters from the constituency how they had voted. Three of the voters said they had voted Conservative. Why had the BBC picked them, they looked like Tories, of course they were going to vote Tory. It didn't mean anything and as for the poll, well, I never trusted the polls anyway.

By the time the early results started to come through I had finished the digestives and started a pack of Garibaldi biscuits. The results appeared to show a consistent swing of around 5 percent to the Conservatives. The experts on the TV said it was almost certain that Thatcher had won. My knees stopped bouncing. I slipped back on the sofa, arms holding my churning stomach. The biscuits were no longer appealing; the currants looked like dead flies that had drowned in the dough.

The Swindon result appeared on the screen without warning. 'Lab hold Swindon.' All our canvassing and leafleting had paid off. I stood up, punched the air and chanted at the TV, "Swindon Town, red and white army! Swindon Town, red and white army!" Come on, we could still do this. Francois and Guillot didn't give up in *Flashing Blade* when things looked hopeless, they succeeded against the odds. Like us they had right on their side.

My belief in a Labour comeback was reinforced when the Tories failed to win Derby North. Where was that panel of Tory voters now? Take that you bastards.

I had trusted the experts when they said Derby North was the seat Thatcher needed to win to become prime minister. But they lied to me. The seats above and below Derby North on the BBC's list were turning blue. Each new result was like a body blow. 'Con gain Anglesey.' 'Con gain Dartford.' 'Con gain Fulham.' 'Con gain Liverpool Garston.' Derby North was left looking like a lonely red island amongst a sea of blue seats as the Tory tide swept in. My stomach heaved like a heavy load in a washing machine. At 3 a.m. the BBC reported that the Labour Prime Minister, Jim Callaghan, had admitted defeat and thanked his campaign staff for their work. I tried to concentrate, to make sense of what had happened. How could the British people have voted for Thatcher?

The big swings to the Conservatives were in the south, luckily most voters held out against Thatcher in the north. Peter Jenkins called it a two nation election with a clear divide between north and south. I was slumped on the sofa but still awake at 3.57 a.m. when the former Liberal leader Jeremy Thorpe lost his seat. Robin Day asked him if his forthcoming trial for conspiracy to murder was a factor in him losing. Thorpe replied, "Put it this way Robin, I don't think it helped."

The professionals were of the view that the Conservatives had won despite Thatcher. I was less sure. Her 'make Britain great again' narrative was a simple story that was easy to understand and repeat. It also resonated with many traditional working-class Labour voters. The Conservatives gained an 11 percent swing amongst the skilled working class and a 9 percent swing amongst the unskilled working class. How could working class people vote for Thatcher? I was bewildered. Seriously, what the hell were they thinking? It didn't make any sense.

At least the people of Swindon hadn't been fooled. More than half of voters in the town had backed Labour; it was a reduced majority but we had won. The *Advertiser* headline was, 'Swindon defies the country as Thatcher comes to power'. I was proud of the town and our campaign. Tessa and I had helped to ensure a Labour victory. Thatcher may have been on the way to a forty-three seat majority nationally but we held firm.

Nile Rodgers of Chic says that the summer of 1979 was the best ever. I beg to disagree. As much as I enjoyed *Le Freak* and

Dance, Dance, Dance. Life was about more than singing Yowza, Yowza, Yowza. I found it hard to enjoy anything knowing Thatcher was prime minister. I wasn't depressed though, the election result galvanised me. I doubled down on my beliefs and convictions. The people of Swindon had shown the way.

9

THE UPPER STRATTON WORKMAN'S REFORM CLUB

"After a nuclear attack, there will be a short period before fallout starts to descend. Use the time to do essential tasks."

In March 1980, just days before my eighteenth birthday, *Panorama* broadcast a documentary called, 'If the bomb drops'. The programme included clips from official government 'Protect and Survive' films which optimistically said you could survive a nuclear war by building a shelter under your stairs. Less reassuringly the films provided guidance on what to do with the dead members of your family. They suggested you wrap their bodies in polythene, tag and bury them. We had little space in our small garden, we would have to dig up the vegetable patch. My dad was worryingly unconcerned that we didn't have large polythene sheets when I asked him.

The films played the sounds of attack and fallout warnings. I tried to memorise them so that I knew which was which. They explained that the most dangerous aspect of a nuclear attack was fallout, as this was carried in the air for hundreds of miles. This meant we were at risk even if no bombs fell on Swindon, though I was sure a sharp-eyed Russian would have added us to the list of targets. We had the railway works and the Pressed Steel Fisher factory.

In the event of an attack we had to shelter under our stairs for fourteen days. I wasn't sure the five of us would fit under the stairs, even if we cleaned out the pantry. We also had to store a minimum of three and a half gallons of water per person; that was seventeen and a half gallons or one hundred and forty pints of water. Seven full milk crates. My parents were seriously unprepared for a nuclear war.

According to a BBC poll, 40 percent of the adult population thought a nuclear war was likely in the next ten years. I was concerned. I might not even make it to thirty. The Conservative government of course said we didn't need to be worried. The Home Secretary, Willie Whitelaw, claimed that even if there was a war, most houses in the UK offered a reasonable degree of protection against nuclear explosions and radioactive fallout. Maybe he had not visited Swindon, or seen the houses we lived in. I can only think he lived in a bunker or more likely that he had a second home in the Scottish Islands.

I paid forty-five pence for a stapled copy of a pamphlet called 'Protest and Survive'. The message was simple, if we wished to survive, we had to protest. Membership of the Campaign for Nuclear Disarmament (CND) grew strongly and I was one of the thousands that joined up. I pinned a new black and white CND peace badge to my jacket.

On my eighteenth birthday my parents bought me a Timex watch and my dad took me to the Stratton Reform Club. He told Mum we were going "over the road" though you reached it by going down the alley next to the school. The club was sandwiched between rows of terraced houses on Beechcroft Road. Dad signed me in at the door and we entered a smoke-filled room that smelt like November bonfires. Under a blue haze men were playing dominoes and cribbage on low Formica tables.

As we made our way to the bar, men looked up and greeted Dad with smiles and shouts of, "Alright Cliffy?" There are people that make other people happy simply by arriving. People whose presence creates behavioural banter and back slapping. People that make the world more cheerful. Dad was one of those people. It was a characteristic my brother inherited but which passed me by.

Standing by the bar were my dad's two best mates Bob and Tony.

"Alright, Steve," said Bob, with a broad welcoming smile. He loomed large above Tony and my dad like a gentle giant. He reminded me of Chewbacca standing over Hans Solo and Luke Skywalker. Tony was small like my dad and reminded me of Nobby Stiles with his receding hairline.

"Good to see you mate," said Tony. "Your old fella has been telling us all about you."

"Don't worry, we didn't believe a word of it," said Bob, beaming at me.

"Must be your turn to get the round in Cliffy," said Tony. "You've got to watch him," he said, pointing to my dad with his thumb. "Make sure the bugger doesn't go home before it's his round." He winked at me and smiled, revealing teeth stained from tobacco.

At the bar Dad explained that rounds were part of pub culture. The basic rule was that everyone in your group has to buy a round of drinks. It wasn't altruistic. If you bought a round of drinks each person was obliged to reciprocate. "You should never leave someone with an empty glass when it's your shout," said Dad. A person who failed to buy their round in the club was viewed as a social pariah. To Dad it was the worst indignity and humiliation a man could suffer. He would often explain to

Mum that the reason he wasn't home earlier was because he had to buy a round. No reasonable wife could expect their husband to leave before they had bought a round.

The culture of rounds was partly responsible for the heavy drinking and alcohol-related illnesses. In 1978, guidelines had been published to encourage reasonable drinking. They recommended men should not drink more than seventy units of alcohol a week, the equivalent of four pints of beer or one bottle of wine a day. But no one in the club drank wine. The beer bellies of the men in the club attested to their reasonable drinking behaviour.

Dad leant on the bar next to a display board where packets of Big D nuts hid the body of a woman in her lingerie. Half of the packets had been removed and you could see down to her navel. "How are you doing Maureen?" Dad asked the woman behind the bar. She reminded me of Sybil Fawlty; her hair was curled like my mum's after it had been shampooed and set. Her gold earrings dangled down to her shoulders. "Mustn't grumble, Cliff." Her voice was deep and husky from years of shouting last orders through the cigarette smoke. "Can you give us four pints of your finest rubbish." Dad saw the confused look on my face and explained that was how you ordered 'three Bs', the local brewery's Best Bitter Beer. "You'll hear some of the guys ask for a pint of sheep's dip," he said, "which means a pint of the club's weakest beer."

Three Bs was the same beer my friends drank from bottles outside Sims Chippy. It was warm, bitter and soapy. It made my body shudder involuntarily at the aftertaste. I asked Dad if I could have a lager as I didn't like beer. A look somewhere between a grimace and disappointment spread across his face. His lips tightened and he slowly sucked in air between his teeth. He made that sound plumbers make before they tell you bad news. He was quiet for a moment and then said under his breath, "What sort of man doesn't drink beer?" He couldn't bring himself to change the order; maybe the shame would be too great. A son that didn't drink beer. No, that wasn't going to happen. We walked back to the table each carrying two identical pints of beer.

"Did you finish getting those carrots planted?" Bob asked Tony.

"Yep, good job the clocks went forward on Sunday," said Tony. "I managed to get them done before the light faded."

The men all had allotments down by Cowleaze Walk, a few hundred metres along Beechcroft Road from the club. They would spend hours sat by their sheds sharing jokes, tips, tools and their crops. We would sometimes go with Dad at the weekend where he showed us how to use the dibber to make holes for the spuds. He would gently push us aside to check our work saying, "Let the dog see the rabbit."

In the corner of the club was a colourful one-arm bandit, where a balding man was pushing coins into the silver slot. There was a ratcheting sound as he pulled the handle down and span the three columns of cherries and crosses.

"It's bloody lovely, having lighter evenings," said Dad. "I never understand why we have to put the clocks back in the winter."

"It's something to do with Scottish farmers," said Bob.

"What's that go to do with the price of tea?" said Tony. "I don't see what difference it makes to them. It's not like the cows can tell the time."

"Did you get the van back alright Sunday?" said Dad.

"Yeah, it wasn't too bad," said Bob, "though my damn back aches from shifting all that gear. It was chockfull of stuff it was."

"Took three of us to get that bloody great wardrobe up the stairs. It was a right bugger," said Tony.

"Pete's missus has more clothes than C&A I reckon," said Bob.

The three men had helped Pete to move house on the

weekend. According to Bob the removal companies charged a fortune and it was easier for them to do it. I was confident that if I ever needed anything, the men from the club would be there to help. They would often have a whip-round for someone who had fallen on hard times. One of the men would walk around the tables with a bucket and chivvy everyone to contribute. They would moan about it but they were generous with their time. In the 1970s they spent their weekends installing central heating at each other's homes. When my parents decided to convert our front and back rooms into a through lounge, a group of Dad's mates turned up to help remove the wall and install an RSJ.

As I sat nursing my beer I was surprised to hear the men talk about the Russian invasion of Afghanistan.

"Bitten off more than they can chew I reckon," said Tony.

The discussion was followed by long rants about state benefits and the cost of fraud. According to Thatcher the rise in unemployment had nothing to do with her government and everything to do with work-shy benefit scroungers. She claimed that £200m was fiddled each year by 'social security scroungers'. I knew the figure was nonsense, something a Tory party strategist had made up. In the *Militant* it said there was no evidence to back up the figure and contrary to Thatcher's claims academic studies suggested the real figure for fraud was much lower. I thought the men would be pleased to know this information.

"The latest studies suggest the real cost of fraud is much lower than £200m," I said.

I surprised myself by speaking; previously I had kept quiet when the men discussed politics. The men were also startled and looked at me. All except Dad, who picked up his pint and drained the rest of his beer.

"No, you got that wrong, Steve," said Tony. "Benefits fraud is a lot higher than two hundred million."

"Yep, I reckon it's way higher than that," said Bob.

"I am telling you it is," said Tony. "Look at that Newsome guy, out gallivanting while claiming benefits for a home and five kids."

He was referring to newspaper stories about a 'super scrounger' called John Newsome who was found guilty of failing to declare his savings when claiming benefits for his family of seven. The papers reported he had jumped the housing queue, got a £200 state handout, free furniture and £50 a week social security. A week later he was hounded out of Rotherham by furious neighbours.

Tony put his pint down on a beer mat, sat back and crossed his arms. "The bastard should be strung up," he said. There was a clatter of skittles from the back room.

Capital punishment for benefit fraud seemed a little harsh but there was a nodding of heads and general agreement around the table that the government's £200m was a severe under-estimate. The men were apparently experts on social security fraud.

I sipped gently at my beer and decided to stay quiet. An old guy in a beige diamond checked jumper, like the ones Val Doonican wore on TV, was playing dominoes on the next table. He said loudly to no one in particular, "We are a soft touch, bloody idiots we are." He then knocked his knuckles on the table to indicate to the other players that he couldn't go.

The men's attitude to fraud was slightly odd given that they often paid cash for items that 'fell off the back of a lorry'. It seemed that stealing from a company and avoiding tax was fair game but claiming benefits you were not entitled to was beyond the pale.

The press stories about scroungers didn't help. It was easy to highlight individual cases and the constant drip, drip of stories was hardening public attitudes. In the spring of 1980, Keith Waterhouse in the *Daily Mirror* said it had become respectable to view people on social security as scroungers, that the unemployed as idlers and most blacks as criminals. I wasn't sure about all his points but from the discussion in the club he was on the money about benefit scroungers.

I thought the men in the club would be enthusiastic about the state benefits system that Tressell had inspired. I was surprised they fell for stories made up by the Tories. They also didn't have the affection for Tony Benn and the Labour Party that I expected. They were probably suffering from something Trotsky had called 'false consciousness'. They were not yet aware of their historic mission to destroy Thatcher and capitalism.

10

IRELAND

The Labour Party Young Socialists was the youth wing of the Labour Party but there were few young people at our meetings. The older comrades that came to speak called themselves Trotskyists and supported the ideas of Militant. They spoke with a Liverpool accent and wore donkey jackets, a thick woollen black coat originally worn by workers on the Manchester ship canal. I was determined to add one to my revolutionary wardrobe.

After our LPYS sessions the comrades would retire to the pub and I started to tag along. One evening Trotsky asked me what I wanted to drink and it took me a moment to reply. I certainly didn't want a pint of soapy beer. One of the guys in Dad's club drank something called rum and black. It sounded like a grown up drink so I asked for a rum and black. This seemed to take Trotsky by surprise, as he asked me again just to be sure.

What arrived was a small glass with a deep red liquid that smelt and tasted a little bit like Ribena. It was sickly sweet but drinkable. Luckily it was also a small drink, not like the pints I had to drink at the club. It wasn't quite like Ribena as following a long night in the pub I found the floor wouldn't stay still and our front door kept moving away as I tried to insert my key into the lock. In bed that night I lay on my back desperately hoping my heaving stomach would settle. I would like to say I made it to the bathroom to be sick but that wouldn't be true. When I finally conceded defeat I simply turned my head to the side and vomited all over the bedroom floor. My mum's reaction was pure fury. It was like the time Dad mistook her wardrobe for the bathroom in a drunken sleep. She was woken by the sound of him pissing all over her shoes.

The carpets in the pub were sticky; each time I lifted my foot it was like tearing Sellotape from the floor. It was sometimes hard to see people across the room through the cloud of tobacco smoke that carried with it an aroma of beer, cheap perfume and aftershave. Once enough seats had been found the comrades would have obscure arguments. One night there was a long discussion about Mike Baldwin and the portrayal of capitalism in *Coronation Street*. On another night we strained to hear Trotsky above Gary Numan on the jukebox, as he criticised the position taken on Ireland by the Socialist Workers Party. A young woman seated opposite me asked who they were. She was either a lot more confident than I was or she hadn't yet learnt the art of nodding knowingly. The discussion that followed was my first glimpse into the Trotskyist family tree, at least the UK part of the family.

I took out my pad to make notes. My advice for any budding revolutionary, or aspiring management consultant, is to always have a notepad and pen handy. I had to write swiftly to keep up as Trotsky talked about the Workers Revolutionary Party, the Revolutionary Workers Party, the Revolutionary Socialist League, the Revolutionary Communist Group and the Revolutionary Communist Tendency. It was easy to get the groups confused; Trotskyists should really be more creative about names. Trotsky told us the RCT were like the People's

Front of Judea in the film *Life of Brian*. They hated other revolutionary groups more than Thatcher.

According to Trotsky the most important group was the Revolutionary Socialist League (RSL) which was formed in the 1950s and led by a guy called Ted Grant. This group became the Militant Tendency, which produced the *Militant* newspaper and ran our Swindon LPYS meetings. I circled the group's name with my pen. Trotsky talked about Grant in hushed tones as though he was a Buddhist Zen master and had the authority to pass down the true Trotskyist traditions.

Trotsky explained to us that Ted Grant and the real Leon Trotsky had agreed in the 1930s that Marxists in the UK should work within the Labour Party. It was a strategy called 'entryism'. Our job was to take control of the Labour Party and to provide a Marxist leadership that would raise the consciousness of working people. This made sense to me; it was like my dad said, when he wasn't singing *Puff the Magic Dragon*, Labour was the party of the working man.

I spent more and more of my evenings and weekends reading the Militant booklets that Trotsky gave me. After a while I became confident enough to ask questions and to engage in discussions at the LPYS meetings. There was so much I didn't understand. The Militant comrades were ambitious educators. Earnest young comrades sought to explain Marx's theories of surplus value and the nature of dialectical change. It was less easy to grasp than the lyrics of The Jam but I was determined to learn.

The more I read the more I became aware of the politics of Ireland. The troubles in Northern Ireland were constantly mentioned on the TV news. In 1972, when I was ten, the IRA started a bombing campaign in England which provided the backdrop to my formative years. In 1973, they exploded car bombs in central London, followed by bombs at Marble Arch, Oxford Street and Horseferry Road. In 1974, bombs destroyed two pubs in Birmingham, killing twenty-one people. A bomb also exploded at the Houses of Parliament. In 1975 and 1976, there were more bombings in pubs frequented by soldiers. In 1977, no less than seven bombs exploded in London's West End. In 1978, when I turned sixteen, the IRA exploded bombs across the country in Manchester, Liverpool, Coventry, Bristol and Southampton.

My dad and his mates hated the IRA. So did Swindon's football fans who, when fed up of attacking the opposition, sang "Fuck the IRA". Who wouldn't hate terrorists that targeted and killed innocent civilians? The carnage, injuries and deaths were covered extensively in the news bulletins. Of course you would despise the people that caused such suffering. I never really understood why the bombing campaign was taking place. The news rarely provided any historical context to dramatic events, focusing instead on the numbers of dead and injured. Front pages carried pictures of victims and raged at the bloody murderers. In March 1976, the *Daily Mirror* had called the IRA 'merchants of death' after a bomb exploded at the Ideal Home Exhibition. The report contained details of dozens of people maimed for life. It seemed senseless; why bomb visitors to an exhibition?

It was left to my new Militant comrades in the LPYS to educate me about Ireland. Sitting in a circle on cold plastic chairs Jim provided us with a history of Irish politics and I took notes in my diary.

"In 1912, James Connolly founded the Irish Labour Party as the political wing of the Irish Trade Unions Congress," said Jim. "He also founded the Irish Citizen Army to defend workers and particularly strikers."

Jim told us Connolly led an armed revolution in 1916, for a

free Ireland, one free from British rule, and signed a proclamation of Irish independence. When the uprising failed Connolly was executed.

"He was too weak to stand for the firing squad," said Jim. "So the British soldiers tied him to a chair and shot him."

This did not seem like the British sense of fair play my dad talked about when shouting at Italian players during the World Cup.

"In 1921, the British partitioned Ireland," Jim continued. "Rather than agree to full Irish independence the government simply drew a line to create Northern Ireland. The six counties in the north."

I had read about the six counties; so that was what they referred to.

"The boundary was gerrymandered," said Jim. "The boundaries were carefully drawn to ensure there was a Protestant majority in Northern Ireland and British control."

He went on to explain that the newly created Northern Ireland was theoretically democratic but by creating an in-built Protestant majority there was effectively one party rule by the Protestant Unionists or what Alexis de Tocqueville called the tyranny of the majority.

"In the six counties there was systematic discrimination against Catholics and nationalists," said Trotsky, who had taken off his greatcoat and put it on the back of the empty chair next to him. "This led to protests and clashes with the Protestant Royal Ulster Constabulary."

He went on to tell us how in 1969, the British deployed the army in Northern Ireland as an occupying force to support the RUC and suppress the Catholic protests. I tried to imagine what it would be like but I couldn't get my head around troops from another country patrolling Swindon's town centre. Just seeing Oxford fans was bad enough and the STAB boys would swiftly chase them to the railway station.

"In 1972, the British army shot dead twenty-six unarmed civilians on Bloody Sunday," said Trotsky.

"Twenty-six unarmed people," repeated Alice, who then paused to let it sink in. After a few seconds she said again, "They murdered twenty-six unarmed people; many were shot in the back. Six of the dead were just seventeen."

I now knew what had provoked the bombing campaign. My sympathy was with the Republicans who wanted to remove the British to create a free and united Ireland. My knees began to bounce up and down. As I thought about it further I felt a tension in my stomach and an expanding lump in my throat. Did that mean I supported the terrorists?

"We support the aim of a united Ireland," said Trotsky. "But we condemn the IRA and their tactics."

I stopped bouncing my foot, leant back in my chair and relaxed. That was good, we condemned the terrorists and their bombings. My dad didn't talk about politics but I knew he would kill me, or at least kick me out of the house, if I got involved with people that supported the IRA. In my relief I spoke up for the first time.

"I agree. It isn't right to blow up people as they enjoy a drink in a pub."

Trotsky looked at me with a grave expression on his face. After a pause he continued, "We condemn the IRA because violence by individuals is no substitute for mobilising the working class."

I nodded in agreement, of course, there was that as well.

My Irish political education sessions, Militant Tendency style, came with homework. Trotsky took me aside and gave me pamphlets to read. He asked me to lead a discussion on terrorism at the next group meeting. I diligently read everything and at the next meeting I reported the Militant line about the importance of uniting workers rather than supporting acts of individual terrorism. It was my first ever presentation.

Shortly afterwards I found myself reading a poem about the Easter 1916 uprising to my 'A' level English class. You might think I had chosen to do this but it was serendipity. It certainly wasn't my choice. There were only seven or eight of us in the class but I wasn't keen on reading aloud to the group. We were studying the poetry of William Butler Yeats and my friend Richard had just finished reading. He was much more confident than I was. He played the piano at school assembly and was the lead in the school performance of *The Mikado*. The middle-class kids appeared to be trained musicians. They came to school with instruments in leather cases and read music, which might as well have been Arabic to me.

Despite keeping my head down I was asked by our bearded English teacher to read the next poem out loud to the class. I squirmed a little and turned the page. There it was, just like that, a poem titled 'Easter 1916'.

I began slowly. As I read each line I began to understand. I knew what Yeats was describing. The more I read the more I was pulled in deeper and deeper. I found I was no longer reading about the uprising, I was experiencing it. Those 'vivid faces' among 'grey eighteenth century houses'. The conversations of those brave men that 'dreamed and are dead'. Those that had sacrificed their lives for a free Ireland. But they had not died needlessly; with the uprising everything had 'changed, changed utterly'. They had achieved something so significant in defeat that it had transformed the world. Their passion for a free Ireland was as beautiful as their deaths were tragic. Again and again and again the verses ended with the haunting words, 'a terrible beauty is born'.

Towards the end of the poem I found myself almost tearful as I read out loud the names of the fallen:

"MacDonagh and MacBride

And Connolly and Pearse."

By the end of the poem I was an Irish republican.

I also became a lover of Yeats. Unbidden by my teacher, I read all of his poems eagerly. I was mesmerised by 'The Wild Swans At Coole' and 'The White Birds'. The writing was magical. I longed to be able to write with such exquisite, precise elegance. I had never written anything beyond my essays at school, in which I had tried many times to capture the joy of catching Chub on the Thames. At one point my teacher specifically asked me not to write any more stories about fishing.

I wanted to seize the words of Yeats and hold them forever. For the first time in my life I memorised poems so they would be with me always. I found the rhythm and cadence of *The White Birds* made it easy to memorise. The words of Yeats became stored inside my head. They became part of me.

I read more about Yeats and learnt that while he supported Irish nationalism he was an observer rather than an activist. But it was not enough to observe, not enough to write beautiful poetry, not even enough to inspire generations of Irish nationalists. It was necessary to act. This was made clear to Yeats by Maud Gonne, who inspired much of his writing, but he failed to heed her advice. If I had any ideology at eighteen, it was that you had to take responsibility, you had to try and change things. As Tessa made clear – you had to fight for what is right.

11

FREEDOM FIGHTERS

"Why do working-class people vote Tory?" I asked Trotsky. "It is obvious that they are the party of the rich. It makes no sense."

We were in a pub near the ABC Cinema. Trotsky had suggested we meet to discuss a pamphlet written by Ted Grant on the way forward for the UK after the election. The writing was dense to the point of being unreadable. I read some paragraphs three or four times, but I still failed to grasp what they meant. Trotsky asked if I had any questions. I did. Why had many working-class people voted for Thatcher? It made no sense to me. It was a conundrum more complex than an Agatha Christie mystery.

Trotsky said it was the lack of a Labour Marxist leadership that led working-class voters to vote Conservative.

"The working class haven't yet experienced a true socialist Labour government which acts in the interests of working people," he said. "The Labour leadership in attempting to manage capitalism undermined workers' living standards. They tried to control pay rises which led to conflicts with the unions and ultimately the 'winter of discontent'. It was these conflicts that brought down the Labour government."

I still wasn't sure why voters disappointed with Labour for being right wing would vote for an even more right-wing government, obviously I was missing something. When Trotsky repeated his arguments at the next LPYS meeting, I was still none the wiser. However, everyone else seemed to happily accept what he said; to them it seemed so obvious as to be axiomatic. I nodded knowingly but inside I remained confused. Clearly there was a lot I didn't understand.

Despite my doubts I started to memorise Trotsky's arguments, much like I had done with the poems of Yeats. I wanted to be able to repeat them when I argued with my school friends and their parents. I found myself increasingly arguing with adults as my friends had little interest in discussing politics.

My first major argument was with Charlotte's dad. He believed in Thatcher's monetary nonsense about balancing the books. I gave him my memorised lines of argument about the benefits of an expansionary fiscal policy and how government spending was needed to offset the fall in private spending. He had no response to my memorised facts and stopped arguing with me. At the time I took this to mean I had won the argument.

"Working people will become conscious of the implications of Thatcherism," Trotsky told us in our LPYS meeting. "Their material conditions will lead them to socialism."

I nodded knowingly. Material conditions? He couldn't mean the stuff Mum ran through her Singer sewing machine. I assumed he meant that people would realise voting Conservative was not in their interests. It was so obvious, I didn't understand why they hadn't seen it already. There was no way they would vote for Thatcher a second time. They would turn to the Labour Party and the unions. Over 50 percent of the population were in trade unions, one of the facts I had memorised, and the Labour Party was the political arm of the unions. It followed that people would turn to Labour. The party just needed the right leadership, a Marxist leadership, which Trotsky and Militant could provide.

At home I lay on my bed and read Grant's pamphlet again. I may not have understood everything but it was clear to me that the fight for socialism had to take place in the Labour Party. Grant had made this point in the very first editorial of the *Militant* newspaper in 1964: "The job is to carry the message of Marxism to the ranks of the Labour movement and to its young people." That was my mission, to spread the word about Marxism. Okay, I hadn't actually read Marx but I would get around to that in time. Much like I would learn Spanish one day.

I didn't grasp all the theoretical arguments Trotsky made, or why working-class people voted Tory, but the demands of Militant were clear. They were also easy to remember and repeat. A thirty-five-hour week without a reduction in pay, reversing public expenditure cuts, nationalising the top two hundred banks and monopolies, and abolishing the medieval House of Lords. Who could call themselves a democrat and support the unelected Lords?

Grant called the *Financial Times* the most serious journal of capitalism and quoted extensively from the newspaper. It made sense; we needed to understand our enemy. It was like understanding the strengths and weaknesses of opposing football teams. I went to the local newsagents to buy a copy but it transpired that the people of Penhill didn't read the *FT*, in fact it seemed that no one in Swindon read the *FT*. In paper shop after paper shop there were piles of red-topped tabloids but no *FT*. When I asked for the paper I was met with blank faces from above the rows of Spangles, Sherbet Dips, Curly Wurlys and Caramacs.

Eventually I found a copy of the *FT* in the local library. It was printed on soft salmon paper, a bit like the *Football Pink*. The paper's writers were concerned that inflation might go to 20 percent by the end of 1980. There were articles about the Iranian revolution and the impact on oil prices. There were also articles on steel strikes in America. It was like trying to understand a world jigsaw puzzle when you only had a few pieces to analyse. I needed an ABC book of global politics.

Tessa, Phil and I started a local campaign about youth unemployment, which was rising sharply under Thatcher. We made some banners and stood outside the Town Hall in Swindon's Old Town to make our demands. Our three-person demo attracted the attention of a local journalist and we were featured in the *Advertiser*. There was a picture of the three of us and the headline, 'Freedom Fighters', but I can't for the life of me recall what we wanted to be free.

I basked in the glory of being a freedom fighter. I wanted to be like Che Guevara. Okay, I admit the only things I knew about Guevara came from the TV sitcom *Citizen Smith*. The image of Guevara, by former fashion photographer Alberto Korda, was prominent on Wolfie's T-shirts and badges. By 1979, it had become an iconic image and the most reproduced photograph in the world. Helen of Troy may have been the 'the face that launched a thousand ships' but Che was the face that drove thousands of teenagers to join Trotskyist groups. He was our romantic hero, literally the pin-up model for all would-be revolutionaries. Unlike other boys who purchased the Athena tennis girl poster for their walls, I proudly bought a two-tone, glossy red poster of Che gazing into the distance.

In the LPYS meetings, everyone knew Militant was a Trotskyist group. The comrades didn't really seem to hide it. Quite the opposite, they were particularly proud of their history, of the RSL and of being the true descendants of Trotsky. However, outside the meetings they argued they were just a group of people on the left of the Labour Party who supported the ideas of the *Militant* newspaper. It was like arguing Schrödinger's cat was both alive and dead at the same time. Revolutionary politics was confusing.

Trotsky was full of praise for my reading and my contributions to the discussions. He gave me a copy of Lenin's *The State and Revolution* to read and discuss with him. It was a difficult read but he helped me understand the key points. The state was a product of class conflict which emerged to enforce the rule of the rich over the working class. I think he was referring to the state as the courts, the army, the police and prisons rather than my auntie Jean who posted vacancies in the Job Centre. Thus if you had a revolution the state would no longer be required as the rich would be dead.

According to Trotsky the revolutionary government would create a new state with their own courts, army, police and prisons to suppress counter revolutionaries and ensure the dictatorship of the working class. I was confused, wasn't this also a state? Trotsky reassured me it would be quite different from the capitalist state.

After more discussion sessions Trotsky gave me some documents which he said were secret internal papers, not be shared outside the Tendency, even with other members of the LPYS, and definitely not with members of the Labour Party. I understood and made sure that I hid the documents from my brother in our bedroom.

There was a lengthy document called *British Perspectives and*

Tasks and another called *What We Stand For,* which set out the demands of the Militant Tendency. I was already familiar with these and agreed with them. Unilateral nuclear disarmament, tick. Nationalisation of the top two hundred companies, tick. Abolition of the monarchy, tick. Reversal of Tory cuts, tick. A minimum wage of £120 a week, tick. Opposition to racial and sexual discrimination, tick. No platform for fascists, definitely tick.

I pinned a badge to my jacket, 'Militant: For Workers Unity and Socialism', and became a Militant supporter. There was no membership application or interview that I recall. One evening Trotsky, Jim and Alice simply asked me to help sell the newspaper and, partly flattered by the attention, I agreed.

A week later I watched as my dad brought his pushbike to a stop at the factory gates. In the early morning drizzle he dismounted and removed his trouser clips. He walked the bike through the entrance with the other men, shoulders hunched over his handlebars, face half-hidden by his cloth cap. I tried to catch his eye but he lowered his gaze and his lips tightened. He didn't acknowledge my presence. Maybe he was disappointed to see me or embarrassed, probably both.

I held copies of the *Militant* newspaper against my chest, hugging them as if they might protect me like a bulletproof vest. Under my chin the aroma of damp newsprint mingled with the misty air. My comrades continued to hawk the paper, walking up and down shouting, "Kick Thatcher out, buy the *Militant.*" Most of the men ignored us but one shouted, "Fuck off back to Russia." He clearly didn't understand that we were Trotskyists not Stalinists. I blamed the education system. There was too much about the Tudors and too little about the Russian revolution.

That afternoon, waiting for Dad to arrive home, I paced up and down the lounge rehearsing what to say in my head. I knew he didn't share my passion for socialism. He was a Labour man but thought politics was not for the likes of us. He believed there was no point making trouble or trying to change the world. You just had to make the best of what you had and not complain.

Unable to sit and watch the TV with my brother and sister, I helped Mum lay the table for tea. On *Newsround* I listened to a report on British plans for elections in Zimbabwe Rhodesia and how two rebels, Nkomo and Mugabe, had resorted to violence. Of course they didn't say anything about colonial racism. John Craven also reported on a panic at Chipperfield's circus where two elephants had charged towards Princess Anne.

When Dad arrived home he sat in his armchair and opened the *Advertiser*. He never said anything, not even when I stood next to him in the kitchen to dry the dishes. He must have been able to hear the thumping of my heart but he just passed me the plates to dry. Maybe he thought it was just a phase and I would grow out of it, much like when I supported Chelsea in the 1970 FA Cup final.

12

SOCIALISTS ARE WEIRD

One of the few record albums my dad owned was *Johnny Cash at San Quentin*. He would often put it on the radiogram and sing along to *A Boy Named Sue*. The song was about a dysfunctional relationship between a father and son. I am not sure dysfunctional is really an adequate description; what do you call a relationship where a son tries to kill his estranged father for naming him Sue and cuts off a piece of his ear?

The good news is that after a bit of biting, gouging and kicking, the father and son in the song become reconciled. Luckily my father never considered naming me Sue or cutting off my ear, though I always suspected that when he sang about the world being rough and a man having to be tough, it was directed at me. I was a disappointment to my father in some ways. I think he struggled to understand how he had created someone so different from himself.

I sensed he was uncomfortable with my presence in the club. I suspected he moderated his language and his jokes in my presence. I wasn't sure he trusted me. When we walked back home after our second night at the club he had said,

"Don't tell your mother about Dave's bit on the side. Best to keep shtum."

One evening I offered to get the first round in, which I could afford thanks to my Saturday job at the Wiltshire Hotel. My parents valued hard work and didn't believe in pocket money. We were encouraged to get jobs to earn our own keep. I was making my first trip back from the bar with two pints when Bob arrived.

"What would you like, Bob?" I asked. "It's my shout."

"Thanks, I'll have a pint of three Bs," said Bob. I didn't really need to ask. He took off his stone coloured jacket. All the men wore similar jackets bought from M&S or C&A by their wives. One night Dad came home wearing someone else's jacket, not that he knew until Mum told him. He had to hurry back to the club as it had someone's house keys in the pocket.

As Bob sat down he said, "Nice to see the young uns buying a round."

When I returned I placed the pint in front of Bob. He picked up the glass and raised it in the air. "Cheers, Steve. That's just the badger."

I raised my glass and did my best not to grimace as I drank.

"How did you get on last night Cliffy?" Bob asked, as he set down his pint.

"We was doing alright until the end," said Dad. "It was close though. Next time we'll get the buggers."

I think they were talking about skittles.

"So you going back to the railways?" said Tony. It was more of a statement than a question.

"I am hoping so," said Dad. "Dave has put in a word for me."

I was surprised. He hadn't mentioned this before. It seemed like the sort of thing that he should have mentioned at the dinner table. I wondered if Mum knew.

"I heard they were taking on more coach fitters," said Bob.

"That'll be strange, going back after all these years," said Tony. "How long has it been?"

"Eighteen years," said Dad. "But Dave's been back for a while and says nothing much has changed."

"You'll be missed in the press shop," said Tony. "And by that blonde bird in the offices who comes down to collect the sheets. I see how she looks at you."

"I don't know what you mean," said Dad. He smiled and reached for his pint.

After a brief discussion of the upcoming darts match, their thoughts on why Bob Smith, the Swindon manager, should be sacked, and a comparison of the legs of the actress Victoria Principal and the newsreader Angela Rippon, there was a pause in the conversation.

"So how do you think our MP David Stoddart is doing?" I said.

The reaction was blank faces. This was obviously not a normal conversation starter. Dad gazed down at his glass, as if he never seen a pint of three Bs before. Bob looked blank and sipped at his beer. Maybe I should have carried on the discussion about Victoria Principal: "I see her new boyfriend is half her age, now there's a lucky guy." Instead I waited, and held my breath. From the corner of the room the one-arm bandit played a jingle as it sought to gain the attention of any nearby punters.

It was Tony that came to my rescue.

"He seems to do a good job. He came to the factory last year during the election and gave us a talk. I always thought he was one of those posh men like Benn, whose dad was a lord, but he said his dad was a miner in Wales. Said he had never seen a bathroom until he moved to London."

"Yep, he was one of the grammar school boys," said Bob. "Passed his eleven plus."

I looked at my dad whose face was impassive.

"Maybe that was why he went on about the importance of education and training," said Tony. "He was a big supporter of the apprenticeship scheme."

"Alan went to one of his meetings in a pub up in Old Town," said Bob. "Only thing he could remember was that Stoddart hates Europe, says that is why he voted for him."

"He used to work on the railways before he became an MP," said Tony, shaking a cigarette loose from its packet. "A railway man and a pub man. You can almost forgive him for being Welsh."

"I wouldn't go that far," said Bob with a laugh as he picked up his pint.

I wiped away the froth from the fledgling moustache on my upper lip. In the sixth form common room Tracey said it made me look like David Wilkie. I think that was the only time I had ever been compared to someone famous and I was happy it was an Olympic swimming champion. I placed my pint down on a beer mat and nervously rubbed my thumb up and down the glass.

"Who do you think should replace Callaghan if he resigns?" I asked.

My Militant comrades had told me his resignation was inevitable and that he was just hanging on to help the right wingers get Dennis Healy elected.

"I don't mind, as long as they don't go for Benn or Foot," said Bob.

"What's wrong with them?" I asked, genuinely curious, as it was obvious to me that Benn was the best choice.

I sensed Dad grimacing to my left but I didn't look at him. There was an eruption of joyous laughter from the men on my right accompanied by the rattle of dominoes and shouts of "You lucky bastard!"

Tony tilted his head back and blew smoke to the ceiling where it mingled and merged with the misty haze that hugged the strip lighting. Looking back down and directly at me he said, "The problem with the likes of Foot and Benn is they want to change the country. They want to give the government more control. They are communists really."

"My missus says she would emigrate if Benn became prime minister," said Bob.

"Ah, that's why you support him," said Dad, and grinned across the table.

"Will never happen," said Tony, tapping his cigarette on the dark blue Arkell's ashtray. "People wouldn't vote Labour if Benn was the leader."

"Why not?" I asked. Dad lowered his eyes to the table and there was a faint shake of the head. Maybe it was my imagination.

"Because he is a bit weird," said Tony. "It's like Derek, the union convenor at our place. Nice enough bloke but he's not normal. He is always going on about Palestine, nuclear weapons and racism. You couldn't talk to him about the football. Spends all his time at meetings and demonstrations."

"He also does them petitions," said Bob. "He was in here the other week asking us to sign something. I think it was about council housing."

"He is also one of them vegetarians," said Tony.

"Yeah, that ain't right," said Bob. "You have got to be a bit betwaddled to be a vegetarian."

"Just barmy," said Dad, definitely shaking his head this time. He could not conceive of what a dinner would look like without meat. At home we only ever ate meat, potatoes and vegetables, normally purple sprouting from the allotment. When I later found out that broccoli was a superfood I looked back more kindly on the amount I had to eat as a child.

"Benn is another of them vegetarians," said Tony. "And he doesn't even drink, he is one of them teetotallers. You can't trust a bloke who doesn't drink."

Around the table there was much nodding of heads. What was life without a pint and something to laugh about?

"I don't know what's up with them," said Bob. "I would be lost without a bacon butty in the mornings."

"You remember them bacon butties we had on that trip to Weston. I reckon they were the best bacon butties we ever had," said Dad, changing the subject.

"That was a good day," said Tony. "I remember how we had to carry Micky back onto the coach."

For the next hour they told tales of boozy day trips and works outings.

As I sat there and listened, I reflected that maybe Orwell was onto something when he said working people didn't object to socialism, they just were not that keen on socialists. Maybe it was true; maybe we were all a bit weird.

PART II

BATH

13

BATH UNIVERSITY

There were just thirty universities in England in 1980. Only one in ten young people went to university and less than 1 percent of the children of factory workers. Nobody in my large extended family had been to university and it had never crossed my mind that I might go.

In the sixth form some of the students had visited universities and talked about a process called UCAA. I didn't pay much attention as my sights were set on a job in the offices of one of the local factories. Not that I wasn't ambitious. I hoped my 'A' levels might get me a trainee management job. I had already started writing letters and sending out my CV. The teacher said we had to address them to the personnel officer. Unfortunately I misheard and sent my letters to the 'personal' officer. I don't recall getting any replies.

The sun was already high in the sky when I walked to school to collect my 'A' level results. Bob, my economics teacher, was standing in the parquet floored corridor outside the school office. He had a fistful of brown envelopes and flipped through them as I approached. He handed me a small manila envelope.

I had achieved an 'A' in history, which goes to prove that

past exam results are not a predictor of future performance, and that it helps if you are a Trotskyist studying Stalin and the Russian revolution. My failure to pass my history 'O' level, if it proved anything, simply showed that spending the day before your exam catching chub and grayling on the Thames was less than ideal preparation. I also got a 'B' in economics and a 'C' in English. I had a lot to thank my socialist educators for.

Bob took me aside and congratulated me. He said I should really think about going to university and apply through something called the clearing process. He handed me a bundle of booklets which I promised to read.

The bundle included pamphlets from the London School of Economics and Bath University. The Bath prospectus for undergraduates had pictures of students sitting around a lake in the sunshine with their books. The LSE one said it offered the chance to study in London and to be challenged personally, socially and intellectually. The prospectus explained the LSE had been set up almost a hundred years earlier by members of the Fabian Society and had a focus on political and economic science. I decided I wanted to be in London studying politics and economics.

Early the next morning I used the avocado green phone in our hallway to ring the LSE and enquire about a place. I sat uneasily on the bottom of the stairs as I listened for the dialling tone, my heart rate racing and with an impending sense of worry about how I would start the conversation. After a faltering start I managed to string enough words together to enquire about a place studying politics and economics. My grades were good enough but unfortunately they were already full. However, they would happily take me the following year if I was willing to defer. I was not keen to spend another twelve months in Swindon sharing a bedroom with my brother. I rang Bath who offered me a place studying economics starting in October. It wasn't London but it was university and the students by the lake looked happy. I accepted immediately.

I had never met a university student but Kevin told me confidently that they were all as "bent as a nine bob note". I had seen *University Challenge* which made me a little apprehensive. The students were scarily knowledgeable. I struggled to answer any of the questions on the show, apart from the odd one they asked about Trotsky. Unfortunately they didn't ask too many questions about radical left politics. That was why a Manchester University team in 1975 made little progress when they answered Marx, Trotsky or Marilyn Monroe to all the questions they were asked.

The depth of student knowledge was incomprehensible to me. The questions were also bizarre, such as, 'Which village near Vienna is the site of the hunting lodge where the Habsburg crown prince Rudolf and his paramour Mary Vetsera committed suicide in mysterious circumstances in 1889?' Surely no one could possibly know the answer, no one in Swindon knew a Prince Rudolf. We knew there was a reindeer. There might also have been a Nazi and a Russian dancer but we didn't know of any Prince Rudolf. Yet immediately the question was read out the students were eagerly pressing their buzzers to answer. The programme was a weekly reminder that I knew nothing, like Manuel in *Fawlty Towers*.

The *University Challenge* students not only knew history, science and literature, they could identify classical music composers. I had never listened to classical music but decided it was clearly something I needed to know about if I was going to university. One Saturday morning I scoured the local record shop for classical records. To my delight they were much cheaper than the best-selling records in the hit parade. I purchased half a dozen. They included Tchaikovsky's *Piano concerto in B flat minor*, I still have no idea what that means, Tchaikovsky's *Swan Lake*, Prokofiev's *Romeo and Juliet*, and

Mozart's Eine Kleine Nachtmusik. I know this because I still have the albums and also because I played them non-stop for weeks as part of my preparation for university. I can still conduct every note, or at least swing my arms in time with the music. It may have been a small collection but it has helped me answer many *University Challenge* questions over the years.

~

1980 was a year of change for me and my family. Dad moved back to the railways. He had never really enjoyed working on the presses and was overjoyed at returning to the carriage works where he did his apprenticeship. According to Mum he was always at his happiest working on the trains. It was good news for me, as he got family 'priv' rail tickets which meant I could travel for free on the railways or at a discount. My brother Andy, turned sixteen and left school to start work as a trainee draughtsman in the Pressed Steel Fisher factory. In September, my eleven-year-old sister, Paula, started at Penhill Secondary School. This allowed Mum to get a full-time job at the local factory sewing 'made in Britain' labels onto the underwear that was shipped in from overseas.

These changes marked a significant improvement in my family's finances. My parents now had two incomes rather than one, my brother was also earning as an apprentice and I was moving away to university on a full maintenance grant. As a result my mum tried to persuade Dad to move house but he had no intention of either taking on a new mortgage or using the savings they had built up. He was happy where he was. What he had, he held. He knew the working-class grim reaper was not far away.

As I packed for my move to Bath, I didn't suspect that my relationship with my family would never be the same once I attended university. That it wasn't simply about leaving home and living somewhere else but about leaving my working-class community and stepping into a new world. I didn't realise that in future my family and I would look at each other differently, that as Yeats might say everything would change, change utterly.

On the 1 October 1980, Tony Benn gave a speech to the Labour Party Conference. He said the next Labour government would nationalise industries, give trade unions more influence, return powers from Brussels to Westminster, and abolish the House of Lords. It was inspiring, though Dad just grunted when I mentioned the speech to him. He could not dampen my enthusiasm. The latest ORC poll put Labour on 49 percent and the Conservatives on 35 percent. The Thatcher government would be short-lived as I always knew it would be. I pinned a 'Tony Benn for Number 10' badge to my denim jacket. My dad and his mates may not have loved Benn but I was sure my fellow students would support him and his socialist policies as much as I did.

The day after Benn's speech, I loaded my belongings into my car, an old mustard coloured Fiat 127, and set off down the M4 for a new life in Bath. I didn't get accommodation on campus as I had applied late through the clearing process. The university housing office found me a top floor attic room in a house located on the Lower Bristol Road. The ceilings sloped on each side and were cladded in pine, making the room resemble a sauna or a ski chalet. I proudly Blu-Tacked my Che Guevara poster to one of the gable walls, put my socialist books and pamphlets on the bookcase, and placed the newly purchased classical music albums underneath my small record player.

Once I had everything set up, I put on my denim jacket,

checked my badges, headed down the stairs and walked into the centre of Bath. The city with its honey coloured stone and flat-fronted Georgian buildings was the antithesis of Swindon. As I placed my hands on the cool stone balustrades and leant over to admire the weir at Pulteney Bridge, I was sure that even the air smelt different.

Away from the main tourist sites I discovered Walcot Street, the artisan quarter of Bath. It was lined with vegetarian food stores, independent cafes, an arts centre and an independent community bookshop called 1985. At the northern end was Walcot Reclamation, which was way ahead of its time in selling reclaimed furniture and goods from baths and radiators to iron gates. Outside a large building called Longacre, the home of Bath CND, a community bookshop had a stall selling radical books.

In the seventies there had been a campaign for Walcot Street's independence, and in 1979, it had declared itself a new independent nation at the Walcot Nation Festival of Independence. The Walcot national anthem was played and each day new rulers were introduced to the public, including Her Excellency Donna Maria Juanita Evita Corleone and General Knitting Patton. I loved the quirky nature of the area and the people in their bright yellow trousers, tie-dye T-shirts and second-hand baggy sweaters. Bath was only thirty miles away from Swindon but it was another world.

I could not help smiling as I walked around. I was rapturously happy. I sat in a cafe and marvelled at the fact they actually ground beans to make coffee. Maybe if I had thought about it, I would have known coffee was made by grinding beans but watching it happen in front of me and smelling the aroma seemed like a miracle. The cafe had posters advertising a myriad of jazz nights, art workshops, CND meetings, poetry readings, exhibitions and nightclubs. It also had free papers, magazines and leaflets advertising events in the city. The wide windowsills were layered with radical anarchist publications, copies of *Bath Spark* and the *Socialist Worker*. I sat by the window with my first proper coffee and a small almond cake. I was not in Kansas anymore.

The cafes I knew in the centre of Swindon were referred to as greasy spoons and everything came with chips. Coffee was made by scooping powder from large tins into mugs and adding boiling water. There were no French Madeleines or almond cakes. There were no papers laid out to read. Occasionally someone might leave yesterday's copy of the *Sun* on the table and sometimes the betting pages were passed around as men decided which horse to back in the three-thirty at Kempton. There was the sizzle and smell of fried bacon, and constant chattering and clattering. Plates and cutlery were banged down on Formica table tops between mugs of strong tea and instant coffee. People shouted orders: two eggs, chips and beans. Eggs, sausage, bubble and tomato. Eggs, mushrooms and fried bread. There were also animated discussions about the latest Swindon game and disappointment at how, despite promising starts, the team always lost their momentum.

In Bath the cafe was silent, apart from the murmur of grumbling coffee beans as they were ground, and the low hiss and gurgle of milk being frothed. As I leafed through the papers I found a copy of *Marxism Today*. On the cover of the magazine was a picture of Tony Benn and some guy called Eric Hobsbawm. I picked it up and felt like a left bank intellectual on the banks of the Seine as I read. I wrote down key quotes and facts from the magazine, which I repeated over and over in my head as I tried to commit them to my memory. It was like I was preparing to be grilled on *Mastermind*. Specialist subject: the October 1980 edition of *Marxism Today*. I wanted to learn but mainly I wanted to be prepared for discussions with the other students.

In his interview Benn was concerned that the Labour Party might forget its working-class roots and be swamped by the middle class. I nodded my head in agreement and took another sip of my expensive coffee. The almond cake was small and delicate but one of the most wonderful things I had ever tasted. The Swindon cafe counters were stacked with huge slabs of sticky lardy cake, originally made by the wives of Wiltshire pig farmers, and turned over after baking to allow the lard to soak through the heavy dough. In Swindon taste always took second priority to size. Even these days a true Swindon lad will rarely spend much time browsing a menu and simply ask the waiter, "What's the biggest?"

I ordered a second espresso and continued to read. Benn stressed to Hobsbawm the critical importance of Clause Four of the Labour Party's constitution which was written on our membership cards. To Benn it represented the party's core commitment to socialism, to the common ownership of the means of production and to democratic accountability.

I ran my fingers up and down the edges of the crisp, slightly stiff paper of the magazine. I caressed it and decided I couldn't leave without it. If I knew where to buy a copy I would have run there in an instant to get one. But I had never seen the magazine before and had no idea where it was sold. It was unlikely to be stocked by the local newsagent. I decided to slip it surreptitiously into my bag. Stealing the magazine from the cafe was surely the sort of thing revolutionaries might do.

I carried the magazine with me constantly during my first few weeks at university, making sure the title was always visible. In seminars I placed it front cover upwards on top of my books. My badges were not enough; I wanted my tutors and others to know I was serious about politics. When people commented on the magazine I would talk knowingly about Hobsbawm, Marxist perspectives and the importance of Clause Four.

I was desperate to read more of Benn's views and bought a

copy of his 1979 book *Arguments for Socialism*. It was a slim paperback, with Benn's face on the cover, which fitted inside my jacket pocket. The book became my bible. On the small desk in my room I would wedge it open and copy out whole passages.

Benn argued Britain should withdraw from NATO, the European Economic Community and Northern Ireland. I noted down his criticisms of the EEC. One: it weakened democracy by passing powers from a parliament you elected and could change, to European Commissioners who were not democratically accountable. Two: The Treaty of Rome enshrined the EEC's commitment to free enterprise and a capitalist economy. Thus the European Court would act to protect global businesses and the free movement of capital against state intervention. I wrote out the arguments in my notepad and underlined them.

Benn wasn't a Marxist but he said Marxism was one of many legitimate strands within the Labour movement. He went further: "The contribution made by Marx to social democracy is widely recognised and admired." I nodded in agreement despite knowing little to nothing about this contribution. I trusted Benn's judgements. In the book he again stressed the importance of Clause Four. I underlined his words: "It remains the clearest and best possible statement of the democratic, socialist faith."[1]

14

FRESHERS WEEK

The main university campus building resembled a spaceship that had landed incongruously in the landscape. It was like a sixties Stonehenge, built in the modernist style of 1964. Future archaeologists may ponder on the purpose of the raised main concourse known as the Parade, which acted as a central thoroughfare with its post office, grocery store, laundry and two banks. At either end were two residential tower blocks some nine or ten storeys high, like huge slabs of bluestone. The student union was located under the block called Norwood House. In the corridor outside the Nightline office someone had put up a black and white poster which said, 'Hang Nelson Mandela'.

I had to stop and read the poster a second time. I blinked; I was sure I must have misread what it said. But there it was, 'Hang Nelson Mandela and all ANC terrorists. They are butchers'. I rubbed the back of my neck. I was no longer sure how my Tony Benn and 'Tories Out' badges would be received. The poster must have been the work of an individual right-wing extremist. I checked there was no one around, tore the poster from the wall and stuffed it into a grey metal waste bin.

The union bar was empty at eleven in the morning. A faint aroma of beer and tobacco, echoes from the previous evening, hung in the air. There was a single pool table, a pinball machine, a Space Invaders game and an Asteroids game. The silence was interrupted by the periodic and lonely bleeping of the machines. I picked up a copy of *Spike*, the student newspaper and browsed its pages.

The headline article declared its opposition to student loans. The Tory Education Under-Secretary, Rhodes Boyson, who looked like a character from Dickens with his big sideburns, had been to the United States to see how a loan system worked. The National Union of Students (NUS) feared loans would deter students from working-class backgrounds like me. There was certainly no way my parents would have let me take on debt to go to university. They spent their life trying to avoid debt. They would not buy things on hire purchase and were even reluctant to buy from catalogues.

I flipped through the other articles. One explained how, while we had been relaxing over the summer, students in South Africa had been shot and baton-charged for opposing the racist apartheid regime. I was relieved to see the *Spike* journalists supported Mandela. The poster had to be the work of a rogue right-wing fascist.

On page four *Spike* said a large student turnout was expected at a demonstration against nuclear weapons on 26 October in London, which I was determined to join. The 'What's On' page listed various gigs and films. There was an all-night film show on Wednesday showing the *Godfather* and *Godfather Two* which started at midnight. Some students obviously needed little sleep. The paper also listed film showings at the local cinemas. The Beau Nash was showing *The Shining*; the Little Theatre was showing *The Deer Hunter* and *Play Misty For Me*, while the Gemini had an *Exorcist* double bill.

Spike also contained a review of a book called *How to Start a Successful Business* but I couldn't make head nor tail of it. The reviewer wrote that while waiting at the Artificial Insemination Clinic he was pleased to see the author had adopted Enid Blyton's style from her existentialism phase. I had no idea what he meant. He observed that as an analysis of the Iraq/Iran conflict the book failed miserably by not mentioning either country. I wasn't sure why he had expected the book to cover politics. Finally, he added the lack of recipes made it valueless as a cookbook. Maybe this was student humour.

It was in the bar that I first met Rob, another first-year student who was on my course. He was older than me, having spent a few years selling advertising for Capital Radio, and drove a Triumph Spitfire. While many of us stood awkwardly at the sides of the room, edging slowly towards other groups of students, Rob simply bounced up and said, "Hello." In his heavy leather jacket with its large fur collar and his clipped moustache, he looked like he had just stepped down from a real Spitfire. When he asked what I wanted to drink, – Rob was always the first to buy everyone a drink – I asked for a rum and black. To his credit he never said a word.

Rob also bought drinks for a group of students in black leathers who were talking about motorbikes. They were engineers and one knew exactly how to fix Rob's Spitfire when it failed to start, which was often. While Rob was being advised to remove his rotor arm at night to stop the car being stolen, I chatted to some students who already knew each other from a place called Charterhouse. I wasn't sure if it was a place or a school. "Oh," exclaimed one of them when learning of my surname, "you must be related to Timothy Raison, the Home Office Minister." I explained that my surname was spelt differently. On learning this and the fact I came from Swindon, they switched their focus to a woman with an Alice band and a large guy wearing a multi-coloured rugby shirt. I listened as they shared stories of sailing holidays in Europe and, after what I considered to be a polite interval, I moved away unnoticed to find Rob again.

~

Later in life I discovered my great-grandfather had been called Raison. According to some ancestry experts Raison was either an old Anglo-Saxon name given to Danish settlers, or a nickname from the Old French given to an intelligent person who gave good advice. I liked the last version best.

The Raison line of my family came from a small village nestled under Ham Hill in Somerset, which was home to the largest Iron Age hillfort in Europe. The village church dates from the eleven hundreds and the square castellated tower was added in the thirteenth century. My ancestor John Raisen was baptised in the church in 1773. When his daughter Elizabeth was born in 1797 his surname was recorded as Rayson but in 1806 his daughter Mary's surname was recorded as Raysan. So who knows what my family name was originally but I am fairly sure it sounded like Raison.

I like to think my ancestors took part in the mass demonstration for higher farm wages that took place on Ham Hill on Whit Monday in 1877. One of the leaflets printed to advertise the event has a picture of a skeleton ploughing a field and a poem with the lines:

> We have starved on ten shillings quite long
>   enough now
> And must have a fair wage for the sweat of our brow
> So come on my Hearties, straight up to Ham Hill
> Three cheers for our Freedom! with lusty good will.

Over twenty thousand people attended and it became an

annual event, taking place just thirty miles from Tolpuddle – where six agricultural labourers had been sentenced to penal transportation to Australia for protesting against low wages.

I am always reminded of Ham Hill when I hear Peter Gabriel's 1977 song *Solsbury Hill*. The song is about a different Iron Age hillfort, the one located just outside Bath, but the lyrics resonate with me.

So who knows, maybe I am related to the Tory Home Office Minister after all.

At the end of my first evening in the student union bar Rob invited a group of us back to his room in Westwood, where each of the accommodation blocks was named after local hills such as Mendip and Quantock. The room was small but functional. It had white painted breeze-block walls on which Rob had Blu-Tacked an *Easy Rider* poster of two guys on chopper style motorbikes. He pulled out a light blue album with an eagle's skull on the cover and placed the record on the turntable. From the black speakers came the voice of a guy singing about crazy old nights.

Another student bought in an armful of his own records including a Rod Stewart album. This did not impress a woman with long red hair called Cathy. She swished her hair over her shoulders and popped out to her room, returning with an album by Fleetwood Mac called *Rumours*. I nodded knowingly as she raved about some woman called Stevie.

I was enthralled and intoxicated by the communal happiness. Cathy and Rob engaged in play-fighting as she refused to let him play the Doobie Brothers, holding the album above her head and away from him. When we finally tumbled out of Rob's room in the early hours there were squeals of laughter accompanied by the Doobie Brothers singing *What a Fool Believes.*

That first evening we didn't talk much about politics but thankfully no one liked Margaret Thatcher. They were a bit lukewarm about Tony Benn, apart from Rob. The guy with the Rod Stewart record was from Barnsley and said he was an anarchist. Despite having spent many hours singing along with the Sex Pistols, I didn't really know what anarchists were. I nodded knowingly, and made a mental note to read about them in the library. As I walked down Bathwick Hill to my flat in the early morning I felt weightless. My senses were in overdrive as I kicked the leaves and sang a medley of Fleetwood Mac and Eagles songs. The air was cold and fresh but inside I was infused with warmth.

The first week at university was known as freshers week, a week with no lectures to enable you to settle in and meet people. During the days we explored Bath and the local country pubs. Rob told me the first week was really known as 'fuck a fresher' week. Just to prove the point he hooked up with a first year Euro studies student whose freckles gave away her Irish ancestry. I was jealous, not of Rob but his girlfriend; I wanted him to spend more time with me.

Rob read the *Guardian* but called it the Gron-e-add, which was evidently a reference to all the typing mistakes in the paper. In the Huntsman pub he told me that if a woman read the *Guardian* she was probably a feminist. Evidently they were quite different to normal women. "They insist on oral sex," he told me. "You have to go down and perform until your tongue gets cramp. You also have to watch out for the squirters." I understood – I once had a girlfriend that drenched me with her brother's water pistol.

"You have to show them you are sensitive," advised Rob. "Tell them you read poetry or are a vegetarian. They love vegetarians. I once spent a month not eating meat but it was well worth it." His moustache curled upwards as he smiled. I was way ahead of him on the poetry. I had also thought of becoming a vegetarian for moral and health reasons, but had not considered the potential sexual benefits.

On Tuesday evening Rob and I attended the Clubs Fair in the main hall. It was full of stalls staffed by students trying to persuade you to join various clubs and societies. The people on the National Organisation of Labour Students stall wore camouflage jackets and red-checked scarves like members of the Palestinian Liberation Organisation. I joined up and wrote down the dates of the upcoming meetings. I also joined the chess club and the ballroom dancing club. Yes, that was a surprise to me as well. I blame Rob; he said it would be a great place to meet women. It was only when he joined the morris dancing club that I started to have my doubts about his advice.

During freshers week James Callaghan finally resigned as Labour leader. Rob, Cathy and I celebrated in the bar. Now the party could elect a new leader, someone young and dynamic who would defeat Thatcher at the next election.

15

PAUL

The 'Hang Nelson Mandela' poster was not the work of a single right-wing extremist as I anticipated but was produced and pinned up by the Federation of Conservative Students. I discovered, much to my disappointment, that Bath was one of the most right-wing universities in the country and had an active FCS membership. Tessa chose more wisely; she went to Essex which had a reputation for radicalism.

Unlike Essex, Bath only had a small social science faculty. It was housed in building 'Three East', where the left-wing students lived. The big courses were in engineering, biochemistry and languages. Most of the engineering students were male. They were sponsored by corporate companies and their courses included a year's placement in industry. Most of them were more interested in rugby, motorbikes and music than politics.

In my class there was a tall, curly-haired member of the FCS called Stuart Warren. The *Spike* student journalists nicknamed him 'Bunny'. During the first few weeks of term he put up FCS posters of a pair of scissors about to cut a woman's bra strap with the words 'support the cuts'. The posters were so controversial a *Daily Mirror* reporter arrived and took pictures of Bunny standing proudly in front of them. The student union committee met to consider the issue and decided, bizarrely, that the posters were not sexist. Buoyed by his victory Bunny put up even more of the offensive posters.

Bunny, like Thatcher, saw tax as something the evil state took from individuals and which penalised his dad for working hard. I didn't pay taxes but I believed they were a good thing. Broadly they took money from those with the greatest wealth and redistributed it through the provision of housing, health, education and benefits.

In the bar I was introduced to Paul, who winked at me. His blue eyes danced as he laughed and joked with everyone. He wore stacked cowboy boots, giving the impression of not being as tall as he wanted to be, and his hair was starting to recede at the temples. He said he was part Irish and part Italian, "so I can take the piss out of the Catholics and the Paddys". He was a few years older than me and had a London accent. He said he came from Rainham, which was "so rough even the Alsatian dogs walk in pairs". Whenever Rob or I gave our views on something he would reply, "I told you a million times not to exaggerate."

Paul held court in the bar telling a non-stop series of jokes that had most of the students around him spluttering in fits of laughter. Not everyone was impressed though. One girl with dark hair remained impassive. There was a studied coldness to her eyes, which were full of derision and disdain. Maybe it was his language or some of the more risqué jokes. Paul looked at her and said, "I might be a cunt, but at least I am not fucking boring." He gave her a broad smile and downed the rest of his pint.

To Paul the worst thing anyone could be was boring. He had

ambitions to be a rock star and had already formed a band called A Shot in the Dark. He joked about renaming the band A2 as the road went through Rainham. Paul and his band performed at a gig in Eastwood a few weeks later. It was so popular not everyone could get in to see them. Stages were invented for Paul and banter was a key part of his act. He had the audience clamouring and cheering for more at the end of the evening.

When the bar closed Paul suggested we play snooker. I am not sure if it was the advent of colour TVs, or the joy and the pain of watching Alex Higgins, but snooker became a huge thing in the early eighties. Over ten million people regularly watched the world championships and over fifteen million would watch the final. Snooker looks easy on TV; the players rarely miss a pot. In real life snooker tables are way bigger than you imagine them to be. You are happy to just hit a ball twelve feet down the table, let alone pot it.

Snooker tables look luxuriously green and soft, but a word of warning if you ever decide to have sex on one. The hard carpets that take the skin off your elbows and knees when you make love on the floor are a joy compared to snooker tables.

The snooker room was at the opposite end of Norwood House from the bar. When we got there the dark green door was locked.

"Fucking hell, what sort of cunt would do that?" said Paul, as Rob tried unsuccessfully to open the door.

I was just about to say we could play another day when Paul simply walked up to the door and kicked it open with his cowboy boots. That was all it took: just one hard kick and the door flung around on its hinges.

Paul didn't stop talking and told jokes constantly as we played.

"Fucking hell, I must be getting old" as he tried to get his leg up on the table to reach a long shot.

"Fucking hell Steve, it's like you never played before" when I missed a ball.

"Bollocks, even the Queen Mum would have potted that one" when he missed a shot.

"Come on. Don't be a greedy cunt, leave some for the rest of us" when I potted two balls in a row.

At one point I was lining up a shot when he walked over and stood next to me. He rubbed his chin with his hand, leaned in and said, "Ever think all this anger you have towards Thatcher is because you want to fuck her?"

When I looked up, he smiled and said, "I wonder what it's like going down on her? Come on, don't tell me you haven't thought about it."

Waiting his turn to play Paul would hold his cue like a microphone and sing to us. When he finished he would say, "Fucking hell, I'm good."

Snooker became part of our evening routine. Once the bar closed we would head past the Nightline offices to the snooker room, where Paul would entertain us. Once having missed a shot he said, "I'd be better off playing with my fucking knob", and to prove the point he took his cock out and feigned potting shots with it. When we had tired of playing snooker, and seen enough of Paul's cock, we would walk the corridors in the early morning tearing down FCS posters.

Paul frequently used words I didn't understand, mostly related to drugs and sex. One Thursday morning he was sat on a grey plastic chair in the kitchen of his accommodation block and strumming his guitar. He started complaining to me about a particularly exhausting bout of sex the previous evening. "She was a dirty one. I should have fucking known when I saw her tattoos," he said. "She had the Ace of Spades on her ankle. That was a fucking giveaway." It wasn't apparent to me what it gave away. Maybe she loved the new Motorhead song, released a few weeks earlier, called *Ace of Spades*. Or maybe she had a predilection for playing bridge. "I had to spend fucking hours on the Hershey highway last night." I smiled knowingly but didn't have a clue what he was on about. I was surprised there was a lot of traffic in the evening.

"I think she might have given me a case of the old Basil," he said.

It was all double Dutch to me but I nodded at him as he began composing a song. The main lyric appeared to be, "My poor fucking todger, been working all night long." When I said I was going to the library he replied, "That's a bit fucking unfair ain't it, studying, think about the rest of us lazy bastards."

To my surprise I was the only student who had bought Tchaikovsky records to college. I wasn't sure how the others were going to answer the questions on *University Challenge*. When my fellow students first visited my room in town, after a night drinking at the Bell, they were bemused to find ballet albums as they flipped through my record collection. My carefully constructed new persona was confusing to the other students. They scanned my room for clues and alighted on my record collection. Browsing through albums was an important student ritual, along with questions such as: What school did you go to? Where do you live? What does your father do?

Album browsing was the equivalent of the sorting hat at Hogwarts. *Bridge over Troubled Water*: Hufflepuff. *Hunky Dory*: Gryffindor. *Black Sabbath*: Slytherin. *Rumours*: Ravenclaw. Tchaikovsky's *Piano Concerto No 1* – what the fuck is this? The other students were unsure what to make of me with my Tony Benn badges and my ballet albums. Rob defended me, saying my musical tastes were really cool, which I appreciated.

It was in Paul's shared kitchen that I came across spaghetti bolognese for the first time. My dad wouldn't eat pasta or rice, anything with garlic or anything foreign. I had eaten pasta before but only spaghetti hoops from a tin. I would easily have believed the BBC's spoof news item on April Fool's Day about harvesting spaghetti trees. At home we ate meat and three veg every day. The meat was typically chicken, liver, chops or faggots. I am sure the vegetables varied according to what was in the allotment but all I can remember is Dad's purple sprouting.

In the kitchen I was placed in charge of the spaghetti while a group of women chopped onions and mushrooms. My job involved slowly forcing handfuls of stiff pasta into a pan as it wilted in the boiling water. Paul told me that the pasta had to be cooked 'al dente' and kissed his fingers. It meant nothing to me. He said you could tell if it was ready by throwing it at the wall. If the pasta clung to the surface it was done. I couldn't see my mum letting people throw pasta at the wall in her kitchen.

On the plate the spaghetti resembled a ball of Mum's knitting wool after the cat had played with it. I was unsure why I had been given a spoon and fork. I held one in each hand and looked around for guidance. The other students used their spoons to twirl and twist small mouthfuls of pasta into neat parcels on their forks. I tried to emulate them, turning my fork and balancing the white strands precariously as I lifted. But each time, just as I tried to put it in my mouth, it slipped and I was left with pasta hanging down my chin.

We washed the pasta down with bottles of sweet-tasting wine as Paul shouted, "Saluti!" He raised his glass in the air and looked at it admiringly: "That is a fucking lovely glass of Calvin Klein." After the pasta Cathy brought out a plate of 'space cakes'. They looked like the fairy cakes Mum made but without the pink icing. Until I arrived at university I had never taken any form of drugs; they were not really a thing at my school. I discovered the middle-class students from the home counties regularly smoked cannabis. I didn't participate. I had never liked smoking since I took a drag on someone's cigarette in the Town End and nearly coughed myself to death. 'Space cakes' seemed a much more enjoyable way to take drugs but they didn't appear to have any effect on me.

I was sleeping happily on the kitchen floor when Cathy woke me and helped me upstairs to her room. That was when I discovered that student beds on campus were very narrow and had uncomfortable wooden edges.

16

THE GREAT MOVING RIGHT SHOW

There were only two Militant comrades at the university. The first was George, a mature student, who actually lived in Bath and had the broadest Bristol accent. He was a large guy with shaggy hair and a beard. He looked more like a Norse god than a student. The second was Matt from Birkenhead. He was tall and thin, with an angular face and black hair, reminding me of Jasper, Cruella's lofty henchman in *One Hundred and One Dalmatians*.

Matt spoke like the Liverpool comrades that frequently visited our LPYS meetings and was much more committed to the cause than either George or myself. On wet afternoons in the city centre he cut a lonely figure in his black donkey jacket trying to sell copies of the *Militant*. Given a choice between having a girlfriend and selling the paper, not that he had a choice, he would choose to sell the paper.

On Saturday mornings George and I would join Matt to sell the paper in the centre of Bath. It was not the easiest sell, even in Walcot Street, which was full of middle-class liberals, peace activists, feminists and hippy environmentalists. They were happy campaigning for vegetarian lifestyles but had little interest in Militant's focus on the working class and trade unions. We sold more papers outside M&S in the main shopping centre than we did in Walcot Street.

Matt would stand stiff and still, like a guard outside a sentry box, holding the paper across his chest. Every now and then he would make passing shoppers jump by shouting, "Kick the Tories out, buy the *Militant!*" After the initial shock most shoppers bowed their heads to avoid eye contact and hurried by with their carrier bags. By contrast George would walk around with a huge smile saying, "Buy a copy of *Militant*, the ideal mother's day present" or "Improve your sex life, buy the *Militant*". George's approach proved to be much more effective. He sold lots of papers, as many as six on some days.

The Labour Students Club at the university was separate from the Bath Labour Party. Matt and I tried to track down the local LPYS meetings and discovered they were run by another Militant comrade called Phil. He was tall, had fair curly hair and wore a camouflage jacket with the obligatory badges. He shared Matt's commitment to Militant; I didn't need to ask if he had a girlfriend. When I say he ran the LPYS meetings I think he was *the* Bath LPYS. He was overjoyed to see us, and we organised regular evening meetings. George's attendance was spasmodic. When he failed to show up Phil would resentfully note his absence in the minutes.

To my surprise, Trotsky also started attending our meetings in his greatcoat and mariner's cap. Bath was obviously part of his regional patch. He was excited and enthused about us building a new Militant branch in the city. We discussed how to grow our membership. Trotsky suggested we included early morning newspaper selling at local factories in our planned activities. I nodded but given my previous experience I wasn't convinced workers would welcome student radicals outside their factory gates. I was more excited by the fly-posting.

Matt and I used a Gestetner duplicating machine in the

local Labour Party office to create our posters. It was a messy process where you turned the handle and the ink-filled cylinder produced smudgy copies of our consciousness-raising posters. On dark evenings we would head out with a bucket of wallpaper paste in a shopping bag and our poorly printed posters folded in my jacket. We became quite adept. Matt would whip out the brush and cover the wall in paste while I unfolded the poster, placed it on the wet wall and smoothed it out. He then pasted over the top, and invariably over my hands, as I held the poster in place. It was messy but we were happy young revolutionaries.

After putting up dozens of posters advertising our meetings, Matt and I would speculate on how many people might turn up next time. The answer was always the same, just the four of us. Apart from one night, when a young woman with mousy hair appeared in the doorway. She appeared unsure whether to step inside. After a while she hesitantly came and sat with us in a small circle of chairs. She held her hands in her lap and said little as we talked about what we did. We asked her a few questions but her voice was so quiet I struggled to make out what she said. She lived in Twerton and said someone had told her about the meeting. Afterwards in the pub Matt was enthusiastic, our first new member, we were making progress. I remember him saying first one person, then two people, then four, then eight and then it would be a flood of new members.

The woman never turned up again. We later discovered George had told her about the meeting. I suspect she was hoping to see him again and was a bit shocked to find earnest and nerdy young men talking about the inevitable collapse of capitalism rather than George joking about Thatcher's sex life.

Matt and I also pasted up Militant posters across the city which were provided to us by Trotsky. They said, 'Smash the Tories, Read *Militant*', and were accompanied by a cartoon of the Conservative minister Norman Tebbit being crushed by a large hobnail boot. The people most likely to read our posters were those tasked with removing them from bus stops, walls and underpasses, and I suspect we were not really endearing ourselves to them.

~

I found, much to my surprise, that the university library had copies of *Marxism Today*. There were boxes of the magazine going back for years. It was like waking up Easter Sunday morning to find so many chocolate eggs you didn't know where to start. I hunted for a 1979 *Marxism Today* article by Stuart Hall called *The Great Moving Right Show*. It had been mentioned by the magazine's more recent articles as a seminal essay and the first to coin the term Thatcherism. I took it over to my wooden cubicle and laid it neatly out in front of me alongside my notepad.

Hall argued Thatcher was trying to destroy the post-war settlement, established by the 1945 Attlee government, whereby people agreed to obey the law, work hard and pay taxes in exchange for a secure job, education, healthcare and a home. She sought to replace it with a right-wing ideology that cast the state as an evil empire – burdening tax payers, hobbling free enterprise and limiting personal freedom.[1]

In my first term Thatcher appeared on a special television broadcast to promote her flagship Right to Buy policy. In her dead dog voice she spoke to us slowly like dim-witted children. "If you have been a council tenant for at least three years you will have the right, by law, to buy your house."

"Not if I can help it," I said.

This appeared to prompt Thatcher to look directly at me, as if she had heard what I said. "People have the right to buy," she said, "and that's that."

I hated Right to Buy. It was like 'Take Back Control', a

perfect slogan. Concise, easy to remember, easy to repeat and incredibly damaging. It was a seductive promise to the millions of aspirational people living in council properties. Thatcher promoted it as an intrinsic human right rather than a cynical ploy to create more Conservative voters. When I tried to argue against the policy, people's response was always the same, "It's our *right* to buy."

At the end of October I joined other Bath students on a coach to London to demonstrate against nuclear weapons. The organisers estimated over a hundred thousand took part though the police said there were only twenty-five of us. It was an eclectic mix of students, hippies, nuns and Buddhist monks. The most exciting moment for me was when Tony Benn spoke. Some people were wearing a badge that said 'Wearing badges is not enough'. I really wanted the badge and spent most of my time walking around Trafalgar Square trying unsuccessfully to buy one. At the demo a band called Killing Joke spent ages making a cacophonous noise tuning their guitars. In New York at a similar demo they had Bruce Springsteen, Carly Simon and Tom Petty. It seemed unfair. However, God was about to level things up.

On Wednesday, 5 November 1980, I woke to the news that Ronald Reagan had been elected president of America. I hadn't stayed up to listen to the results. I knew it was unlikely that Jimmy Carter would win but the scale of Reagan's victory shocked me. He won 489 seats, 90 percent of the electoral college. Seriously America? What the hell were you thinking? A sixty-nine-year-old former actor? I hated Thatcher but at least she was a politician. The Republicans also won the Senate for the first time in twenty-six years. They were now in full control. I didn't want to leave the comfort of my bed. Thatcher was delighted of course. I pulled the covers over my head as she spoke on the radio but could still hear her muffled voice saying Reagan shared her values and philosophy. Yeah sure, I shouted under my duvet, rule by the rich for the rich.

The Thatcher-Reagan romance was based on a shared love of tax cuts, reductions in social spending, deregulation, and increases in military spending. All the things I hated. Nancy Reagan called them "political soulmates", fighting for freedom against the terrors of communism. I could hear Reagan on the phone: "Margaret, I think this is the beginning of a beautiful friendship."

I refused to believe the election of Thatcher and Reagan reflected the shifting nature of politics and the rise of social conservatism. How could the world shift ideologically to the right? It had to be obvious to anyone with a brain that Thatcher and Reagan were the dark side. I comforted myself that it was just a temporary phenomenon. After one term of Reagan and Thatcher, people would realise that what they really needed was radical socialism.

I couldn't understand how Americans could elect Reagan. It was ridiculous. It wasn't just that he was an actor. He was born in 1911, and older than my grandparents. It was like asking my nan, God bless her, to run the country. She was already shaking with Parkinsons in her sixties, something I first noticed when she was pouring condensed milk over our tinned peaches.

The more I saw Reagan and how people responded to him, the more I came to realise that not being a traditional politician was probably an asset rather than a hindrance. While Carter had concentrated on the details of government policy, Reagan had focused on making his audience laugh. People liked him; he may not have had much of a grasp on policy, in fact no grasp at all, but given a choice of who to have a beer with, Reagan won hands down. All political leaders had to pass the beer test, something Benn would probably fail as a teetotaller.

I despised Reagan but I had to grudgingly admire how he used humour to communicate with the public. It was not an accident. He kept a box of index cards stacked with jokes written in his own hand. He would embellish the speeches drafted for him not with policy adjustments but his favourite one-liners. He had better timing than most comedians. His humour was self-deprecating and devastatingly effective. He made constant jokes about his age. In his first state of the union address he quoted a speech George Washington had made in 1790 and added, "Let me say I did not actually hear George Washington say that."

It was just a taster of what was to come. When Democrats criticised his work rate Reagan replied, "It's true that hard work never killed anybody, but I figure, why take the chance?"

When they said he often fell asleep in the afternoons he responded by saying, "I have left orders to be awakened at any time in case of a national emergency, even if I'm in a cabinet meeting."

The public lapped it up. I didn't see the funny side but I came to learn that it is hard to lay a glove on someone so skilled at self-deprecating humour. While many Americans viewed Reagan as the kind and amusing grandfather they always wanted, the reality was terrifying.

Reagan saw the world as a binary conflict between good and evil. He called the Soviet Union, "the focus of evil in the modern world". He abandoned the strategy of nuclear deterrence which had kept us safe. Instead the psychopath tasked his advisers to find a way to win a nuclear war, including a Star Wars missile defence system that would shoot down missiles before they reached American shores. He believed America could win a limited nuclear war in Europe, a thought which made my legs wobble like Mum's jelly.

Before Reagan's election CND had been almost a quasi-religious protest group. In Bath the most active members were the Quakers, who staffed a stall every Saturday morning outside of Bath Abbey. Suddenly there were queues of people wanting to join. CND membership rocketed and it became a mass movement led by a Catholic priest, Monsignor Bruce Kent. Almost everyone I knew was wearing a CND peace symbol badge.

Along with many of my friends I Blu-Tacked a mock *Gone with the Wind* movie poster on my wall. It had a picture of a young Ronald Reagan carrying Margaret Thatcher in his arms. The poster promised an 'explosive' love story. At the bottom it said, 'She promised to follow him to the end of the earth. He promised to organise it'.

Just days after Reagan's victory Labour elected Michael Foot as the new leader of the party. The right might have been winning elections in the UK and America, but I was happy the Labour Party was moving to the left. With Foot as our leader we were sure to defeat Thatcher. In the bar Paul was less convinced. "He looks older than my fucking grandad." Okay, he was sixty-seven but Reagan had proved age was no barrier to winning elections. While we were drinking Bunny came over and congratulated me on gifting the Conservatives the next election. "Fuck off!" shouted Rob, and we toasted the bright new chapter in Labour's history.

17

CHRISTMAS 1980

On 9 December 1980, I woke in my top floor room to the news John Lennon had been assassinated in New York. People say they can remember where they were when JFK was killed. I can remember clearly the radio alarm waking me at 7 a.m. and the BBC leading with the news. Radio stations played Lennon's song *Imagine* non-stop for days afterwards. I was the dreamer in his song, an internationalist who didn't believe in countries or religion, who wanted to live in a world of peace.

At the end of the year Thatcher's 'make Britain great again' narrative was taken up by British Leyland. They launched a new car, the Metro, with the slogan, 'A British car to beat the world'. The jingoistic TV advert showed invading foreign cars coming across the channel in landing craft, just in case we didn't get the reference to the war. They were bravely seen off by a band of Metros on the top of white chalk cliffs. The car was no Ferrari but my dad and his mates were incredibly proud of it. British Leyland was making Britain great again. My dad was still driving a Metro when he crashed into the garage wall in his seventies and decided to finally give up driving.

Unemployment was soaring as my first term at university

ended. In December 1980, the number of those officially jobless increased to two and a quarter million people. A rise of nearly one million since Thatcher was elected. So much for 'Labour isn't working'. The Tories were wrecking the lives of families across the country and particularly those in post-industrial towns. My opposition to the Conservatives was vindicated and I added a yellow 'jobs not bombs' badge to my denim jacket.

As I packed up and headed home after my first term at university my mood was boosted by a Mori opinion poll. Labour were on 56 percent and held a 24-point lead over the Conservatives. Thatcher had become the most unpopular prime minister in history. I was more confident than ever that a left-wing Labour Party under Michael Foot would win the next election. Thatcher's reign was going to be a short one.

Things in Swindon were fairly much as normal when I got home. The fake Christmas tree was up in the lounge along with the paper chains. While summer holidays were organised by my dad, Christmas was my mum's domain. She pegged Christmas cards onto strings of wool and hung them on the walls. Ticking off who had sent cards was my mum's annual ritual. "We haven't had a card from Uncle Eric," she said disapprovingly.

Mum bought the Christmas editions of the *Radio Times* and the *TV Times*, and highlighted various films and programmes for us to watch. At university I didn't watch much television but in Swindon the TV was the heart of the household. In the lounge was a new twenty-six inch colour TV. It was huge and dominated the room. Between programmes the adverts encouraged us to eat fresh cream cakes, 'naughty but nice', to 'pop a tic tac', 'pick up a Penguin' and not to leave home without an American Express card. I was more taken with the

Calvin Klein advert for jeans. Brooke Shields, her legs akimbo, pouted at the camera and whispered seductively, "You want to know what comes between me and my Calvins? ... Nothing." Mary Whitehouse would not be happy. My dad generally ignored the adverts but even he paid attention when Brooke Shields appeared. He also sat up when he heard the sounds of *Rule Britannia* and saw four landing craft on the screen heralding the advert for the British Metro.

My parents had also purchased a chest freezer while I was away. It was in the garage with our bikes and fishing gear. We were lucky as in 1980 only half of UK households had a freezer but sales were growing as was the range of frozen food. For Christmas my parents gave me a boxed set of Old Spice talc and aftershave. It was 'the mark of a man' according to the TV advert which had a guy surfing to the dramatic stirring sounds of Carl Orff's *O Fortuna*.

In the evenings, between watching the programmes Mum had marked out in the TV guides, we played cards. Dad would take charge of the pack, taking out the jokers and checking the suits. Mum would make sure everyone had a drink and place large bowls of nuts and chocolates on the table. We played various games but mostly Chase the Lady and cribbage. When we were ready to start my mum would always ask to be reminded of the rules. Almost every time someone played a card Dad would jump in saying, "Fifteen two". He was as sharp as a tack. He pegged his points on the cribbage board and never neglected to score 'one for his nob' when he held the jack.

If you lost to Dad at cards he would smile across the table and say, "That's a shame." He loved playing, almost as much as he hated losing. When we were kids Mum once asked him to let us win. He refused saying we had to learn to win. He wouldn't even let his three-year-old grandson win at arm wrestling, though he would at least fake how much he had to struggle to win. Dad was competitive; he didn't think there was any point playing a game unless you wanted to win.

When the *Advertiser* was delivered my mum would bring it in from the hall and start by browsing the announcements column. She would let us know who had died, got married or given birth recently. She also read out articles about an open day at the railway works and how Swindon's very own Diana Dors had a role in *The Two Ronnies*. I was disappointed that Dad had started having the *Sun* delivered in the mornings rather than the *Daily Mirror,* though he was not the only one switching newspapers. Sales of the *Daily Mirror* had been declining since the 1960s. The paper had lost over one million readers, and by contrast sales of the *Sun* were up by over two million.

At the end of 1980, the *Sun* overtook the *Daily Mirror* to become the UK's best-selling newspaper and its owner, Rupert Murdoch, appointed Kelvin MacKenzie as the new editor. I detested the *Sun* and its topless page three girls. The paper portrayed women as objects of lust. They were described as food for men. There was 'luscious Linda', 'scrumptious Sandra', and 'tasty Tracey' amongst many others. It also published a topless picture of a sixteen-year-old girl, Samantha Fox, who was voted 'Page 3 Girl of the Year' for three consecutive years. *The Sun's* picture desk had tried to place an advert in *Spike* for their 'university challenge'. They said they wanted to find the girl with the cutest curves to graduate on the nation's favourite page three. *Spike* printed their request and everyone agreed the *Sun* could fuck off.

MacKenzie appealed to his reader's lowest base instincts. He claimed his typical reader wanted "to send the wogs back, buy his poxy council house, is afraid of the unions, afraid of the Russians, hates the queers and the weirdos and drug dealers".[1] Despite her low poll ratings MacKenzie and Murdoch were staunch supporters of Thatcher, who later said they were the people that stood by her in the dark days.

In exchange for his support Thatcher helped Murdoch to gain control of *The Times* and *Sunday Times*. She met him for lunch at Chequers on 4 January 1981, to discuss the acquisition. A meeting which she denied took place. She continued to lie about it for thirty years until it became public with the release of government papers. She made sure Murdoch's acquisition did not get referred to the Monopolies and Mergers Commission, even though it meant he would control 40 percent of the British press. After the acquisition I vowed never to buy *The Times* or *Sunday Times* again.

In Swindon I missed the *Guardian*, which had become my regular newspaper at university. The newsagent, where I had worked as a paperboy, didn't stock the paper but I managed to buy a copy at the newsagents down at the crossroads. The shop also stocked *Cosmopolitan*, or Cosmo as it was called by female students on my course who frequently challenged us to do its personality quizzes in the refectory. The December edition of *Cosmopolitan* ran a front page headline, 'Surviving Your First Christmas After Divorce'. Divorces were not listed in the *Advertiser* but they were growing and the subject of much discussion behind the net curtains of Merton Avenue, where my parents lived.

In the Club after Christmas the men discussed the Health Education Council's new guidelines for healthy drinking.

"Did you see that article in the *Sun* this morning? The government says we should only drink three pints a day," said Bob.

"You are just trying to avoid buying your round," said Dad with a grin as he emptied his glass and placed it on the table.

Tony folded his arms across his chest. "Bloody typical of the government. They will take away all the pleasures we have left," he said.

"I am not sure you can trust these experts," said Bob. "Look at Dave, he has six pints every night and he's still Highworth's top scorer."

"Hollow legs, that bugger," said Dad.

TV advertising campaigns stressed the positive benefits of drinking alcohol with straplines such as 'Double Diamond works wonders' and 'Heineken refreshes the parts other beers can't reach'. However, the HEC was growing increasingly concerned that rising unemployment was exacerbating social problems and alcohol abuse. During the 1960s and 1970s alcohol consumption had steadily increased. There had also been a surge in underage drinking. It seems it was not just the kids from Penhill buying booze from the offy and drinking while they sat on the wall outside the chippy.

The HEC lowered the recommended units of alcohol a week from seventy to fifty-six, and employed Saatchi and Saatchi, Thatcher's favourite advertising agency, to raise awareness of the new guidelines. They produced a poster of a tearful young girl above the text, 'Eight pints of beer and four whiskies a day are not doing her any good'.

I was quietly pleased that alcohol guidelines were being lowered. At university there was huge peer pressure to drink. "Come on, don't be boring, have another one." The organisers of rag week had put on a 'drink the pub dry' evening, followed by a disco at Charlie Brown's club. During rag week all shorts in the union bar were priced at thirty pence to encourage more drinking, not that any encouragement was needed. I used driving as my excuse for not drinking. It seemed to be the one acceptable reason for refusing drinks.

In the club Bob and Tony were also animated about Thatcher's Right to Buy policy.

"Me and the missus have decided to buy our place," said Bob, resting his fingers on the edge of the table as if wanting to hold it steady.

"It's the one good thing Thatcher has done," said Tony. "And about time. You've probably paid for it twice already with all that rent you have paid the council."

I wasn't sure why Tony was so excited; he didn't live in a council house but further down the street from us. He then revealed he was planning to help his mother to buy her place.

"If we wait a little longer she'll be entitled to a fifty percent discount," he said, clapping and rubbing his hands together.

It was the best council houses that were going to be bought, like Bob's semi. Those relying on council housing would have less choice and increasingly be ghettoised in the areas where no one wanted to buy.

I had only been away at university for three months but at home that first Christmas I was distant from my family. I sighed loudly when my mum switched channels to watch the film special of *Are You Being Served*. I sighed equally loudly when my parents said they wanted to watch the *Terry and June Christmas Special* and the *Mike Yarwood Show*. I didn't sigh all the time. I enjoyed *The Likely Lads*, a story of two streetwise working-class lads in the north east whose main interests were football, beer and women. James Bolam, who played Terry, looked like my dad and reminded me of him.

My brother accused me of being 'up myself'. He was right. I was frustrated we had cheap instant coffee, sliced white bread, watched sitcoms and had the *Sun* delivered. I was frustrated at my parents lack of ambition and their lack of interest in politics. I was particularly frustrated when my mother said all politicians were the same. How could you think Thatcher and Tony Benn were the same?

I loved my family, even my brother. Okay, maybe not when he sat on my chest, pinned my arms to the floor with his knees and dribbled on my face, but I loved him most of the time. I also loved playing cards with everyone. I knew my parents were proud of me but they didn't really understand me. I travelled back to university before the holidays were over, despite my mum's protestations, explaining I had studying to do in the library. I was eager to get back to my new life.

18

ALISON AND THE SDP

In January 1981, I made my first speech at the university Labour Club. I argued in favour of Benn's campaign to democratise the Labour Party and extend the franchise for electing the party's leader. It was blindingly obvious that MPs were not representative and only fair that individual members and trade unions should also have a vote.

I pointed out that in 1979, only 3 percent of the MPs elected were women. Just 3 percent. There were no black or ethnic minority MPs at all. Not a single one. Over half of the MPs were aged over fifty. That was way older than my parents. Many Labour MPs were older than my grandparents for God's sake. It was ridiculous to think these old men, two hundred and thirty-two of whom had served under Callaghan, could lead the drive for a socialist Labour government. Yes, it was true that Tony Benn was also an old man and a minister under Callaghan but he was different.

After a short debate, and a show of hands, the Labour Club passed my motion to support Benn's campaign. Later in the month a special Labour conference passed a similar motion. In future the leader of the party would be selected by an electoral college composed of 40 percent trade unionists, 30 percent party members and 30 percent MPs. This was a major victory for Benn, and for me. I had won my first political campaign, well I am not sure the party paid that much attention to a motion passed by Bath University Labour Club but still, I was on the winning side of a political debate.

The old people were furious. A gang of four ex-senior Labour ministers were particularly appalled. The reactionary pensioners argued it was dangerous to let party members choose the leader. It was a ridiculous argument; how could democracy possibly be dangerous?

The gang of four decided they were not going to stay in a party where members like me could vote in the leadership election. They also argued that the Militant Tendency was damaging Labour and destroying the party's electoral prospects. They clearly hadn't learnt from the last Labour government. They needed to read Ted Grant's articles explaining how the party, in trying to manage capitalism and constrain wages, had been in constant conflict with the working class.

If the old people wanted to leave, good riddance. They should go and take others with them. They were clearly wrong about Labour's electoral prospects. Under our new left-wing leader, Michael Foot, Labour held a 16 percent lead over the Tories. Okay, it was down from the 24 percent lead Labour had held before he was elected but I was sure the more the public saw of Foot the more they would like him.

In March, the old people launched their new party, which they called the Social Democratic Party (SDP). This was ironic as they were neither socialists nor democrats. They were led by Roy Jenkins, an old guy that belonged in the past. He was sixty but epitomised an even older generation with his slicked hair, thick glasses and dull suits. He had a form of rhotacism and was unable to pronounce his Rs. This somehow made him seem very posh and very old. He belonged to the age of black and white TV.

As far as I was concerned the UK didn't need a new party; the rich had the Tories and the workers had Labour. The old people should simply join the Tories. The British public, not for the first time, disagreed with me. A poll in the *Observer* found that 45 percent of people actually liked the idea of a new centre party. The public were clearly not yet aware of the benefits of a Marxist-led Labour Party. Why would working people abandon Labour when it had Michael Foot as its leader, and policies such as unilateral disarmament and increasing income tax to invest in public services?

I enjoyed the ballroom dancing classes at university more than I thought I would. I even managed a passable foxtrot. I particularly enjoyed the sensation of female breasts against my chest, as we skipped around the room doing the Viennese waltz. Rob was wrong about me finding a girlfriend there but I did dance regularly with Astrid, a blonde Euro studies student. I managed to avoid stepping on her toes and we laughed as we learned to dance together. I found myself looking forward to the Wednesday evening classes and the sweet smell of her perfume.

Astrid spoke at least three languages fluently which made me feel inadequate. She had gone to school at an institute in Switzerland which had its own stables. I sensed the stables were more luxurious than the mobile portacabins at my school. She discussed the countries she had visited, including Italy, India and the south of France. I had never travelled further than Barry Island or Margate. These were major holiday expeditions as far as my dad was concerned. He would check the tyre pressures and the oil in the car before we left in the early mornings to miss the traffic.

Astrid was bubbly and adventurous. She went horse riding, skiing, scuba diving and skydiving. I had not been on a plane and I wasn't sure I wanted to throw myself out of one. When I tried to talk about politics Astrid said, "Why would anyone want to be a politician, it is just so dull." The more we talked the more it became apparent we came from different worlds. I liked the sound of her world; it was exotic and reminded me of James Bond films. I wanted to know more and asked lots of questions. She seemed less interested in learning about Swindon. She had never heard of the town and to my surprise had never watched a game of football.

As the weeks progressed we saw less of each other. By the end of the second term she had found a new partner to dance with. One evening in the union bar Astrid introduced me to her new boyfriend, a large guy in a pink shirt. He joked about being a Euro stud, which he found hilarious. I got it, an abbreviation of European Studies, I didn't laugh. I was polite though. I feigned interest as they told me of their upcoming skiing holiday and shared anecdotes about hot chocolate, black runs and things I didn't understand such as moguls and glühwein. I didn't see her much after that.

At the Labour Students meeting I met Alison. She had shoulder length peroxide blond hair and wore a multi-coloured, quilted jacket. Her lips pouted naturally like Debbie Harry's and her smile revealed a perfect top row of white teeth. Occasionally when thinking, or considering an argument, she would suck in her cheeks and press her tongue against her teeth. She hated Thatcher even more than I did. This probably dulled her critical faculties when it came to boyfriends as she would listen to me for hours talking about Tony Benn's plans for a socialist society.

Much to my surprise I found myself one spring afternoon lying naked on her narrow university bed in Norwood House and looking up through the window at a clear blue sky. The Average White Band was singing *Walk on By* on the record player and the air smelt of fresh lemons. That afternoon we worked our way through her record albums, including Stevie Wonder's *Hotter Than July* and Dire Straits *Making Movies*.

At one point Alison stood up and put the Bill Withers album *Menagerie* on the turntable. I was captivated by her nakedness, the curves of her breasts as she leaned over. She lay back down and rested her head on my chest. I traced my fingers through her hair, lifting the strands and watching as they slipped through my fingers. Exhausted by our exertions we lay there and watched a passing cloud as the sounds of *Lovely Day* meandered across our bodies. I savoured the warm feeling of skin on skin. After a long while Alison sat up. The sun streamed in through the large glass window and her hair glowed like Blondie's when singing *Sunday Girl* on *Top of the Pops*. She passed me a glass of apple juice. Sunbeams danced through the transparent golden liquid as Alison played *Muskrat Love* on the record player. It was the best apple juice I had ever tasted.

We held each other for hours as the sky became peach and purple. As the light faded we listened to the birds singing along with Minnie Riperton on *Lovin' You*. Alison joined in singing "la-la-la-la-la, la-la-la-la-la", and promised we would live each day in springtime.

"Did you know Elvis Costello wrote a song about me?" said Alison.

"No, were you a member of Oliver's army?"

She kissed me on the nose.

"Don't be silly, monster."

I am not sure why my pet name was monster but I liked it. I watched as she sat up naked and pulled out a checkerboard album cover with Costello framed in a yellow square. It took her a few goes to get the needle in the right place but then I heard the song *Alison* for the first time.

Later I sat up in bed and read her Winnie the Pooh stories. When I finished, Alison smiled up at me with a mischievous grin on her face.

"Do you know the wonderful thing about Tiggers?"

Before I could answer she jumped on top of me shouting, "They are bouncy!"

Alison and I agreed that institutions like marriage were social constructs created by capitalism. When I tried to explain this to my mum she just offered me another helping of crumble. Alison and I were determined to be free thinkers who challenged conventional thinking. We both became vegetarians. Rob's advice was still echoing in my ears and I was anxious to continue having sex in the afternoons. Or at any time for that matter. Sex was still new to me and it was an experience I was keen to keep exploring.

We both got part-time jobs at a hotel opposite the park on Henrietta Street, which was once owned by Tom Jones and Engelbert Humperdinck. We were lucky to have grants but their value was declining rapidly with inflation in double figures, and despite living off lentils and vegetable curries, it was necessary to work to make ends meet. Like my parents, Alison's mum and dad expected her to work. Her dad owned a number of fish and chip shops, where she also worked sometimes, and he was a passionate believer in the virtues of hard work.

Alison scared me off bacon for life by telling me they used

artificial salt containing sodium and potassium nitrate which caused cancer. It was 'nonsense', according to my mum, who declared the experts didn't know anything. It had never done her any harm. Some thirty years later the World Health Organisation declared artificial salt to be carcinogenic. I missed the smell of fried bacon rashers, which reminded me of caravan holidays when I would wake to the smell of Dad cooking breakfast. He would get up early to pick mushrooms which he would put in the pan along with the bacon and fried bread.

Alison and I bonded over our hatred of Thatcher and what the Conservatives were doing to the country. Company bankruptcies were rising rapidly. The unemployment rate continued to soar. In March 1981, it passed 9 percent. It had almost doubled since Thatcher was elected but she seemed completely unmoved by the plight of people whose livelihoods were destroyed. She ploughed on relentlessly with her austerity drive. Over three hundred economists wrote to *The Times* criticising Thatcher's policies. Despite this the government agreed further sweeping public sector cuts which would push unemployment still higher. As the recession grew deeper Thatcher's popularity declined sharply as I always knew it would.

Alison suggested I should henna my hair and one afternoon I found myself with my head over the sink while she massaged a soft paste into my head. Forty-five minutes later my hair was a deep wine red. When I took Alison home to Swindon, my parents loved her but were unsure about my new look. Dad didn't invite me over to the club.

Mum struggled with the concept of vegetarianism. At Sunday lunch she served us small portions of meat and extra vegetables because, as she explained, she knew we were vegetarians. In the kitchen I tried to explain why Alison wouldn't eat the meat but my mum was upset and didn't understand: "I only gave her a small piece." She was particularly affronted when we refused suet pudding; she was adamant there was no meat in her spotted dick.

Back at university I walked around in a warm glow, like a 'Ready Brek' kid. I was getting a grant to study something I loved, I was reading literature by Zola and Dostoyevsky, I was studying politics, I was living in a beautiful part of the country, and I was having afternoon sex. The world was a wonderful place. On many days I forgot that Thatcher was in power.

One weekend Alison and I drove to see her mother in Berkshire. Or rather Alison drove us in her white Fiat 126. Her parents had divorced a few years earlier and it is fair to say her mother hadn't taken it well. One afternoon when she was driving in Camberley town centre she spotted her ex-husband with his new partner. In a fit of rage she tried to run them down and probably would have succeeded if a lamp post hadn't intervened. I am not sure Cosmo's advice on dealing with divorce would have helped her.

We turned off the road into a gravel drive with 'in' and 'out' gates. It was the largest house I had ever visited. The only detached house I had been inside was a neighbour's in Swindon, who invited us in to watch the 1970 World Cup match between England and Brazil on his colour TV. This house was different; it was in the centre of its own plot of land, it wasn't in a street like normal houses. Clearly there was money to be made in fish and chips.

Alison's parents were not alone in getting divorced. On 24 March 1981, the *Daily Mirror* headline was 'Decade of Divorce'. In the ten years since the Divorce Reform Act in 1972 the number of divorces had trebled. The *Daily Mirror* claimed Britain had the worst divorce statistics of any country in western Europe. Anne Robinson reported on Court 34 of the London Law Courts where in less than ten minutes the names of a dozen couples were read and divorce decrees announced. The paper also reported on the Newham Solo Club where recent divorcees went to have a Babycham and find new partners.

Alison's mother was anxious, always getting up and moving around to find things to worry about. When Alison was younger her mother was concerned that her ears were too big and had taped them to her head so they didn't stick out. I was on my best behaviour and we got on well until I took out my Tony Benn book. Alison's mum went white. To my surprise she was physically trembling. She told me she was not going to have communist books in her house. I tried to deflect her anger by saying I was studying politics and it was a set book. This helped calm things but she insisted it would be better if I took the book out to the car and left it there. She seemed worried that the book might infect her house like a virus. I decided it was probably best not to talk politics over dinner.

It was not the first time I had come across strong reactions to Tony Benn. When I was seventeen I went out for a few months with a girl called Debbie, who, inspired by Blondie's *Picture This*, promised to let me watch her shower. Her father hated Benn and didn't think I was a suitable boyfriend for his daughter. It was probably as well that he didn't know about our afternoons in their shower. Once, while I was still in the room, he told Debbie that socialists were losers and she should never marry one. He said if she married a socialist she would condemn herself to travelling on a bus for the rest of her life. Luckily I was not considering marriage or asking for his consent. He was happy when we broke up and she started dating someone who, rather than arguing with him, agreed with his view that we should never trust the French.

I was elated in the spring when XTC came to play at the university. I told everyone how they came from my school, which was not quite true but close enough. The father of the bassist, Colin Moulding, was the caretaker at our school. I bought a black and white XTC badge where the letters combined to create a picture of a face. It didn't make coming from Swindon cool; nothing could do that, but it was something.

In the student union elections, Bunny stood unopposed for the position of union secretary. His manifesto said students should vote for him as he was the only person willing to take on the work. It was a fair point. He was elected, just managing to scrape over the required quota. It was almost as close as the winning margin in the Eurovision Song Contest later that month. Buck's Fizz won by four votes with their travesty of a song *Making Your Mind Up*. It was hard to disagree with the French who said the competition had become "a monument to drivel" and refused to enter a song the following year.

In the student presidential election Alison and I campaigned for Helen, a member of the Labour Club. *Spike* published her campaign manifesto below a photograph of her holding a cigarette and wearing leather boots. In the election she comfortably defeated her opponents Captain Birdseye and Jimmy 'Guitar' Watson to become the first woman president of the student union. I saw it as a major political victory for those of us in Badgeland. A sign the times were changing.

I also supported Alison's campaign for a proper vegetarian counter at the Norwood refectory, rather than a token counter that did baked potatoes and omelettes. To my surprise the university agreed. It was yet another victory. They even employed a proper vegetarian chef, Vikki Lodder, from a restaurant in Truro that Egon Ronay had recommended. The number of students eating at the refectory doubled after her arrival. Our generation was going to change the world, one nut loaf at a time.

Alison and I were driving in her car when BBC radio

reported that Labour were ten points ahead of the Conservatives. Despite all the hype, the old people's new SDP party was only polling at 15 percent. We celebrated by punching the air and playing Stevie Wonder's *Happy Birthday* at full volume. It was only a matter of time before we had a socialist government.

19

HUNGER STRIKES AND RIOTS

In January 1981, gunmen from the Red Hand Commando, a small Ulster Loyalist paramilitary group in Northern Ireland, smashed down the front door of the MP, Bernadette McAliskey with sledgehammers. They shot her three times but she survived. On the same day two gunmen walked into a customs office in Warrenpoint, South Down. They forced the staff to line up and asked for Ivan Toombs, a part-time member of the Ulster Defence Regiment. When he stepped forward they shot him dead. In the same week a parcel bomb addressed to the prime minister was intercepted by a sorting office worker. The troubles in Northern Ireland were reaching breaking point.

In March 1981, Bobby Sands began a hunger strike in support of the IRA's campaign to be treated as political prisoners. Thatcher, who would never forgive them for murdering her friend Airey Neave, was unmoved by the campaign. There would be no concessions; if they wanted to die of hunger that was their choice. To Thatcher the IRA, like Nelson Mandela, were terrorists not political prisoners.

Four days after the start of the hunger strike the MP for

Fermanagh and South Tyrone, Frank McGuire, died and the Republicans seized on the by-election as a way to raise the profile of the hunger strike campaign. Despite being in jail Bobby Sands was chosen as the new Republican candidate. It was a bitterly contested election which only had two candidates, Sands and an Ulster Unionist. On Thursday, 9 April 1981, Sands won the election with 51 percent of the vote.

The *Daily Mirror* claimed the election victory was a major propaganda coup for the IRA and a boost to their hunger strike campaign. The paper also said Sands, who had not eaten for eight weeks, was growing weak. His pulse and blood pressure were dangerously low. The paper said the new MP was likely to die within weeks if the prime minister did not intervene. Thatcher remained unmoved. She insisted the IRA were criminals. "There can be no question of granting political status."

Bobby Sands died on 5 May 1981. He was only twenty-seven. Over a hundred thousand people lined the route of his funeral.

He was not mourned in Swindon. My dad was only disappointed that the Home Championship, an annual football tournament, was cancelled when the English and Welsh teams refused to travel to Northern Ireland citing security concerns. Over Sunday lunch I told my parents we needed to understand why the IRA was pursuing its campaign, and gave them an uninvited and unwanted history lesson on Ireland.

My family ate quietly as I talked. When I finished Mum asked if we wanted Angel Delight for pudding. Frustrated at the lack of response I ratcheted up my anger, becoming deliberately provocative and melodramatic while Alison maintained a diplomatic silence. I said I was a staunch supporter of a united Ireland and if I were a nineteen-year-old Catholic in Northern Ireland I would support the IRA. There was a glint of cold anger in my father's blue eyes that I had never seen before. He cut across me and told me to shut up. It was like a Rottweiler baring his teeth, warning you not to take another step. I had finally roused his rage and was fearful of what might happen next. He stood up and I flinched. He picked up his plate and walked to the kitchen. I went quiet and we never discussed Ireland again.

Nine more men died as the hunger strike continued but Thatcher remained unmoved. By the summer relatives of the hunger strikers were intervening to stop their husbands, sons and brothers dying. The government made some minor concessions but effectively the IRA capitulated on terms that had been offered to them five months earlier and Thatcher went to the top of the IRA's death list.

In England there was a growing sense of despair in the inner cities and in former industrial towns as unemployment continued to rise. The Trade Secretary, John Biffen, stupidly said this was a good thing as the dole queue had replaced overmanning. The Thatcher government was ridiculously out of touch. Ten percent of working adults were unemployed. UB40's song *One in Ten*, said it was a statistic of a world that didn't care. The song reached number seven in the charts.

Alison and I spent a weekend in Essex with Tessa and Phil. Over lunch Tessa was furious that in places like Birmingham unemployment amongst young black men was over 30 percent and as high as 48 percent in some areas due to racial discrimination. Phil said Thatcher was throwing oil on the fire by giving the police new powers to question black people about their immigration status and that in London the Metropolitan Police were increasingly targeting black people to combat rising street crime.

Tessa was particularly agitated about increasing attacks on black people by right-wing gangs, including fire bombings of black shops and houses. Thirteen young black people died when a house in New Cross was petrol bombed. No one was arrested and the slogan, 'Thirteen dead and nothing said' came to symbolise the community's growing anger at indifference to their plight.

Like other towns Swindon had an active National Front group and racist attacks were common. On Friday, 10 April 1981, racists stabbed and murdered a black youth, Malcolm Chambers, in Swindon town centre. Mum said it was very sad. I replied it wasn't sad, it was a racist murder and people had to start fighting back.

The fightback started in Brixton. The simmering resentment at racism, police harassment and the criminalisation of black communities exploded into violence and rioting. Over one weekend fifty-six police vehicles were burnt out and over two hundred police officers were injured. They got what they deserved according to the youths that took part in the uprising. The Metropolitan Police had to deploy over two and a half thousand officers to quell the rioting. Newspapers called it the 'battle of Brixton'. In Dad's *Daily Mirror,* Enoch Powell said, "You have seen nothing yet", and warned of a racial civil war.

The Brixton uprising was followed by major riots in Toxteth and Moss Side, where more than a thousand people besieged the local police station. As we moved from spring to summer riots broke out in more than thirty-five towns and cities across Britain. They included Birmingham and Bradford, Blackburn and Bedford, Leeds and Leicester, Portsmouth and Preston, Sheffield and Southampton, Newcastle and Nottingham, Edinburgh and Ellesmere Port, Wolverhampton and Wycombe.

Tony Benn attacked the rioters saying, "The Labour Party does not believe in rioting as a route to social progress nor are we prepared to see the police injured during the course of their duties." What else were young black people supposed to do to call attention to the racism they were experiencing? The riots mainly caused damage to property not people, and they worked in terms of getting attention. The hated SUS law, where the police stopped, searched and arrested people if they suspected they intended to commit an offence, was repealed on 27 August 1981. The government said the repeal had been in the works for some time but I was convinced it was the riots that hastened its demise.

The single *Ghost Town* by The Specials, topped the charts over the summer and captured the sense of urban decay. It was music as social commentary, like The Jam's *A Town Called Malice* which had also topped the charts earlier in the year. Both songs gave voice to the growing tensions and increasing anger behind the violence on the streets of Britain's inner cities.

For the middle classes in the suburbs and country villages the riots were something they watched on TV. They lived in a parallel universe of nostalgia, country houses, royal weddings and cricket. At the cinema they watched *Chariots of Fire*. A film about patriotic, upper class British athletes striving for success at the 1924 Paris Olympics, with slow motion shots of athletes running across a beach in white shorts to a moving musical score by Vangelis. Britain had become two countries. I found myself in the Britain of villages, cricket and morris dancing.

At the end of the summer term I moved into a large old house in Freshford, with Rob, his girlfriend Florence, and Alison. Freshford was a small village on the other side of the campus from Bath reached via Brass Knocker Hill which twisted and turned down past Monkton Combe. Our house was a three-storey Georgian building built in Bath stone with wooden shutters. There was a large open fireplace in the lounge but it lacked central heating. At the end of the road by the church was a red telephone box that I would use to call home occasionally. I wasn't great at calling home. I suspect the whole of Freshford voted Tory though there may have been a few Liberals amongst the white, elderly population. It was like living on a Merchant and Ivory film set. We were surrounded by chocolate box villages like Limpley Stoke and walked in picturesque countryside near the Dundas aqueduct where the canal passed over the river Avon.

There were no riots in Freshford, and nothing to disturb our tranquil river walks. I still went to LPYS meetings and sold the *Militant* outside Bath Abbey but afterwards I would drive back to our life in a world of English fetes and morris dancing. Rob would clank down the stairs with bells strapped below his knees and wave his white handkerchief as he drove off in his Triumph Spitfire. We would often join him and watch from a safe distance drinking scrumpy, as his morris troop hopped and bashed their sticks together on village greens. On late summer evenings we walked along the canal path and across the toll bridge over the river Avon at Batheaston.

In July, Ian Botham led England's cricket team to a remarkable victory over Australia at Headingley. I was conflicted. I wanted England to win but I was concerned that winning would be good for Thatcher.

At the end of the month Prince Charles and Lady Diana Spencer got hitched at St Paul's Cathedral. It was a bizarre arranged marriage because evidently protocol demanded that Charles had to marry a virgin. Diana was nineteen when she sat next to the thirty-two-year-old for their engagement pictures. Arranged marriages of younger women to older men was a thing in the upper reaches of society. The newspapers spun a fairy tale of romantic love and more than thirty million people watched the wedding on television.

In Freshford we held a 'Not the Royal Wedding' party and cheered Ken Livingstone, the leader of the Greater London

Council, when he declined his invitation and instead declared his support for the abolition of the British monarchy. I loved him for that even though it upset my mum. My parents were not really royalists; we rarely ever watched the Queen's speech on Christmas Day, but Mum would hear nothing said against her.

The wedding was good business for the romantic book publisher Mills & Boon, who was soon selling over two hundred and fifty million romantic novels a year. Princess Diana was like one of Barbara Cartland's heroines who had to be virgins and have a ring on their finger before they went to bed with a man. For Cartland a sexy man was one "fully clothed and preferably in uniform". Films and TV programmes celebrated the new aristocratic fashion. Princess Diana with her strings of pearls, turned up collars, and Hunter wellington boots became a style icon celebrated in the *Sloane Ranger Handbook*, which sold over a million copies.

Aristocratic fashion was also celebrated by Granada TV in their adaptation of *Brideshead Revisited*. Using new high quality cameras the programme created beautiful, sumptuous images of England as it followed the lives of rich people living on a country estate. The programme became aspirational viewing and found an enthusiastic audience. There was a surge in people wearing Barbour jackets, buying flowery fabrics from Laura Ashley and visiting country houses. The membership of the National Trust doubled as people wandered country estates dreaming of floppy-haired young men in linen suits, sipping champagne on the lawn.

The summer newspapers carried dramatic photos of inner city riots and burning cars alongside sunny images of the royal wedding, cricket fields and country houses. It was a portrait of a divided Britain.

20

TONY BENN FOR DEPUTY

'Tony Benn: Is he Mad or just a Killer?'

K elvin MacKenzie's headline in the *Sun* on 22 May 1981, provided for no other possibility.

Benn had decided to challenge Denis Healey for the deputy leadership of the Labour Party and published a manifesto where he said he was committed to abolishing private schools and private health. Unlike other Labour MPs Benn did not send his children to private school. Alison and I enthusiastically agreed with Benn. Health should be provided on the basis of need not wealth. It was obscene that rich people pushed poorer people down the queue for healthcare. How could you defend such things? To my nineteen-year-old self it was simply wrong. I pinned a 'Tony Benn for Deputy' badge to my denim jacket.

MacKenzie argued that if people voted for Benn they were voting to live in Eastern Europe. The *Daily Express* compared Benn to Adolf Hitler, because his promise to abolish private education was obviously the equivalent of murdering six million people.

The election was to be the first vote to take place under the new electoral college which I had helped to create. The *Daily Mirror* reported that Michael Foot was pleading with Benn not to stand and ran a front page saying 'Don't Do It Tony'. Foot was worried there would be six months of internal party fighting which the press, the Conservatives and the newly created SDP would exploit.

Peter Shore, the Shadow Chancellor, criticised Benn for creating a 'betrayal' theory of Labour history. What nonsense, the working-classes *had* been betrayed. I rallied to Benn's support as did my Militant comrades. The Labour MP, Neil Kinnock, denounced us as raving mad, saying Benn's manifesto insulted one's intelligence and should be treated with the derision it deserved. He argued the manifesto guaranteed disappointment. Why? Why couldn't you abolish private education and private health? How could you be a socialist and support such things?

The Yorkshire miners' leader, Arthur Scargill, argued Kinnock and the Tribune Group of Labour MPs were sabotaging socialism. I agreed. They said they wanted change but in reality they were committed to keeping the existing system with its establishment and its inequalities. I wasn't sure who the establishment were but I was pretty damn sure they sent their kids to private schools and jumped the queues for medical treatment.

In the summer I attended a Militant weekend school. George was also supposed to come but we were not surprised when he failed to show up as we waited for the minibus. I travelled with a dozen Militant supporters including Trotsky, in his mariners cap and greatcoat. During the drive he told us Militant had become so threatening to the establishment that the police would already have installed spies in the group.

"It is highly likely that one of us on this minibus is a government spy," he said.

I didn't know why he was looking at me; I would make the world's worst spy. Just Trotsky looking at me made me feel guilty. I was almost ready to admit it was me. I broke his gaze, suddenly finding something interesting on the floor of the van. Phil was excited by Trotsky's comments and leaned forward saying, "That's right, MI5 are bound to be tracking what we are doing."

If there was a spy in the Bath LPYS meetings it had to be one of the three of us. My money was on Matt. He was a textbook revolutionary in his donkey jacket and with his scouse accent.

In the first session of the weekend Ted Grant told us, to great applause, that the establishment were worried because we had become the biggest threat to the capitalist system. Were we really that threatening? I looked around at the faces in the lecture theatre. Were there really MI5 spies in the room? Surely it wasn't the sallow youths at the front chewing through doughnuts like they had not eaten for a week and dropping food down their revolutionary jackets adorned with badges. I began to wonder if the comrades were losing their grasp on reality.

It turned out that Trotsky was right. During the Callaghan era, MI5 identified Militant as the main subversive threat in the UK. They were concerned its successful 'entryist' activities were subverting Labour Party democracy, and planted thirty secret agents within Militant's ranks. So maybe there really were MI5 agents in the lecture room.

I enjoyed many of the talks but I was troubled by Militant's certainty. The comrades predicted with absolute confidence that capitalism was about to collapse, just as the real Trotsky claimed it would. They seemed untroubled by the fact Trotsky's claim was made before the Second World War. After which we had never had it so good. In Swindon people were painting their houses in Dulux soft tones, placing twenty-six-inch colour TVs above Betamax video recorders, and decorating their walls with holiday souvenirs from Spain. It was not how I imagined a pre-revolutionary period.

Despite encouraging debate, if someone challenged the Militant line the comrades would double down on their views. The miscreant would be educated to see the truth of the situation. In the bar there was a discussion of revolutionary groups and the decision of the Revolutionary Communist Tendency to rename itself the Revolutionary Communist Party. Senior comrades were dismissive of their guru, Frank Furedi, a lecturer in sociology at the University of Kent, and his clique of middle-class revolutionaries. They were equally critical of the Socialist Workers Party and its apparent theoretical blunders about the character of the post-Stalinist period.

On the Saturday evening we had to sleep in small dormitories with bunk beds. I was uneasy about communal sleeping. I had shared a bedroom with my brother but that was different. In the night I was woken by some of the comrades staggering into the room in the darkness. As they passed my bunk I could smell the alcohol and cigarette smoke. There were sounds of fumbling as they tried to undress. The air became sour and sweaty, like the kitchen at home when Mum boiled cabbage to death on the cooker. There was then the unmistakable sound of someone pissing, followed by screaming. The lights went on and a drunk comrade was standing over a lower bunk; he had urinated over the head of an unfortunate young guy sleeping there. There was pandemonium, punches were thrown and the pissing comrade fell to the floor with his trousers around his ankles.

I didn't sleep much after that and got dressed early to leave the dormitory. I walked alone in the fresh air. It was so good to be outside. I debated heading back to Bath and missing the second day. I finally went to the large open room where breakfast was served. There was much excited chatter and laughing as news of the incident bubbled through the room. I joined Matt for coffee. He had already heard. He explained that disciplinary action was going to be taken against the drunk comrade. At the start of the first session one of the Militant leaders made a speech that didn't refer to the incident directly but made it clear the Tendency strongly discouraged drug taking and excessive alcohol.

At the end of the second day Peter Taaffe spoke and urged us to contribute money to enable Militant to take the fight to the Tories. He asked for donations from the audience. One person stood up and spoke emotionally about how we needed a socialist society. He then pledged to give Militant five hundred pounds. I was amazed. I supported the group's aims but I wasn't handing over five hundred pounds. It didn't occur to me at the time that he may have been a plant. The fundraising was like an auction in reverse: "Who will contribute fifty pounds", "who will donate twenty pounds for a socialist future", "who will give ten pounds to help us fight the Tories". Each time I kept my hand down. Finally Taaffe said he wanted to see "a forest of green" by which he meant hundreds of hands holding up one pound notes. I fished out a note from my pocket and held it aloft while comrades walked around and collected the money. On the way back Matt talked enthusiastically about the event. I didn't join in. I think he sensed my deflation.

After the weekend I wasn't sure MI5 needed to worry much about Militant. The tactics they adopted might be effective but they were so earnest and dogmatic. I no longer saw them building a mass movement. It seems MI5's agents drew similar conclusions. They reported back to Thatcher that Militant was not having a significant impact on events. While Thatcher feared a revolution and Militant promoted one, most of the population were actually at home happily watching *The Two Ronnies*.

There was a lot of bad feeling about Benn's opponent Denis Healey and claims he had betrayed the working class. I knew he was on the right but I didn't understand the degree of hatred. Healey had been a communist but said the actions of Russia in Hungary and Czechoslovakia in the fifties and sixties had made him pro-NATO. He criticised left-wing politics as "rhetorical candy floss" and was as scathing of Militant as they were of him. I began to see why Foot was nervous about the contest.

In the summer my parents got on a plane for the first time to fly to Spain. I was jealous of my younger sister who went with them. My parents were not alone in expanding their horizons beyond Margate. Following the death of Franco in 1975, the Spanish government had been heavily promoting tourism and at the start of the 1980s there was a huge growth in Spanish package holidays. The Lunn Poly shop near the Brunel Centre was packed as people visited the travel agent to book plane tickets for the first time. Foreign holidays were such a novelty that neighbours were invited to sit around slide projectors and eat vol-au-vents, while admiring the highlights of David and Barbara's trip to Benidorm.

Despite Thatcher's personal views on thrift and the virtues of saving, her government backed the expansion of personal credit which fuelled a travel and shopping boom. Personal debt rocketed in the 1980s as people visited the new shopping malls and equipped their homes with freezers, video recorders and computers. Thatcher personally opened the Milton Keynes shopping centre with its sub-tropical trees, six department stores and one hundred and thirty shops. Beryl Bainbridge called it a cathedral to the credit card, a place where people paid their respects to the new consumer society.

Thatcher and Reagan's promotion of free, unbridled capitalism was being enthusiastically embraced by major corporations. In August 1981, Jack Welch, the new CEO of General Electric, made a speech in New York about "growing fast".[1] His view was that companies should focus ruthlessly on shareholder value to the exclusion of everything else. He promoted offshoring jobs to lower cost locations around the world to save money. He was seen as the new God by the business community who enthusiastically supported his philosophy.

Welch agreed with Milton Friedman, Thatcher's favourite economist, that a company had no social responsibility to the public or wider society. According to Friedman a company's only responsibility was to its shareholders which meant increasing profits. Thatcher and Reagan agreed. Companies should focus on making profits and the invisible hand of the market would ensure everything in society would be just dandy. They were appalled by the idea that businesses should be constrained by social or environmental considerations. Sure. Don't worry your shareholders about environmental damage, the staff that die from asbestosis or the communities destroyed when businesses relocate to lower cost locations.

Welch was also a psycho who fired the bottom 10 percent of his company's managers every year regardless of their performance. Despite this he was named 'Manager of the Century' by *Fortune* magazine whose investors benefited from his focus on shareholder returns.

To encourage CEOs to act solely in the interests of shareholders new compensation packages were designed. The focus was on driving up share prices. If the share price increased, CEOs made obscene amounts of money. CEO salaries, despite being disgustingly high, were becoming insignificant relative to their bonuses and share options. When Reagan and Thatcher were elected CEOs earned around thirty times more than the average worker. This would grow to three hundred and sixty-eight times in less than a decade.

～

In the middle of 1981 the SDP entered into an alliance with the Liberals. The two parties agreed to work together and form a coalition government if they won a majority of seats in the next election. They were clearly living in an alternate reality; there was no way people were going to vote for them. Not now we had Michael Foot as leader and potentially Tony Benn as deputy leader. It was a socialist dream team, one that would inspire working-class people to vote Labour.

Unfortunately my enthusiasm was not shared by the public.

At the start of September the SDP-Liberal Alliance was polling ahead of both the Conservatives and Labour. Buoyed by the polls the Liberal leader David Steel, famous for his striped shirts with white collars, told delegates at their party conference in Llandudno to go back to their constituencies and prepare for government. The SDP supporters at university became unbearable, parading their smiley enthusiasm like born again evangelists.

On Saturday, 19 September 1981, there was a Labour rally against unemployment in Birmingham where both Tony Benn and Denis Healey spoke. I wasn't there but the following day the press was full of reports that Benn supporters wouldn't let Healey speak. Despite appeals by Michael Foot the crowd continually chanted "Tory" at him so loudly he was forced to sit. The *Sunday Mirror* front page headline read, 'Healey gagged by Benn mob'.

I didn't like Healy but I didn't see the point of shouting him down. By all means heckle and make your objections known but surely stopping him speaking only reinforced the press claims of left intolerance. But it was difficult to reason with some on the left, particularly those that pissed on people while they were sleeping.

At the end of September the deputy leadership contest finally took place. It was the first Labour Party election to use the party's new electoral college system. When all the second ballot votes were initially tallied and counted Benn was in the lead by less than 1 percent but on the recount he lost by less than 1 percent. I was suspicious of the recount but Benn accepted it. The soft left Labour MPs abstained rather than voting for Benn. Neil Kinnock was one of the abstainers. It was unforgivable. How could you abstain? You had to choose a side.

The result was so agonisingly close. It was like Swindon being relegated by a single point but Benn was not depressed. He claimed his campaign had been a victory for those of us on the left as we had won the argument. He added we had to fight for socialism over and over again, "so toughen up. Bloody toughen up". Ken Livingstone agreed. He told the *Socialist Organiser* that the vote was a major achievement for the left and the transformation of the Labour Party into a socialist party was now clearly irreversible.

21

TARQUIN BISCUIT-BARREL

I was watching the Conservative Party Conference when a Birmingham councillor called Edwina Currie stood at the rostrum waving handcuffs in the air. I think she was making some point to Willie Whitelaw, the Home Secretary, about locking more people up. The Tories liked locking people up. I suspected that many of the older Conservative men were not thinking of law and order but rather dreaming of Currie chained to a bed. Or more likely dreaming of her chaining them to a bed.

The biggest conference cheers were for Norman Tebbit when he blamed people for being unemployed. He said his father didn't riot when he was unemployed. Instead, "He got on his bike and looked for work and he kept looking until he found it."

On 24 October 1981, I travelled with members of Bath CND to a rally in Hyde Park. On the coach I sat behind an old lady called Mary, who had grey hair tied up in a bun. She told us that in the early 1960s she had marched from the atomic weapons establishment in Aldermaston to London on some of the first CND demonstrations.

When we arrived I had never seen so many people. It was like the world had descended on London. The sight almost brought tears to my eyes. I was not Cliffy's boy with the strange views, I was part of a mass movement. We were going to do this, we were going to change things. I bought two red badges that said 'Together we can stop the bomb, 24 October'. I gave one to Mary and hugged her, much to her surprise.

There were thousands of banners from grand embroidered trade union flags held up between wooden poles, to homemade placards saying, 'Fall out with Thatcher'. Our chants were a little repetitive, such as 'Maggie, Maggie, Maggie, Out, Out, Out', and lacked the creativity of football chants such as, 'He's fat, he's round, he bounces on the ground'. But I couldn't stop smiling and had to resist embracing everyone.

The rally was so much bigger than the year before and had to be held in Hyde Park rather than Trafalgar Square. There were over a quarter of a million of us though according to the police there were just two of us and a dog. Tony Benn and Michael Foot both spoke against the insanity of nuclear weapons, though I couldn't really tell you what they said. Their muffled voices had faded across the open park before they reached me.

In November, Michael Foot attended the Remembrance Sunday ceremony at the Cenotaph in his best overcoat. The press attacked him as a scruffy old man who hated our armed forces and wore a donkey jacket that disrespected the war dead. It was not true but there was no counter-attack from Labour portraying him as a patriot in a smart overcoat he had bought from Harrods. An overcoat that the Queen Mother had complimented him on. Britain simply accepted MacKenzie's donkey jacket version. Facts were not allowed to spoil a good story.

On 26 November 1981, the traitorous Shirley Williams, wearing a bizarre oversized red, white and blue flower rosette, won a by-election in Crosby. She overturned a Conservative majority of twenty thousand and gained almost 50 percent of the vote. I had no problems with the Tories losing but Labour's vote fell off a cliff. The party lost their deposit and only narrowly beat the Raving Loony Party's candidate Tarquin Biscuit-Barrel, a student who had changed his name by deed poll in homage to a *Monty Python* election night sketch. It was the SDP's first election victory and Williams declared there was no longer a safe seat in the country.

The day after the election Williams was pictured celebrating by drinking champagne in the Blundellsands Hotel. Support for the SDP surged and everyone lost all sense of proportion. The *Daily Mirror* said the SDP-Liberal Alliance were now, "the punters' favourite to be the largest party at the next election". The *New York Times* said they were likely to become the next government. I comforted myself that Americans knew nothing about British politics.

The following week I read my copy of *Militant* with growing despondency. The paper argued the fall in the Labour vote was because the public wanted more radical policies. I didn't understand. Why, if people wanted a more left-wing candidate, would they vote for Shirley Williams?

At the end of the month there was an 11 percent fall in Labour's support. It didn't make sense. The party was now polling lower than at any point in the previous ten years, despite our new leader and our radical policies. Maybe the public didn't realise we were promising nuclear disarmament and higher taxes to fund better public services. It had to be a rogue poll. Labour's support couldn't fall 11 percent in a month.

Alison and I spent most of Christmas in front of the TV in Swindon. Top of the Pops was opened by Teardrop Explodes and followed by Kim Wilde singing about *Kids In America*, Clare Grogan singing *Happy Birthday* and Kirsty MacColl telling us *There's a Guy Works Down The Chip Shop Swears He's Elvis*. I would like to say it was a great time for music but also in the charts was Cliff Richard singing *Daddy's Home* and Julio Iglesias singing *Begin the Beguine* in Spanish.

After lunch we slumped soporific in front of the TV. Bizarrely Mum took the opportunity to update her Green Shield stamp books while Dad slept through most of *The Two Ronnies*, though he claimed he was just resting his eyes. He woke up for his new favourite show, *Only Fools and Horses*. It was John Sullivan's follow-up sitcom to *Citizen Smith*, which tracked the ups and downs of the market trader Del Boy and his brother Rodney. Alison declined a fourth glass of Blue Nun and Mum made her tea. It came in a royal wedding mug, with Charles and Diana smiling inside a gilt oval.

In January, Alison and I moved into a room in a shared house in Bath city centre. The house in Freshford was lovely in the summer but in the winter it was a nightmare. The roof leaked, it was damp and it was cold. There was no heating other than the open fire in the lounge. Rob got increasingly angry at the landlord for not fixing the leaks and shortly after another altercation we left.

The National Union of Students was becoming increasingly unhappy about the declining value of our student grants and launched a campaign for an increase of 17.4 percent. You had to give them points for precision. Surely Thatcher would recognise that we couldn't survive on 17.1 percent. The NUS asked student unions across the country to organise a week of protest actions to support the campaign.

In Bath our radical actions included street theatre, a teach-in and a music concert, which we were encouraged to attend to show the strength of our feelings. Thursday was designated as a day of rest to enable us to recover from the exertions of our protests and to catch up with our studies. Surprisingly Thatcher was not persuaded by our street theatre, and the government announced that student grants would be increased by just 4 percent later in the autumn.

February's edition of *Spike* carried an edited picture of Bunny with a Hitler moustache and his arm raised, as if in a Sieg Heil salute. Under the title 'Bunny's lust' it made unfounded allegations about his sex life, including inviting women back to his room to 'watch television'. They also said he denied being a Tory wet after having a bucket of water tipped over him. I was increasingly uncomfortable at his treatment. It seemed childish, unnecessary and did nothing to enhance political debate. The newspaper also asked why people had started colouring their hair and if there was a vermillion burgundy lookalike contest. I thought maybe my henna hair had to go.

In the union elections Paul was elected as social secretary and took even more time off his studies to organise events. Following his elevation, Paul's band, A Shot in the Dark, got some high profile exposure supporting groups that came to play at the university. I am sure it was just coincidence. I went to one gig featuring a lanky frontman for a band called Pulp who, as far as I could tell, was singing about the crabs that killed Sheffield. I must have misheard.

I was no longer that interested in music unlike the students that read *The Face* and talked about bands like Talking Heads. When the Thompson Twins came to the university I was surprised to see there were seven of them and had to be informed that the band's name came from the bowler-hatted Thompson Twins in *Tintin*. I even missed seeing The Jam play at Shepton Mallet, a market town about fifteen miles from Bath. I am not sure how it got added to their tour schedule. I couldn't imagine someone saying London, Manchester, Birmingham and oh, Shepton Mallet, must make sure we reach our fans in Somerset. The review in *Spike* called the band's rendition of *A Town Called Malice* a 'magnificent howl of outrage at Thatcherite Britain'.

Once, in fear of missing out, I bought a copy of *The Face* which had a picture of Spandau Ballet's Martin Kemp on the front cover. I browsed through the pages. It was like a stylish advertising magazine, more *Marxism Today* than *Militant* or *Socialist Worker*. It seemed more style over substance to me. It was full of photographs, large typography and edgy graphics that promoted a form of Thatcherite individualism. The images and graphics didn't hold my attention. I flicked from one page to the next and decided I wasn't that interested in fashion. Surely you couldn't go far wrong with lime green trousers and a denim jacket full of political badges.

Despite the initial hype about the SDP-Liberal Alliance, their vote share in the polls had started to fall back. People were coming to their senses. Thatcher remained the most unpopular prime minister since polling began and was losing her touch. In the House of Commons Denis Healey made a devastating speech on how her broken promises had resulted in rising unemployment and crime. Thatcher became flustered, lost her place in her notes and admitted she had her facts wrong. The journalist Simon Jenkins said she was undeniably in trouble and could not last much longer.

A week later the Tories lost a by-election in Glasgow Hillhead, a seat they had held since its creation. Roy Jenkins of the SDP won with a 14 percent swing against the Conservatives. There was another swing against Labour but I reasoned it was due to tactical voting to get the Tories out. The result was a disaster for Thatcher. It had taken three years but she was finally finished.

Then everything changed.

22

KINTSUGI

I am willing to bet that at the start of April 1982, more people could sing the words of *Begin the Beguine* in Spanish than place the Falkland Islands on a map. Mind you, most people couldn't place the Isle of Man on a map. The Falklands were over eight thousand miles from the UK and had a population of less than three thousand people, primarily the descendants of British settlers.

The Argentinians had historically laid claim to the islands, which they called the Malvinas. After decades of diplomacy Thatcher's government, concerned at the costs of maintaining the islands, had started discussions on handing back sovereignty to Argentina. Before any final decision could be taken the Argentine President General Leopoldo Galtieri ordered the invasion of the islands.

It was a classic political ploy by Galtieri. He wanted to divert attention away from his country's domestic economic and political problems; and stir up Argentine nationalism. Given the discussions to hand back control of the islands he did not expect a military response from the United Kingdom. Unfortunately for him, Thatcher had even greater economic, social and political problems at home. Encouraged by Admiral Sir Henry Leach, the Chief of the Naval Staff, she enthusiastically took the decision to go to war to free the islands.

I was disappointed when Michael Foot backed Thatcher's decision. I supported Tony Benn, who opposed going to war, and called for the United Nations to intervene. Benn argued Thatcher was risking the lives of servicemen and said the British people would oppose the sending of a task force. He was wrong. Within days the UK was brimming with nationalist sentiment at the idea of saving the Falkland islanders and their sheep. There were suddenly Union Jacks everywhere.

As the Task Force sailed to the Falklands, I broke up with Alison. The cause was Céline, a petite French student, who traced her fingers up the inside of my thigh and whispered in my ear the things she would like me to do to her.

I think it was a Greek philosopher who first said that the male libido was like being chained to an idiot. They were right. Céline's fingers led me to make one of the most stupid decisions of my life. Jane Austen should have said, "It is a truth universally acknowledged that a man whose cock gets hard loses all reason and makes reckless decisions." I would like to say it is a truth that only applies to young men but it also applies to presidents and prime ministers.

On the third day of my 'relationship' with Céline, I lay on her narrow campus bed dog-tired after a long night of sex, little sleep and almost nothing to eat. Céline seemed to survive on a diet of black coffee and nicotine. The room began to glow as the morning sun streamed through the red curtains and we started to talk, something that we had not found time for over the previous two days.

Céline sat above me, one elbow resting on her wrist, holding a cigarette out between the first two fingers of her upturned hand like Brigitte Bardot. She then proceeded to tell me how French people could never be vegetarians. I was still reflecting on this when she said, "I really admire Margaret Thatcher."

I thought she was winding me up. I waited for her to punch me in the arm and say, "Ha, got you." Instead she said, "Things are terrible in France, Mitterrand is working with the communists to introduce a ridiculous wealth tax." Not even her sexy pronunciation of 'ridiculous' could lessen the impact of her words. I was sleeping with a reactionary conservative. I didn't understand; surely she had seen my badges. I lay completely still and gazed at the ceiling, which was already yellowing with tobacco stains.

We only lasted another few days as I tried, and failed, to persuade her about the evils of Thatcher. In less than a fortnight I was breaking up with a girlfriend for the second time. Céline was angry and sought to wound me with her gesticulations. She put her thumb under her chin and pushed it out towards me. Then she tilted her head, placed an index finger under her eye, pulled down her cheek and stared at me. I hadn't the foggiest idea what it meant in French but it was disturbing.

The day after my break-up with Céline I sat in my room, hands clasped between my thighs, lips pressed together and stared at the floor. Suddenly I was back in the headmaster's office, I could hear his words, "I am so disappointed in you." My eyes were wet with tears. I watched them drip from my cheeks to the carpet below.

I hadn't given any consideration to Alison's feelings. It was only when she dumped all my stuff on the concourse outside the library that I knew things were not good. What had I expected? I hadn't even thought about it. In the rain I had avoided the looks of other students as I picked up my damp clothes and records from the concrete floor.

I hated myself. I was so self-absorbed and driven by lust that I hadn't thought about how our break-up might affect Alison. I didn't think about what it had taken for her to move in with me, whether she was still fragile after her parents' divorce, that she probably felt humiliated when I arrived in the bar with Céline, that our split could possibly cause her to leave university and that she might never trust men again.

Alison was lovely. She was kind, fun, slightly mad at times admittedly, but we fitted together in a way that Céline and I never could. Alison had been my dream, a woman who looked like Debbie Harry and hated Thatcher even more than me. I had left her for someone I knew absolutely nothing about.

Was it possible to mend things once they were broken? I thought of the Japanese practice of Kintsugi, or golden repair. The art of repairing broken pottery with a lacquer mixed with powdered gold. The idea that with love and care something could be more beautiful after it had been repaired than it was before the damage. A mature person would acknowledge how badly they had behaved, apologise and try to mend things.

I was not a mature person. It would mean facing up to the terrible thing I had done. Maybe it was to protect my sense of self but rather than confront my behaviour I ran away. I chose a strategy of avoidance rather than atonement. I was ashamed of myself. Unable to face people I travelled back to Swindon for the weekend alone. Maybe I wanted the comfort of familiar surroundings. I explained to my parents that Alison and I had broken up – but lied when I said it was a mutual decision and we were both happy.

On Saturday afternoon I went to the County Ground with

Kevin to watch Swindon play Lincoln. The STAB boys had a new chant: 'If you hate the fucking Argies, clap your hands'. It was one of those rare chants where the opposition fans joined in. The team won 1-0, their first win at home for a month. As we walked home Kevin talked constantly. He said I was a lucky charm and I should go to every game but I wasn't really listening. I was still thinking about Alison and how I had lost her through my own stupidity.

~

The Swindon-Oxford rivalry continued on Saturday, 4 May 1982, when we beat Oxford by three goals to two at the County Ground. The Oxford keeper claimed he was left unsighted for the third goal by a smoke bomb thrown by Swindon fans. It was typical of Oxford, making any excuse when they lost. We didn't complain about the farmer's field they called a pitch at their Manor Ground. When the referee rightly permitted the controversial Swindon goal he was pelted with coins by Oxford fans and needed treatment after being hit in the eye. In the following melee police officers were hurt in the fighting and crowd barriers were torn up. The violence made the national news and Swindon were ordered to a face a Football Association disciplinary committee following the crowd trouble.

The following day I walked to the club with Dad and Andy, who had turned eighteen in March. I was conscious of the banter between them as we made our way down the alley. Andy already played in the same football team and had now joined Dad in the darts and crib teams. Andy signed me in to the club with his gold membership card which had 1982 in seventies *Top of the Pops*-style lettering on the front. He had joined on his eighteenth birthday. He told me the sons of members could automatically join when they turned eighteen. This was something I was unaware of, and which Dad had not mentioned to me when I turned eighteen.

In the club Dad refused Bob's offer to buy us a drink.

"No, I'll get them. We can only stay for a couple as we have to be back for dinner." At university I had learnt to call the midday meal lunch but in Swindon it was still dinner.

"No, I insist," said Bob, who was beaming under his floppy fringe like a demented Chewbacca. He told us he was celebrating the purchase of his semi-detached council house.

"Bloody bargain it was," he said. "My missus is chuffed to bits." He stood between Andy and I, and hugged our shoulders with his large arms pulling us into his chest. "What you having boys?"

Bob's purchase was one of one hundred and seventy-four thousand Right to Buy sales in England in 1982. He was still smiling when he set our drinks down on the table.

Andy lifted his pint glass and glugged back most of it in one long swig. As he returned the glass to the table he let out a deep and gratifying sigh. He reminded me of John Mills savouring his cold beer after weeks in the desert in the film *Ice Cold in Alex*. I sipped at my beer; maybe they had changed the formula as it didn't taste as sour as I remembered.

"You still going to buy your mother's place?" said Dad.

"Yep, two of her neighbours have already bought theirs," said Tony. "She's been in that house in Pinehurst nigh on fifty years. Her and my old man never lived anywhere else. Never wanted to. I was born in the front bedroom. Bloody good job I was a boy, as otherwise they were going to name me after the midwife. Mildred."

The men laughed and Tony looked lost for a moment as if trying to remember something. Finally he continued. "Lot of memories in that house. Feels right that we're going to buy it."

"Yeah," said Bob, putting a hand on Tony's shoulder. "So you can sell it in a few years and make a tidy profit."

"Damn right," said Tony, lifting his pint from the table. "Be wrong not to. Never look a gift horse in the mouth and all that."

Pinehurst was Swindon's first council estate. It had been built in the 1920s under the 1919 Housing and Planning Act, which had been promoted by Christopher Addison, who became Swindon's first Labour MP in 1929.

"Has your brother told you how he got on at darts last week?" asked Bob, looking at me.

I stared across the table blankly.

"I blame Father's darts," said Andy as he stretched his arm and mimicked throwing a dart.

"He needed double top to win the game," said Tony, "but the thing hit the wire and bounced out."

"One of them boomerang darts it was," said Bob with a grin. "It almost got Cliffy in the leg."

The guys laughed and Andy's eyes flashed a smile as he finished his pint.

"They're a bloody lucky team, that Blunsdon lot," said Tony, shaking a cigarette from its packet. "Next time we will have them."

"Too right," said Andy, and nudging Dad added, "I just have to get some decent darts first."

"You bugger off," said Dad. "There's nothing wrong with my darts."

"A bad workman always blames his tools," said Tony, as he lit up his cigarette.

"I never blame my tool," said Bob. "Always works perfectly."

The men laughed again and raised their glasses.

In the silence that followed, I asked, "So what do you think about this Falklands conflict?"

I saw Dad shift a little uncomfortably in his seat. It was barely perceptible and it wasn't visible to the others. Maybe I imagined it.

"We're giving them Argies a bloody good hiding," said Tony.

Bob and Andy nodded in agreement.

"I reckon they only invaded them islands to get revenge for 1966," said Tony.

"1966?" I wasn't sure what he was referring to.

"They never accepted their defeat in the quarter-final," said Tony.

"Yeah, they reckoned Hurst's goal was offside," said Bob. "Was it buggery."

"Was that the game where their captain refused to leave the pitch after being sent off?" asked Dad.

"Yeah, had to escorted off by a police officer," said Bob.

"Bloody right too," said Tony. "They never got over that game. I reckon that's what this is really about."

It wasn't a theory I was familiar with. To be fair the Argentinians referred to the game as 'the theft of the century' and the England manager Alf Ramsey did not allow his players to swap shirts, describing the Argentinians as animals. Still, it didn't seem plausible that Galtieri had invaded because of a football match sixteen years earlier. But Tony was wedded to his theory and nothing was going to shake him.

"Good job we have Maggie as prime minister and not that Michael Foot," said Bob.

"Or Tony Benn, he says we shouldn't have sent the taskforce," said Tony. "Says we should talk to Galtieri – look what happened when we tried that with Hitler."

Bob nodded in agreement and I decided to stay silent.

In May the Argentine ship, the *General Belgrano*, was sunk by torpedoes fired by the British nuclear-powered submarine, *HMS Conqueror*. Kelvin MacKenzie at the *Sun* ran a jingoistic headline 'Gotcha!' He was criticised for celebrating the deaths of Argentine sailors but stood defiant saying he was proud of his headline: "The fact that the enemy were killed to my mind was a bloody good thing and I've never had a moment's loss of sleep over it."[1] I suspected the men in Dad's club agreed with him.

At the end of the month the Tories won a by-election in the safe seat of Beaconsfield. It wasn't a surprise but the Labour vote halved as voters switched to the Liberals. The Labour candidate, Tony Blair, lost his deposit. Bunny teased me about the result which I wrote off as an unrepresentative by-election. But Thatcher was suddenly popular in a way that didn't seem possible previously. She was defying political gravity. Unlike Michael Foot, whose personal ratings were sinking faster than the *Belgrano*.

The press attacks about Foot looking like Worzel Gummidge were damaging. He also refused, or was unable, to adapt to the media. In interviews he peered through his bottle bottomed glasses and looked around as if he was lost. He failed to get across his points in short sound bites. Instead he made long rambling speeches. I started to have doubts about Foot leading the party to victory in a general election.

The war was over in ten weeks. The TV news reported a white flag flying over Port Stanley and an army officer said it was "bloody marvellous". A Mori survey found that 85 percent of the public were satisfied with Thatcher's handling of the Falklands crisis. It was incredible, 85 percent. The conflict had stirred up working-class patriotism; people loved the way she stood up for Britain.

Men on the Penhill estate flew the cross of St George from huge flagpoles in their front gardens. By the end of the war the Tories had a twenty-point lead over Labour and Thatcher's personal favourability ratings reached 59 percent, almost double her ratings in February. It was an unprecedented swing in opinion. Politically the war had changed everything. The future was not what it was.

23

KEN LIVINGSTONE

"Ken Livingstone is an IRA-loving, poof-loving Marxist."[1] Bunny put down the copy of the *Daily Express* from which he had been reading and added, "I think you can say that the journalist John Junor is not a fan."

"Thank you, Stuart," said our tutor, Elizabeth, in her soft Scottish accent. She had tasked us with analysing press coverage of Ken Livingstone, the new leader of the Greater London Council. The flip-up wooden tablets attached to the side of our chairs were full of newspapers. There were constant rustling sounds as we took turns to find articles and read to the group.

"The council is now going to be run by a left-wing extremist," said Rob holding up the *Daily Mail*.

Outside there was a break in the clouds and the room was illuminated by sunshine streaming through the metal-framed sash windows.

"Livingstone's election means full-steam-ahead for red-blooded Socialism in London," said Cathy, taking her turn to read from the *Sun*.

"Let's hope they're right," I said.

I hadn't heard of the Greater London Council before Livingstone. To be fair neither had many Londoners. A substantial number thought the London County Council still existed despite it having been abolished and replaced by the GLC in 1965. No one paid much attention to the tiers of local government, and councils rarely made national headline news. That all changed following Livingstone's election as the leader of the council.

There was general agreement in the seminar room that the press were whipping up fear about 'Red Ken' and a socialist GLC. Our tutor pointed out that even the County Hall building, the council's headquarters, was being personified as a swaggering monster drunk on power with its one thousand rooms and twelve miles of corridors.

"I think it's great he has agreed to boycott goods from South Africa," said Alison. It was something she had also advocated at the student union meeting. I nodded my head in agreement. We hadn't spoken since she dumped my clothes outside the library in the rain. Every time I saw her something inside me died but I made a point of acknowledging her with a nod of my head, a raised hand or a smile. She had begun to acknowledge me back, which I took to be a positive sign. It was more than I deserved.

"The press hate him because he's a real socialist," said Rob. "Unlike other champagne socialists he lives in a bedsit with a shared toilet. He's also refused the limousine normally provided to council leaders and says he will only travel on public transport."

This confirmed to Thatcher, Bunny and the press that he was a loser.

Livingstone had promoted women and black people to run key council committees, and set up monitoring to track how many women and ethnic minorities were employed, and at what levels. Kelvin MacKenzie said it was a ridiculous left-wing obsession. What did it matter how many women and black people were employed? MacKenzie was particularly upset that Livingstone had appointed a young black man, Paul Boateng, to be in charge of the police committee. As far as he was concerned it was like putting a fox in charge of the henhouse.

"This MacKenzie bloke is convinced Livingstone is a few sandwiches short of a picnic," said Paul, putting down a copy of *The Sun*.

MacKenzie believed that Livingstone, by promoting equality for black people, women and God forbid, gay people, was mentally ill. He engaged three psychiatrists to analyse Livingstone's behaviour. They concluded that as an only child he was simply saying outlandish things about gay rights to crave attention.

"You have got to admit, it does seem like the lunatics have taken over the asylum," said Bunny. "Declaring London a nuclear-free zone is just mad and refusing to take part in civil defence exercises is irresponsible. That's why the press are calling them the 'loony left'."

He didn't say it but Bunny was convinced, like MacKenzie, that those of us supporting socialist ideas were so deranged we represented a danger to decent society.

Even the *Guardian* was ridiculing the GLC's women's committee that had been set up to oversee policy development and ensure women's views were adequately represented. The chair person was Valerie Wise, a prominent Tony Benn supporter and a frequent target of press criticism. The committee had paid for crèches to allow women to attend policy meetings which, according to the *Daily Mail*, was pure lunacy.

The press were increasingly obsessed by Livingstone's personal life. The *Daily Mirror* rang up his father-in-law in a search for salacious details on the break-up of his marriage and the *Daily Mail* offered his ex-wife £10,000 to tell the inside story of their relationship. Meanwhile outside Livingstone's home so-called journalists fought over his refuse sacks in their hunt for stories about his private life. In the absence of material they simply made stuff up such as Livingstone having a vasectomy, a story which Paul enjoyed retelling.

"They are saying he is a Jaffa after the old flip and snip," said Paul.

"For God's sake Paul," said Cathy, raising her eyes to the ceiling.

"What?" said Paul, holding his hands up in mock innocence. "I am only reporting what they are saying about his old Dickory Dock."

Livingstone was defiant and stood up to the press attacks. The *Daily Mirror* called him the rebel with a cause saying he wanted to create ten thousand new jobs, build one thousand five hundred new homes, and create more nursery schools. The more I read about Livingstone, the more I liked him.

When I returned home at the end of June, I was surprised by the number of new housing estates, factories and offices. Swindon was benefiting from its road and rail connections, and its central location between Bristol, Birmingham and London. The town was growing rapidly; another forty thousand people were now enjoying the delights of the Oasis and the Brunel Centre. A huge area to the north and west was earmarked for expansion to accommodate the growth. The first enlargement had been at Toothill in West Swindon. I knew the estate because my girlfriend Debbie had lived there. We used to play Pong before walking to the top of a small hill near her house where we would lie next to each other on the grass like in *Gregory's Girl* and watch the stars. Once after ten fruitless minutes of fumbling under her mohair jumper and running my hands along her back to find the clasp, she informed me it was front fastening. Why had no one ever told me such bras existed? I had spent hours extensively studying the lingerie pages of catalogues and I swear I had never seen such a thing.

In 1982, a mile or so north of Debbie's house, a new award-winning building designed by Norman Foster was unveiled. Okay, it was only the Renault distribution centre but it won awards for its distinctive style which they said was characteristic of the British high tech architectural movement. The building had an external steel structure painted in yellow to echo Renault's corporate colour. It resembled a giant alien grasshopper with yellow legs. I wasn't an admirer. Still, award-winning architecture in Swindon.

In the summer our football team was relegated to Division Four and British Rail announced plans to cut its engineering workforce. The company was losing export orders as it couldn't compete with lower cost overseas locations. While other countries treated their rail industries as national assets Thatcher was happy to outsource the UK's railway engineering to foreign companies. The works at Shildon and Horwich were to be closed, while in Swindon they were to be reduced in scale with the loss of a thousand jobs and the closure of the apprentice training school.

Thousands of people in the town took part in a march against the loss of the railway jobs. At the rally our MP, David Stoddart, said, "This is not only the railway's fight, this is Swindon's fight. Because what happens to the railways will affect the livelihoods and well-being of every other person in Swindon." Despite the campaign the job reductions went ahead.

∽

"You wouldn't have put your money on Villa to win the league this year," said Tony.

"Great pairing, Gray and Withe. They bulldoze the opposition defenders," said Bob.

"They have some skill as well," said Tony. "That goal by Morley against Everton was beautiful. He was just like you Cliffy, sprinted down that left wing like a dog after a rabbit."

"I can't believe they only used fourteen players in the whole season," I added.

Statistical interventions were my strong point. I had realised this while watching *Gregory's Girl*. Clare Grogan had said, "Why are boys obsessed with numbers?" Were we obsessed? Surely everyone knew Labour needed 326 seats for a majority in Parliament and that Swindon had been relegated with fifty-two points, just one point from safety.

Tony was in a celebratory mood after helping his mother buy her council house. "Bloody great deal it was," said Tony. It was difficult to disagree with him, it wasn't often you got a 50 percent discount on a house. A cynic might even suggest the Tories were trying to buy votes.

"We're off to Benidorm Saturday," said Bob. "Can't beat it. Sunshine every day. Great Irish pubs and they do better fish and chips than Sims Chippy."

"You just like them topless sunbathers," said Tony.

"Nah, it was just coincidence I chose that spot by those young women last year," said Bob, as a big grin spread across his face.

"Can't see my missus going topless," said Tony. "Her tits are down past her knees these days."

"What about you Steve, where do you students spend your long summer holidays?" asked Bob.

"I'm flying to Athens in a couple of weeks," I said.

I was flying to Greece with friends on Monarch Air. I had never been on a plane before but the airline sounded grand, fit for a king. I spent the two weeks before we left working out in a new Swindon gym, my aim being to become Charles Atlas in fourteen days. The previous gyms I had visited were full of grunting sweaty men. In the new place there were mirrored studios where women, wearing pink and yellow lycra, copied routines from Jane Fonda's workout video. On the gym wall were TVs playing *Eye of the Tiger* with clips of Sylvester Stallone skipping, jogging and exchanging punches with Mr T from *Rocky III*. The song was the UK number one for four weeks that summer but remained the gym's favourite for about ten years until it was replaced by Right Said Fred's *I'm Too Sexy*.

At the end of July I got on a plane for the first time. I was excited and a little nervous as we sat on the runway before take-off. I gripped the hard plastic armrests firmly as we hurtled down the runway. I was pleased we didn't have seats in the smoking section at the back of the plane. On arrival in Athens we made our way to the port of Piraeus where we slept in a square with hundreds of other students. In the morning we ate doughnuts as the sun came up and we waited for a ferry. We had no accommodation booked. On arrival at an island people would clamour to rent us a room. We would negotiate a price, without seeing the place, get in a car with people we didn't know and be driven miles away to their house. We would have been ideal kidnap victims.

In one place a family gave us ripe pears on arrival. I still remember the sheer joy of biting into them and the juices flowing down my chin. We spent the days getting our bottoms burned and our evenings drinking cocktails, as we watched the sun descend over the sea. I don't think I had ever watched the sun go down before; sunsets were not big in Swindon. On the way back to Athens we slept on the deck of a ferry. I couldn't sleep but I watched the stars. I think that was when I understood that life does not come to you, you have to go and find life.

24

CHANNEL FOUR

In September 1982, we had to relive the Falklands all over again as the aircraft carrier *HMS Invincible* sailed into Portsmouth. Unfortunately it was a glorious day – I had prayed for rain – and thousands of people, including hundreds of bare-chested men, lined the harbour walls waving flags, carrying red, white and blue balloons and wearing plastic Union Jack hats. There was almost enough bunting to sink the battleship. The press contrasted the actions of our brave boys with Ken Livingstone, who they falsely claimed was attending the Gay Olympics in San Francisco.

In October, I unpacked and lined up books on the shelf above my desk in Norwood House which had a view over the main university concourse. It was becoming a ritual, setting up my workspace for another term. In the shared kitchen there was a copy of the *Daily Mirror* and *Spike*. The *Mirror* headline was 'The boy who doesn't mind being called a girl'. It was about Boy George who said he liked dressing up and fell in love with people of both sexes. When asked about the controversy surrounding him he replied, "It's great, it's all good publicity." He was right. The band's single *Do You Really Want To Hurt Me* went to number one in the charts. Cross dressing and androgyny amongst musicians was not new but it was becoming mainstream and popular.

Spike had a pullout 'Freshers Guide' that recommended new students get familiar with Charlie Browns, the Island Club and the Huntsman pub. It was strange to think that every year new students went through the same process, exploring the places we had discovered in our first term. *Spike* reported there had been fourteen thousand applications for the eight hundred first-year places available. I was pleased I had arrived two years earlier; it didn't sound like there would be much chance of getting in via clearing this year.

Spike also carried a pen portrait of Paul. He was styled as the Union Exec's lovable sex symbol, the resident joker with his witty repartee and the lead singer for his renamed band, After the Dark. All this was true and more. I could hear Paul saying, "Fucking hell, is that all! Why didn't they mention the size of my knob?"

I decided against cooking, probably as well given the lack of food in my cupboard, and walked down to the Norwood refectory. Paul and Alison were sitting at a table on their own.

"I see they reinstated the vegetarian food bar," I said, as I put my bag down on the chair next to them.

"They also upped the fucking prices," said Paul.

Alison's hair was lighter, sun bleached; maybe she had also been away somewhere warm.

"How is the food?" I asked, looking at Alison's empty plate.

"It's okay," she replied. "Not as good as mine though." She gave me a thin smile across the table.

"Three hundred and sixty glasses have gone missing from the bar, can you fucking believe it," said Paul, scratching his head. "I mean, what the fuck is going on?"

"You finally given up on those green trousers then?" said Alison.

"Yeah, and the henna," I said, brushing my hand through my hair.

"They also stubbed out their fags on the new carpet," said Paul. "Fucking kids today. They don't fucking think. That's why we can't have nice things."

I didn't envy him being social secretary. There were probably also students who kicked down the door of the snooker room.

"They seem so young, don't they?" said Alison, looking across at a gaggle of new students. One excited young woman was wearing a recently purchased Bath University sweat top.

"That was us two years ago," I said. "We are older and wiser now." It was subtle but I hoped she would get the meaning. If she did, she ignored it.

"You coming to the Labour Club meeting?"

"Yes, if you'll have me." I was aware that Alison was now the chair or secretary, or something important. I had stayed away from most meetings since our split.

"As long as you don't give us all that Militant stuff."

"I've given up on them," I said.

"About time you became Captain Sensible," said Paul.

"Sounds good, maybe you can help out at the Freshers' Fair?" said Alison.

"Sure, happy to help."

"I don't know why you two bother," said Paul. "The Labour Party is completely fucked."

I didn't tell Alison that the Militant comrades were not happy that I no longer went to their meetings. In June, Trotsky had come over from Bristol specifically to speak to me. He asked why I wasn't attending meetings or selling the paper any more. I mumbled something about being busy with exams. He managed to extract a promise from me to attend the meetings but it was one of those promises you make with absolutely no intention of following through. Like saying you will probably see someone on Saturday when you know you will be somewhere else. Sometimes it seemed easier to tell people what they wanted to hear. I learnt later in life that this is not always the case.

"On the bright side, my band is going to be on that new TV channel," Paul said.

Paul had Del Boy optimism. There was always a scheme that would propel him to stardom.

I looked at Alison.

"It's true. They wrote to me as social secretary and asked about the best new local bands. They want to showcase them on a programme called *The Tube*."

"Hmmm. So you recommended your own band?" I said and tried to keep the smile from my face.

"Well, I couldn't fucking lie could I?" said Paul. He beamed across the table. "Come on, there's got to be some benefits to being social secretary beyond the free booze and the women."

"Wow, that's great," said Alison. "You were saying all you needed was some exposure."

"So, when are you going to be on?" I asked Paul.

"Not sure. They said the show is being broadcast live from Newcastle, which is fucking miles away. I nearly said to them 'Haven't you fucking heard of London?'. Nothing back yet but Simon's mate knows one of the presenters, if you know what I mean."

He tapped the side of his nose.

"This is the break we have been looking for."

For the first twenty years of my life we only had three TV channels and the BBC dominated viewing hours. Thatcher loathed the corporation. She viewed it as bloated, bureaucratic, and full of liberal lefties. In her first Queen's speech in 1979,

Thatcher pledged to introduce more competition and more advertising-funded TV. The result was Channel 4, a public service broadcaster part-funded by advertising. The new channel commissioned programmes from dozens of small production companies, as it sought to develop a new ecosystem of entrepreneurial producers.

The irony was that Thatcher's creation of Channel 4 provided a platform for more radical voices. The commissioning editors wanted to present Britain as it really was. When the channel was launched on 2 November 1982, I sat perched on the end of my bed with a pack of Bourbon biscuits. On my small black and white portable TV I watched Bobby and Sheila Grant move from a council house into their new home in *Brookside*. While they were stepping up in life, another couple, the Collinses, were moving to the estate after the husband had been made redundant. The programme echoed the changes taking place in Thatcher's Britain.

I was still making my way through the biscuits when Channel 4's new comedy, *The Comic Strip Presents*, came on the TV. It featured a new generation of comedians including Alexei Sayle, Dawn French, Jennifer Saunders and Rik Mayall. They were quite different from the comics my parents loved such as Dave Allen and Benny Hill, and those that starred in *Carry On* films with Barbara Windsor. This new generation were political, and consciously avoided sexist and racist material.

Three days later Channel 4 broadcast the first edition of *The Tube* which featured The Jam and Heaven 17 performing live from Tyne Tees Studio Five. After our discussion in the refectory Paul never mentioned the show again and I decided not to ask.

A week after the launch of Channel 4 the BBC broadcast *The Young Ones* which also featured Rik Mayall. It became an instant university hit. Hundreds of students would watch together in the coffee area. Some sat on chairs but most sat on the floor or stood at the back with beer in plastic glasses. The show was chaotic, featuring explosions, puppets, South African vampires and even a blow up sex doll. It resonated because it was different; it wasn't *Hi-de-Hi* or *Terry and June*. It was an anarchic show about students in Thatcher's Britain. They were caricatures – the hippy, the punk, the cool guy and the vegetarian student anarchist. But there was enough truth in the characters to be recognisable.

The show was also overtly political, referencing the racism of the police. In one episode Alexei Sayle played Mussolini working for the Metropolitan Police. In another episode *The Young Ones* went on *University Challenge* to represent Scumbag College against the Oxbridge Footlights. When Rick asked the host, Bambi, if he would let them win, the reply was, "The posh kids always win, everybody knows that."

TV drama was also becoming political. On BBC2, *Boys from the Blackstuff* highlighted the impact of unemployment on working-class men. Almost one in seven of the working population was unemployed; it was like the 1930s. The programme, created by Alan Bleasdale, followed five unemployed men searching for a job in Thatcher's Britain. Bernard Hill played a poignant character called Yosser Hughes. The episode *Yosser's Story* was broadcast appropriately enough on Halloween.

Many men like Yosser were finding themselves unemployed for the first time. They had lost the dignity of work and were not prepared to enter a competitive labour market. The baby boom of the mid-1960s meant that over a hundred thousand extra teenagers were looking for jobs in 1982. The 'young uns', as Dad called them, didn't have families to support. Instead they had computer certificates and were prepared to work for less money. The men being made redundant were not office people; they had worked with their hands.

Yosser like many working-class men was increasingly in

despair at being out of work and struggled to keep his three children from being taken into care after his wife left him. He reminded me of Terry in the club. Yosser pleaded with everyone he met to employ him. "Gizza job. Go on, gizza job. I can do that." The story was harrowing, almost unbearable. The system was incapable of helping him. Finally, his kids were forcibly removed by social services and he was evicted carrying nothing but a picture of his three children.

~

Fed up of eating cheese omelettes and ploughman's lunches I gave up being a vegetarian. The ploughman's lunch wasn't even a real thing but something created by the Milk Marketing Board to sell more cheese in pubs. Unlike Alison I didn't have jars of lentils, beans and grains in my kitchen, or make nut loaves for Sunday lunch.

At the Labour Club Alison and I put ourselves forward as candidates to represent the university at the upcoming NUS conference in Margate. The elections were based on a transferable vote system with ranked vote choices. The Labour Club had a slate. Alison was the Labour Club's first preference. Neil with the black curly hair and red-checked PLO scarf was second, and I was third.

I created my own leaflets for the campaign about the need to fight capitalism and racism. Helen, the former president of the student union, said helpfully that my leaflets would ensure I got no votes. She was wrong. I managed eleven first place preferences and scraped into the seventh and last conference place after the transfer of votes. Neil, the union president came first but he only beat Alison by a single vote to be the university's delegation leader. Bunny came fifth with eighteen first place preferences.

Our delegation travelled to Margate together on the train,

which felt like trekking to the other end of the world. I chatted for hours with Neil and was surprised to find he was a kind and gentle man despite being a Tory. He never got angry even when we fiercely disagreed. Maybe it is easier to be a nice guy when the world is as you want it to be.

The NUS conference was not what I was expecting. There was a complex bureaucratic process of constructing motions which involved a constant moving of amendments and voting on composites. I was often confused as to what we were actually voting for. I kept my head down and shrunk into my chair when we voted, as mandated by our university students, against a motion on nuclear disarmament. Thankfully Bath University in the early 1980s was not representative of wider student opinion, only two other universities voted against, and the main motion passed easily.

In Swindon at Christmas I was back to sharing a room with my brother. Despite his complaints that only old people listened to BBC Radio Four, I turned the dial until I found the Today programme. The Pope won the award for 'man of the year' but the surprising runner up was Ken Livingstone. It was quite difficult to fathom but it did seem Ken was able to put across socialist policies in a way that resonated with a significant segment of the population.

On the TV my parents watched the BBC's *Sports Personality of the Year* which was won by Daley Thompson. He was the personification of a new Britain, born to a Nigerian father and a Scottish mother. When I look back at our family Christmas pictures from 1982, I am struck by how old my parents look. They were only forty-two. I think it was the way they dressed more than anything. Maybe it was the slacks. A good rule for everyone, not just old people, is never wear slacks.

Margaret Thatcher had been a contender for *Time Magazine's* person of the year but was beaten by a computer. The magazine reported that 80 percent of Americans expected that, "in the fairly near future, home computers will be as commonplace as television sets or dishwashers". In America they had proper PCs such as the Apple II and IBM PC, not small boxes you plugged into your TV. I was most surprised about the dishwashers. In 1982, I had only seen a dishwasher in the Wiltshire Hotel. I didn't know a single family that had a dishwasher. America was truly a different country.

I visited Glynn who proudly showed me his new Sinclair ZX Spectrum personal computer. Computers such as the Sinclair ZX, along with the Commodore 64 and BBC Acorn were 1982's most wanted Christmas presents. The basic version of the ZX had 16 KB of RAM memory, though you could buy an upgrade to 48 KB for an extra £50. It was difficult to conceive that you would ever need more than 48 KB of RAM.

One of our lecturers at university was enthused by the new IBM personal computer and something called a spreadsheet named VisiCalc. He predicted that it would be essential to all businesses and that we should all learn how to use spreadsheets. The *Financial Times* was suddenly full of articles about the potential of computing and how it might change the way we lived, worked and studied.

At the start of 1983, Britain had a greater level of home computer ownership than any country in the world, including America. The WH Smith shelves were full of computer magazines like the *Home Computer Course*, *Sinclair User* and *Your Computer*. A new generation of teenagers, the generation below me, were growing up with computers. I was definitely being left behind. I vowed that once I was working I would buy a proper computer, one with spreadsheet software.

25

BERMONDSEY

In the great depression of 1930, two and a half million people were unemployed. At the start of 1983, there were over three million. Despite this economic and social catastrophe the Conservatives were, quite incredibly, polling at 44 percent. A full nine points ahead of Labour and the SDP-Liberal Alliance. Thatcher had become 'our Maggie' and her personal poll ratings were off the scale.

Rob put it all down to the Falklands. "Marx got it wrong," he said. "A patriotic war is the opium of the masses not religion."

Thatcher continued to milk the war by undertaking a five-day visit to the Falklands which was covered extensively by the press. There were pictures of Maggie wearing an army T-shirt, Maggie congratulating British troops, Maggie in the turret of a tank in a yellow headscarf, Maggie sat with soldiers in black berets, and Maggie in a camouflage jacket.

According to Rob it was all part of her plan for an early election. "It's just one long series of photo opportunities," he said, holding up a picture of Thatcher as Gunner Maggie firing a large gun at an empty island.

"A woman with a gun," said Paul, resting his guitar on his lap and giving us a wink. "The squaddies will be bashing the bishop to that one."

Rob and I both looked at him.

"I'm just saying," he said. "She's not my type, I prefer Princess Spanner, I bet she's a right dirty bird."

We continued to look at him confused.

"You mean Diana?"

"No, you slow bastards," he said. "Princess Spanner, because she tightens my nuts."

Paul started strumming gently on his guitar and singing, "Princess Diana". He sang quietly, almost as though singing to himself. When he sang he was tender; there was a vulnerability, a fragility that belied his bravado.

I had spent the last three years longing for an election and the chance to get rid of Thatcher. Now I hoped she would wait another year, or at least until memories of the Falklands had faded a little and Labour's poll ratings had recovered.

At the start of the year inflation was running at 10 percent and the NUS argued we needed to take stronger action to secure an inflation-linked grant increase. They suggested we organise occupations and sit-ins. To Neil, our Conservative president, this was all a step too far. It was the sort of thing that Trotskyites, wearing red-checked tablecloths, would do at universities like Essex or the LSE. So instead he proposed a twenty-four-hour 'work-in' because it was more constructive.

Yes, that was the masterplan. We would study in the library for twenty-four hours. The government must have been trembling. To be fair that wasn't the only plan. If the 'work-in' didn't bring the Education Secretary, Sir Keith Joseph, to his senses he would be subject to a mock trial by the theatre group in Bath city centre.

Despite the strength of our protest, and our threat to keep revising until Thatcher caved in, the government announced a few months later that the student grant would be increased by just 4 percent.

I had given up on Militant but despite losing my active support, the Tendency's influence continued to grow. At the start of 1983, the group had complete control of the LPYS. They had an estimated five thousand Militant supporters and over two hundred full-time paid organisers, which was more than the Labour Party could muster. Militant was increasingly visible and making news headlines. By 1983 it had become the most successful Trotskyist group in Britain.

To counter Militant's influence Labour expelled Ted Grant, Peter Taaffe and three other members of the Militant Editorial Board. The party also established a register of acceptable groups which, to no one's surprise, did not include Militant. When I met Matt he proudly wore a badge on his donkey jacket saying, 'I am an unregistered socialist'. He complained furiously about Labour expelling Militant supporters and, though I nodded my head in agreement, I thought maybe they had a point about entryist groups trying to take over the party.

In February 1983, there was a by-election in Bermondsey. The local Labour Party selected Peter Tatchell as their candidate. He was a passionate advocate of gay rights and a supporter of direct action. I wasn't surprised to hear that Militant opposed his selection. Matt said it was because of his activity in the Gay Liberation Front but I suspected it was because he didn't support the Tendency. It was typical; Militant wouldn't support him because he wasn't one of them. The Labour Party was also not enthusiastic about Tatchell and tried to persuade him to stay quiet about his homosexuality. The press though, led by Kelvin MacKenzie, made sure it was at the centre of the campaign.

The Sun falsely claimed Tatchell had attended the Gay Olympics in San Francisco along with Ken Livingstone. They also sent young boys to his flat to try to get compromising pictures of him. The *News of the World* published a cartoon image of Tatchell with plucked eyebrows, lipstick and eyeliner. Soon the walls in Bermondsey were full of offensive graffiti with slogans such as 'Tatchell is queer' and 'Tatchell is a communist poof'.

The Liberals, who had previously finished third in the seat, selected Simon Hughes as their candidate. They ran a homophobic campaign with their male canvassers wearing 'I've been kissed by Peter Tatchell' badges. Liberal leaflets were circulated asking, 'Which Queen do you support?' They also promoted Hughes as the straight choice. Labour lost the by-election, their vote collapsing from 63 percent in 1979 to just 26 percent. *Gay News* called it 'the dirtiest and most notorious by-election in British political history'.[1]

During the campaign Tatchell received over five hundred hate letters, thirty death threats and warnings his flat would be firebombed. He was also physically attacked over a hundred times. There were real consequences to the hate campaign run by the press and the political parties, but they simply didn't care.

A month later at a by-election in Darlington, the Labour MP Roy Hattersley was reportedly overheard saying, "Thank God there are no poofs in this by-election." What was the point of the Labour Party if they were not going to defend fundamental principles like equal rights? What was the fucking point? I was angry with the right of the Labour Party, I was disillusioned with Militant, I detested the SDP, I despised the Liberals, I loathed the press and I was also angry with the voters in Bermondsey. If this was British politics I wasn't sure I wanted anything to do with it.

26

SHOTGUNS AND KNIFE FIGHTS

In April 1983, women at Greenham Common held a mass protest which involved forming a human chain around the American airbase. Tens of thousands of women joined the protest creating a fourteen-mile human chain. It stretched past the Aldermaston nuclear research centre to the ordnance factory in Burghfield. CND claimed that eighty thousand people took part. The police in their usual way halved the numbers and told the BBC there were just forty thousand.

I was determined to prove the police wrong by calculating how many people it took to form a fourteen-mile human chain. Fourteen miles was around twenty thousand metres, two people a metre was ... forty-thousand people. I decided calculations proved nothing.

I spent most of the month writing up my dissertation on political violence and the suffragettes. My thesis was based on Ted Gurr's psychological theory that violence is caused by feelings of relative deprivation. The suffragettes certainly had a case for feeling relatively deprived.

I spent weeks in the Fawcett Library in East London researching the actions of the militant suffragettes. They destroyed the contents of letterboxes, cut telephone wires, and broke the windows of thousands of shops and offices. They slashed paintings in art galleries and vandalised exhibitions at the British Museum. They also planted bombs and set light to the houses of politicians. To many men their most heinous crimes were burning down cricket pavilions and damaging golf courses.

In Dublin in 1912, Mary Leigh hurled a hatchet at Prime Minister Asquith. It only narrowly missed him but hit the Irish MP John Redmond. Later that afternoon they set fire to the Theatre Royal during a performance attended by Asquith. In 1913 and 1914 it was estimated the suffragettes caused up to two billion pounds of damage. Hundreds of women were jailed as a consequence and began hunger strikes.

As part of my research I read *Hidden from History: 300 Years of Women's Oppression and the Fight Against It* by Sheila Rowbotham and *Beyond the Fragments* edited by Rowbotham, Lynne Segal and Hilary Wainwright. *Hidden from History* provided a socialist perspective on women's rights and celebrated stories of working-class women working with trade unions. The concept of women being hidden from history resonated with me; most history was written by men. It didn't address the issues faced by women. All history is written from a particular perspective and influenced by cultural values. I agreed with Rowbotham; you have to be sceptical and challenge what writers set down in their books.

In *Beyond the Fragments* the authors argued socialists had to look beyond the traditional and hierarchical male forms of organisation, and embrace the experiences of the women's movement and feminism. They argued that the struggle against male domination and patriarchy was as important as the struggle against class oppression. I wasn't sure but felt I wasn't in a position to judge. I did agree with the authors that individual campaigns, whether for women's rights or racial equality, were weaker without the backing of the labour movement.

My studies limited my role in the local council elections to a few evenings canvassing with George in Twerton, where Labour was defending two seats. The evening of Thursday, 5 May 1983 was depressing. The Conservatives gained over a hundred council seats nationally. This wasn't supposed to happen. After four years in power governments were supposed to lose council seats not gain a hundred.

On Sunday, 22 May 1983, I visited my parents in Swindon and joined my dad and brother in the club before lunch. Most of the discussion was about the previous day's FA Cup final. The match between Manchester United and Brighton and Hove Albion had finished two each and a replay was scheduled for later in the week. Replays were big in the eighties.

"United were bloody lucky yesterday," said Tony, setting down his pint.

"Yep, that chance Smith missed was an absolute sitter," agreed Bob.

"Bet he's feeling gutted today," said my brother, before getting up to buy another round. My glass was still half-full while the other pint glasses on the table were empty. The drifting cigarette smoke settled on my clothes; I would have to wash them when I got back.

"Brighton have missed their chance now I reckon," said Dad.

"Not so sure," Bob replied. "Might be worth putting a quid on them for the replay."

"Nah, not a chance," said Tony, dismissively waving away the suggestion with the cigarette in his hand.

Tony was right. Brighton were battered 4-0 in the replay.

You have to take your chances in this world and Thatcher wasn't going to miss her chance. After gaining a hundred seats in the May council elections, the Tories held a twenty-one point lead over Labour. She called a general election for the 9 June 1983.

"I reckon Maggie will win by a mile," said Bob.

"Yep, old Stoddart is in a bit of bother I reckon," added Tony.

My dad was silent as always when politics was discussed.

"What do you think Steve?" asked Bob. "You're the politics student."

I held my breath and gazed at him. I brought my hands together and steepled my fingers as my professors had done when considering a difficult question. I tried to be optimistic.

"I'm not sure," I said. "I think it will be close."

The men ridiculed my suggestion.

"People won't vote for Foot," said Tony. "The old fool says he will give up our nuclear weapons. Bloody mad. Do you think the Russians will give up their weapons?" It was a rhetorical question as he answered himself immediately. "No, they'll think we are damn idiots. You have to take a knife to a knife fight."

"No," said Bob, as Andy put more beers down on the table, "you should take a shotgun!" The men laughed in agreement.

"Too bloody right," said Tony.

It was clear they didn't see Foot as a leader that would defend their nation, what Benedict Anderson called an imagined community.[1]

My dad stayed silent. I couldn't believe he would support the Tories particularly following the recent the job losses at the railway works.

The conversation was interrupted by my brother's friend Rod. He squeezed past me and sat down next to Tony on the bench seat that ran along the wall.

"Sorry I'm late. I had to take the missus and the babber over to her mum's place."

"Where's that to then?" enquired Tony.

"Over in West Swindon. She was bloody furious about something."

" 'ark at he,' said Bob 'You should know by now that behind every angry woman is a bloke who has no idea what he's done wrong."

The men nodded their heads in agreement. Magically my brother appeared and handed Rod a pint. No order had been placed, no words exchanged, it was telepathy.

"Thanks mate," he said. "That's just the badger."

There was no more discussion of politics but if the men's feelings reflected those in the country as a whole it was going to be a difficult campaign.

At the end of May the papers were full of pictures of Thatcher holding up a copy of the Conservative manifesto with a red, white and blue Olympic torch on the cover. The manifesto claimed the Falklands War was just the first step in the 'make Britain great again' campaign. The Tories proposed to accelerate the privatisation programme, including the sale of British Telecom, British Airways, Rolls Royce and most of British Steel and British Leyland. They also proposed abolishing the GLC to get rid of Ken Livingstone.

I was nervous about fighting an election so soon after the Falklands but at least we would be fighting on a true left Labour manifesto. The party's commitment to unilateral nuclear disarmament was given top billing. Michael Foot had been a founder member of CND in 1958, and he was a passionate believer in the policy. It was his life's ambition.

The Labour manifesto also promised:

- No more sales of council houses.
- Higher taxes for the rich.
- The abolition of the House of Lords.
- Re-nationalisation of privatised industries.
- Withdrawal from the European Economic Community, as the European Union was known at the time.

Labour had been split about Europe in the 1975 referendum. Tony Benn, Barbara Castle and those on the left had argued Britain should come out of the EEC, while those on the right argued we should stay in. This time there was no ambivalence; the party position was to leave. The Tories by contrast were united in wanting to stay in Europe.

The Labour manifesto was unusually long. The right wing of the party decided that Labour couldn't win the election so wanted to use it to discredit the left. Rather than discuss the myriad of policies put forward for inclusion, they deliberately adopted every policy in the manifesto without any debate. They wanted enough rope to hang Tony Benn when the election was over. Immediately the manifesto was launched the right of the Labour Party joined in with the Tories in denouncing it. The former Labour Prime Minister Jim Callaghan criticised the policy on disarmament and Gerald Kaufman called the manifesto "the longest suicide note in history".[2]

Despite the criticisms I thought the Labour manifesto was wonderful; so did Thatcher. She carried a copy with her everywhere.

27

THE 1983 GENERAL ELECTION

I decided to spend most of the election in Bristol campaigning for Tony Benn. Labour was never going to win in Bath, where the main employer was the Ministry of Defence. Benn's old seat had been abolished and he was fighting a newly created constituency with less favourable demographics. One morning he spoke to us before we headed out to canvass. He was much taller than I expected. He held a huge mug of tea and enthused us about the radical nature of the Labour manifesto. This was our chance to defeat Thatcher and elect a true socialist government.

I was eager to start knocking on doors and led the way, striding to the first council estate on our list, my heart full of optimism.

It didn't last long.

On doorstep after doorstep council tenants proudly said they were going to support 'our Maggie'. They were certainly not going to vote for that pacifist Michael Foot. Give up our nuclear weapons and leave us naked; what the hell was he thinking? After a while I stopped mentioning the policy and focused on privatisation. Surely they would agree that privatising British Telecom was going to be a disaster.

No, they didn't. They were frustrated at waiting months to get a telephone installed or get hold of an engineer. The company should have been privatised years ago. It was the same when I discussed housing; they were adamant people should have the 'right' to buy their council houses. The Labour Party was trying to take away their rights. The more I canvassed the more I seemed to be highlighting to people what they disliked about the Labour Party. I wasn't sure this was how it was supposed to be.

Why couldn't they see Thatcher was changing Britain forever and not for the better? There would be more privatisation and cuts in services to fund lower taxes for the rich. What was not to understand? They were not listening. Or maybe I was not listening. People were telling me on the doorstep what they disliked about Labour and I was trying to persuade them they were wrong.

Every time a door opened during canvassing I would hear Spandau Ballet's *True*. The song was number one and played constantly on the radio. On Top of the Pops the band, previously called the Gentry, had a rather aristocratic and romantic look that was being copied by high street fashion chains. In the song's video Tony Hadley appeared to have dressed for a posh country wedding in his zoot suit, crisp white shirt and pocket handkerchief. The white trousers, blazers and floppy hairstyles of *Brideshead* and *Another Country* were being reinvented by pop stars and adopted by a new generation.

Thatcher argued there was no space for the centre ground in the election. I agreed; this was a battle between right and left. She called the Liberal Alliance with its two leaders a miscellaneous mishmash and said the SDP people who didn't have the guts to stay and fight in the Labour Party. I agreed with Thatcher, we were the real opposition.

A number of celebrities came out to support the Tories including the swimmer Sharron Davies and the Arsenal manager Terry Neill. This just confirmed my loathing for Arsenal. The world snooker champion Steve Davies also supported the Tories. Alex Higgins said he hated Davies and now I knew why.

At a Tory youth election rally the radio DJ Kenny Everett provided the entertainment saying, "Let's bomb Russia" and "Let's kick Michael Foot's stick away" to loud applause from the pimpled youths in their suits and pearls. The young Conservatives were the worst sort of Tories in my view. I wasn't normally a violent person but I was full of visceral hatred towards them.

Two days before the election Neil Kinnock made a powerful speech in Bridgend. He warned the British public against electing the Conservatives. His words resonated.

"If Margaret Thatcher wins on Thursday
– I warn you not to be ordinary
– I warn you not to be young
– I warn you not to fall ill
– I warn you not to get old."

It was the sort of speech we needed from our leader. Instead Michael Foot mumbled endlessly about nuclear disarmament from behind his bottle top glasses. He hobbled through crowded town centres with his stick receiving abuse and jeering as he went. Foot was an old style campaigner but the influential political medium was TV and it was one that didn't suit him. He didn't adapt. He literally stood on soap boxes on street corners making long rambling speeches as people walked past and shouted at him. Kelvin MacKenzie slaughtered him. He ran a front page headline, 'Do You Really Want This Old Fool To Run Britain?' with a photograph that made Foot look much older than his seventy years.

Labour's campaign struggled to adapt to the new media age. Their TV adverts were so bad that Patricia Hewitt, who later became Labour MP for Leicester West, said that had she seen the ads during the campaign she would have resigned.

Thatcher's campaign by contrast was slick and professional. Thatcher's love for Reagan extended to his style of presidential campaigning. Her rallies were designed to be like US presidential conventions; there was warm up music and Union Jack flags were provided for everybody to wave. As Rob predicted there was also extensive use of the staged pictures of her trip to the Falklands, just in case people didn't get the message. The events were also ticketed and 'invitation only' to ensure they went smoothly. The hand-picked audiences of devotees ecstatically applauded her speeches like zombie penguins.

Conservative private polling found that Thatcher was their greatest asset. It was astonishing. Before the Falklands War she had been the most unpopular prime minister in history. Still, the Tories left nothing to chance. One of her advisers Christopher Lawson even consulted industrial psychologists and behavioural psychiatrists before choosing the curtains for the Conservative press conference. By contrast the Labour Party press and communications team was mired in bureaucracy. They had to get approval for all decisions from the party's campaign committee. A group of forty, yes forty, inexperienced people who knew nothing about communications and who couldn't agree on anything. Roy Hattersley described it as ludicrous and it was difficult to disagree.

Spike conducted a survey of three hundred and forty-eight

students after a hustings election session. The SDP candidate came top, closely followed by the Conservative MP for Bath, Chris Patten. The Labour candidate was a long way back in third place. It was not an encouraging sign, even if our university was not representative of students nationally.

The bookies stopped taking bets on a Tory victory as Labour's support continued to ebb away. During the last week of the campaign the Conservatives were so confident they cancelled their planned advertising four days before the election. There was no point wasting money. Opinion polls suggested the Tories would beat Labour by a full twenty points. The polling experts said it was going to be a disaster for Labour, who were likely to finish third. The election had become an existential threat to the party and could end the two-party system.

In the last days of the campaign I found many people on the doorstep were no longer hostile but sympathetic at my plight. Poor you canvassing for Foot and that bunch of incompetent losers. Their commiseration and condolences were crushing, much more so than those that simply told me to "Fuck off!" Our last day of canvassing in Bristol was conducted in light drizzle. We walked the streets like condemned men. George no longer tried to lighten the mood with his jokes. We didn't say anything but we all knew what was coming.

On the day of the election the *Daily Mirror* published an article by Keith Waterhouse. He said it might be the day when those with a job voted to look after themselves and say 'up yours' to the seven million people living in poverty.

During the morning Thatcher and her entourage were flown to the Isle of Wight by four military helicopters. While she was being photographed with her arms outstretched in front of a large Union Jack flag, I was in Bath with George, knocking on the doors of those that had said they would vote Labour and helping to drive them to the polling stations in a university minibus.

At around nine-thirty in the evening we returned to the Labour committee room. We had done all we could; there were no more prospective voters to ferry to the polling booths. Some people paced up and down, some distracted themselves by doodling or straightening piles of leaflets. Others smoked cigarettes with shaky hands. I ate vol-au-vents that one of the women had made, and sat in a caramel coloured leather chair like an extra at *Abigail's Party*. Time seemed to slow down as we waited for David Dimbleby to appear on TV in his pink tie.

We didn't have to wait long for the bad news. Just after 10 p.m. Peter Snow forecast the Conservatives would win 398 seats and Labour just 208. George and I looked at each other. That couldn't be right. We had won 269 seats in 1979; we couldn't lose another 60 seats. That would be a landslide and give Thatcher the ability to rip up society as we knew it.

As we waited for the results the former Blue Peter presenter Valerie Singleton popped up to report on the election in Torbay. I fully expected her to say, "Here is the result we made earlier." As the evening progressed the updated projections from David Dimbleby and his colleagues were unrelentingly miserable. Someone switched channels to ITV, maybe in the hope they had more optimistic news. They were interviewing Jim Mortimer, the Labour Party General Secretary. He tried to put a positive gloss on things, arguing the industrial heartlands were still voting Labour. God help us if they were also voting Tory.

Around midnight George and I walked over to the Bath election count at the Guildhall. The Labour team in the hall were not optimistic; the piles of Labour votes were reportedly very small. At ten minutes past two in the morning the Returning Officer walked to the rostrum to announce the result. The chatter in the room hushed and was replaced by an expectant silence. A solitary cough echoed in the hall. Below the stage a group of middle-aged women stood hesitantly with blue rosettes pinned to their Crimplene jackets. They resembled a bunch of smiling blue hydrangeas and filled the air with an aroma of blue rinse lavender. Their hair had been sprayed and sculpted for the evening's count. They rippled with nervous excitement as if they had just been offered a voucher for tea and cake at a garden centre.

The Returning Officer cleared his throat.

"I hereby give notice that the total number of votes cast for each candidate was as follows:

Malcolm Dean, Social Democratic Party, seventeen thousand, two hundred and forty votes.

Christopher Francis Patten, Conservative, twenty-two thousand, five hundred and eighty-five."

There were loud cheers from the hydrangeas who swirled about, as if caught by a summer breeze.

When the cheering calmed down, the Returning Officer continued.

"Adrian Pott, the Labour Party, seven thousand, two hundred and fifty-nine."

A group of men and women holding red clipboards drifted away in silence to the edges of the room. One man slumped down and sat on the polished wooden floor, his legs out in front of him, like one of the wounded you see propped up against a wall in war films.

We moved to an adjoining room where people were grouped around a TV. George passed me a can of beer in silence. He took a swig from his already open can and wiped the froth from his moustache. It was as bad as we feared; after four years of Thatcher, our vote had dropped 8 percent. Four thousand voters had switched from Labour to the SDP Alliance. It was to be a familiar pattern.

"It was always going to be tough in Bath," he consoled me. "Even the bloody dogs wear blue rosettes."

In seat after seat returning officers stood on stage to announce Conservative victories. The night got worse when the Swindon result came through. David Stoddart had lost but the people in Swindon hadn't turned to the Conservatives, who received less votes than they did in 1979. The Labour vote had been split by the SDP traitors which gifted the seat to the Conservatives.

When the SDP's Shirley Williams lost her seat to the Conservatives, we punched the air in celebration, though I wasn't sure if we should really be celebrating a Tory win. Another of the gang of four, Bill Rodgers, also lost his seat to the Labour candidate in Stockton North. I cheered ironically like a Swindon goal when we were already 4-0 down.

The BBC cut to the announcement of the result in Bristol East. Benn had been the Bristol MP for thirty-three years but I knew the boundary changes would make it difficult. Despite our best efforts he lost by just over a thousand votes. The SDP-Liberal Alliance was again to blame taking ten thousand votes from the Labour Party. In his concession speech Benn said people would continue to fight for socialist ideas inside and outside Parliament. "Bloody right we will," George shouted at the screen.

We took comfort from isolated pockets of good news. Two prominent Militant supporters, Terry Fields and Dave Nellist, were elected as MPs. George was jubilant that for the first time in history there would be Trotskyist MPs in the House of Commons. The two MPs would give Militant a voice in Parliament. They had stood on the principle that a worker's MP should be paid a worker's wage and promised to take just 40 percent of the normal MP's salary. The IRA's Gerry Adams was also elected as MP for West Belfast, just two years after Bobby Sands had been elected while on hunger strike, though he vowed not to take up his seat.

The Tories won thirteen million votes, the same as in 1979. But the opposition was now split. Labour and the Alliance each received around eight million votes. Former Labour voters had switched to the Alliance causing the party to lose over 60 seats. It was a landslide; Thatcher had a majority of 144 seats and it was all the fault of the SDP.

On the morning of 10 June 1983, I managed to drag myself out of bed before lunchtime. The newspapers were depressing. The *Guardian* headline read, 'Tories hail a massive majority'. *The Sun's* headline was simply, 'The Great Maggie Massacre'. Just to rub my nose in it, there was also a sub-headline, 'Benn gets boot'. I didn't buy a copy.

I met Rob in the union bar. We sat quietly for a long time.

"I blame the SDP," I said. "They split the opposition vote."

The SDP-Liberal Alliance claimed they had broken the two-party system. They hadn't but they had come close. The Alliance gained 25.4 percent of the national vote just shy of Labour's 27.6 percent. Labour was saved by the country's 'first past the post' electoral system. The party won over 200 seats while the Alliance won just 23. Labour had an MP for every forty thousand votes, while the Alliance needed three hundred and thirty-eight thousand votes for each of their MPs. The system was a travesty; it was not democracy. The Alliance won a quarter of the votes cast but were rewarded with just 3.5 percent of the parliamentary seats. Still it was what they deserved for splitting the anti-Conservative opposition.

I studied my pint in silence, rubbing my thumb up the side

of the glass and creating patterns in the condensation. We were jolted upright by the arrival of Paul.

"Come on, cheer the fuck up," he said. "It ain't so bad."

"It's a disaster," I said. "Thatcher is going to completely change Britain. We won't be able to stop her cutting public expenditure, reducing taxes and privatising services." I shook my head and muttered, "It's so depressing."

"Well, ain't you a cheerful cunt," said Paul, slapping me on the back. "Come on it could be worse. You could have had a stroke last night and woke up this morning speaking Welsh."

Rob laughed but I sat stony faced.

"Don't look at me like that," said Paul. "I ain't racist. I get on well with the Welsh, the proddies, the Jews, and the Muslims. You know why? Because we all gang up on the Eskimos. The igloo-building cunts."

I tried and failed to stop the smile that was forming on my face. Paul was barking mad, even dangerous at times but so absurd and ridiculous that somehow he always made you laugh.

"There you go," he said. "See, I told ya, it ain't so bad." With that he strolled over to the bar as if to say 'my work here is done' and put his arm around a woman in a cheesecloth dress.

Despite Paul's efforts at cheering us up, the reality was worse than bad. It was even worse than Swindon being relegated from the football league. Only 30 percent of men had voted Labour, compared to 40 percent in 1979. The Falklands War had a lot to do with it. There was something macho about fighting a war. Even worse was that 41 percent of those aged 18 to 24 voted Conservative, with only 31 percent voting Labour. How could my generation vote Tory?

I spent the next week in mourning. It wasn't just the election. My days at university were almost over and there was a constant ache in my chest. When I arrived back in Swindon I was lethargic and listless. It was the hottest summer on record and with psychic foresight Paul Weller's new band, The Style Council, released a single called *Long Hot Summer*. In Badgeland we sang along to UB40's *Red Red Wine*, like a melancholic political hymn.

As we shared our war stories of canvassing I discovered my experience on the doorsteps of council flats was not an aberration. The proportion of working-class people voting Labour had fallen from 62 percent in 1959 to 38 percent in 1983. Thatcher had won more working-class votes than Labour. The world no longer made any sense.

PART III

LONDON

28

THE GREATER LONDON COUNCIL

The ghost of Victor Hugo hung heavy over the campus during my final year at university. One by one student radicals morphed into besuited, aspiring trainee managers. They attended 'milk round' interviews as the country's leading blue chip organisations sought to recruit the 'cream of the crop' to their management schemes. There was no 'milk round' for Trotskyists, no graduate scheme for aspiring socialists, but there was the Greater London Council, which was the next best thing.

In 1894, Lord Salisbury described the London County Council as, "The place where collectivist and socialist experiments are tried and where a new revolutionary spirit finds its instruments and collects its arms."[1] At the time the GLC's predecessor had been run by a coalition of independent socialists, trade unionists and radical liberals. Almost a hundred years later County Hall was regaining its revolutionary spirit under Ken Livingstone and embarking on a new socialist experiment. Thatcher was winning nationally but Labour was winning in London.

Livingstone lifted my spirits; he was everything that

Michael Foot was not. He was young, dynamic, and media savvy. He drew on creative designers to develop a fresh radical aesthetic for the GLC that was contemporary and modern. He was also winning elections by building a wider, less partisan coalition in support of socialism. Writing in the *New Left Review* he said the Labour Party's almost exclusive concentration on the employed white male working class was a weakness.

To transform society Livingstone argued you needed, a broad coalition including skilled and unskilled workers, unemployed, women, and black people, as well as sexually oppressed minorities. It was the fresh approach the party desperately needed and represented the future of socialism.

Inspired by Livingstone I applied for a place on the GLC's graduate management scheme. Okay, yes, the GLC graduate programme was another elite scheme but I couldn't be accused of careerism by joining a council that Thatcher had just promised to abolish in her manifesto.

I don't recall anything about the recruitment process. I have been told it was a two-day selection event, so you think I would recall it but I can't. Maybe I was still in a state of grief. My friend Matt says we were sent a case study of the Thamesmead housing project to review. It sounds vaguely familiar but nothing else comes to mind. Evidently there were eighteen hundred applications which indicates there was either a shortage of graduate jobs or that most applicants didn't read the news.

I was at home in Swindon at the end of August 1983, frowning at the newly framed graduation photo of me hanging on the wall in the lounge, when the letter from the GLC arrived. Unable to sit down, I walked from room to room. I must have read the letter a hundred times. My application had been successful and I was going to live in London. I wasn't Dick Whittington, I didn't believe the streets of the city were paved with gold but it was still a mythical place. The land of black cabs, red Routemaster buses, the Monopoly board, Old Kent Road, Marylebone Station, Mayfair, Trafalgar Square and free parking. Well not exactly free parking.

My parents had taken me to London once when I was young. I can't recall the trip but there is a black and white photograph of my brother and I outside of 10 Downing Street. There is also one of my father with his hand out feeding pigeons on the bridge in St Jame's Park. My sister isn't in the pictures, so I am assuming it must have been the late sixties. The second time I went to London was in 1977. I was on a school trip which I mainly remember from the coach journey. It was a hot June day and the sun warmed my face through the window as I marvelled at the shops and buildings. The driver had the tennis from Wimbledon on the radio and I remember Virginia Wade was playing.

I boarded an intercity 125 train from Swindon to London and sat by the window with my London A-Z. It was the Google Maps of the 1980s, said to have been invented by Phyllis Pearsall after she got lost on her way to a party in Belgravia in 1935. I wasn't going to get lost, I had already marked the page where I was going to work. In the A-Z just above Westminster Bridge were the words 'London County Hall'. Below the bridge were the words 'Houses of Parliament'. My chest swelled; I was going to work in the political heart of the city. I turned the pages imagining the places I might live. I was going to be paid six thousand pounds a year, so I was confident of finding somewhere nice. Roads close to County Hall on the map were marked 'The Mall', 'Birdcage Walk' and 'Victoria Street'. It would be good to live in one of those streets so I could walk to work.

When I stepped off the train at Paddington I was immediately intoxicated by London. The bustling people, the constant noise, and the air which smelt of cigarettes, brake dust and stale beer. I bought a copy of the *Evening Standard* and turned to the 'Rooms to Let' column. I ran my finger down the lists and circled suitable places with my pen. I didn't know the geography of London and spent some time looking up addresses to find out where places were. To my disappointment none of them were close to County Hall; there were no rooms to let on The Mall. Armed with a pocketful of coins I went to a phone box and rang the numbers I had circled. I arranged to see a room in a shared three-bedroom flat by Tooting Bec common. All I knew about Tooting was Wolfie Smith and the Tooting Popular Front, so it seemed appropriate.

The door was opened by Chris, a tall guy with fair hair. In the lounge a dinner place setting had been glued to the ceiling. There was a red rose in a vase and a cigarette in an ashtray from which trailed a cotton wool thread that resembled smoke. It looked like the cover of the Bill Withers greatest hits album. When Chris caught me looking up at the ceiling he explained that it was his creation. He was an art student and he had been experimenting. I liked it; I would never have thought of anything like that.

The other flatmate Jane bundled into the room. She was a small energetic, young woman with red hair. She bounced onto the sofa next to me and pulled her legs up under her, like she was adopting the Lotus position ready to start some yoga. "So let's hear all about you," she said. I really liked them but I was not like them. As I travelled back to Swindon I reflected that I was too straight, too square and took life too seriously. I didn't glue crockery to my ceiling.

To my surprise Jane rang the same evening and said they would be happy for me to live with them. I moved in three days later and discovered my new flatmates had a cannabis plant called Boris. They would regularly say, "I am just off to visit Boris." I didn't join them; it wasn't really me. I wasn't entirely sure why they chose me as a flatmate.

On my first weekend Jane and Chris invited me to a party. As everyone was getting ready the buzzer went. I opened the door to a woman with a shock of big hair who beamed at me.

"Hi, I'm Izzy." She pushed past me saying, "Sorry, I am dying for a piss."

I explained Jane was in the bathroom but would be out shortly.

"Okay, no problems, I will use the sink."

While my brain was still wrapping itself around this idea, she had made her way to the kitchen. Without hesitation she lifted her skirt, pulled down her red panties to her knees, placed her arms behind her on the edge of the kitchen sink and jumped up. She was sitting there holding her skirt up under her arms, her red panties around her legs and grinning at me. Then there was the unmistakable sound of her pissing which continued for a long time. During which she smiled and chatted to me as if this was the most normal thing in the world. London was really not like Swindon; in Swindon guests didn't piss in your sink. I found it both disturbing and somewhat erotic at the same time. I would like to say I took it in my stride and thought no more of it, but that would not be true.

One of my first tasks in London was to join the local Labour Party. Neil Kinnock had been elected as the new party leader and I found I was still unable to forgive him for not voting for Tony Benn. I also shared Bryan Gould's concerns that he was a lightweight. On the morning he was elected, Kinnock was walking with his wife Glenys across the pebbles on Brighton beach when a wave caught him by surprise. As he tried to back

223

up the beach he stumbled, lost his footing and fell on his backside becoming engulfed by the water. It didn't look prime ministerial. It was played on all the news channels. It was probably the first time many people had heard of Kinnock and their abiding memory would be him falling on his bottom into the sea. It was a gift for the Tories and Murdoch. The *Sun* said he was a born loser and utterly out of his depth.

There were no Militant supporters in the local party, or at least none that attended the ward meetings. I no longer had to learn and repeat the Tendency's positions on Ireland or South Africa. I didn't have to worry about confusing the Tendency's position with that of the SWP or RCP. However, I found life is more complex when you don't have a position to repeat. When I was free to make up my own mind I had far less certainty about the world. I wasn't sure what my position was on most things. I also changed my mind on a regular basis.

At my first ward meeting I sat next to Mark who was a similar age to me. He was small, with round glasses and carried a large satchel. In the pub I discovered he was a maths teacher and was trying to change the world one lesson at a time. He invented math problems for his pupils that showed the costs of nuclear weapons and got them to plot the rising numbers of unemployed people on their graph paper. He was the sort of teacher Norman Tebbit hated.

Mark brought along copies of the *Labour Herald* to sell at the ward meetings, which was rumoured to be the newspaper of the Workers Revolutionary Party. When I asked Mark about it, he told me they simply shared some of the same ideas. It reminded me of Trotsky bringing along copies of the *Militant* to our LPYS meetings in Swindon. Mark also told me the WRP was not to be confused with the Revolutionary Workers Party, who believed we should welcome aliens as our liberators.

A week after my first local Labour Party meeting Mark and I joined over three hundred thousand people on a march to

Hyde Park to oppose the deployment of US cruise missiles in the UK. Across Europe three million people joined the protests. I purchased a black badge with yellow writing, 'October 22nd, I was there'. Seeing so many people lifted my spirits. I was somehow taller, stronger, more confident. It was good to be back in Badgeland. I took a deep breath and filled my lungs. I was ready to take on the world. Thatcher may have won the election but millions of us were preparing to oppose her government and pinning new badges to our chests. The real battle was about to commence.

Neil Kinnock spoke at the rally in Hyde Park, despite his concerns about unilateralism. He didn't think Labour could win an election on such a platform. I wouldn't admit it publicly but I was beginning to think he was probably right. I was conflicted. It didn't seem right to abandon a policy you believed in, simply because the public wouldn't vote for it. Isn't that what political leadership means, trying to persuade and lead opinion rather than follow it? On the other hand, what was the point of having principled policies if you never got elected?

29

COUNTY HALL

Mum insisted that I 'look smart' for my new job. It was important I made a 'good impression'. I ironed my M&S shirt as she had shown me, rotating it around the ironing board. I also polished my black shoes as she had instructed me. I worked the polish into the leather before swapping brushes to buff up the top of the shoes until they were shining. As I left for work that first morning I put on a grey overcoat, also a purchase from M&S, as none of my student jackets looked right over the suit. Finally, I picked up my black plastic briefcase, a gift from my parents, and left for work. I hoped my suited and booted image said I was hard-working, ambitious and reliable.

Outside Tooting Bec station I picked up a copy of the *Guardian* and made my way down to the platform. I held the rubber handrail as it bumped along. It was like descending into a dystopian film set as the escalator fell away under the curved ceiling. From below there was a warm breeze and the sounds of distant rumbling which reminded me of The Jam's *Down in the Tube Station at Midnight*.

It was a short walk to my new office from Waterloo. 'The County Hall' was carved in gold lettering above the main entrance. I climbed the stone steps, pushed open the large wooden doors and stepped into the main lobby, and into the world of work.

I was rounded up with other new graduate management trainees and briefed in a room on the ground floor. A portly woman informed us that we were Admin A's. The A referred to our grade. We were at the bottom of four management grades that went up to D. She didn't say what was above D but she explained that at the very top was the Director-General, Maurice Stonefrost. As graduate trainees we were in a separate lift to the executive officers. Our lift had a fast track to the higher floors like those in posh hotels. Our lift went to the very top.

I was allocated to the new Industry and Employment Branch, which was responsible for drawing up socialist local economic strategies. I was to provide support to recently recruited activists and academics including Robin Murray, Irene Bruegel, Sheila Rowbotham and Hilary Wainwright. I felt slightly light-headed at the prospect of working with people whose books I had studied. I was almost too excited to think, my brain couldn't catch up with my thoughts as they raced and tumbled over each other.

My new office was on the raised ground floor and had a view overlooking the river and Westminster Bridge. It was a long way from the press shop in Swindon where I did my work experience day. I couldn't have told you then that this was what I wanted, that this was the pinnacle of my ambition but as I gazed across at the Houses of Parliament I realised this was everything I ever wanted.

That first afternoon I was reluctant to leave the office. I stayed long after everyone else had gone. I watched the sky fade into a deep blue then black. Big Ben became illuminated and gleamed against the night sky, and the underside of Westminster bridge glowed green. When I finally left the building I walked down the South Bank. This was it, my new home, my new manor. I jumped up onto one of the raised benches and looked across to Whitehall. I was the king of the fucking world.

~

The next morning I was inducted by Brian, who worked through a checklist. He outlined to me the structure of the council, and the role of elected members and committees. He also said if I felt like not coming in one day I should just call in sick. It was like an extra leave category, a 'can't be bothered today' allowance of ten days a year. I frowned inside, it didn't sit right with me. I was proud of my protestant work ethic even if it was the force behind modern capitalism. I valued diligence, discipline and responsibility. Values Thatcher would also have been proud of. Despite the advice I never took a day's sick during my time at the council. Brian also advised me to join the Staff Association. This was effectively like a trade union but just for GLC staff which was affiliated with the National Association of Local Government Officers.

At around eleven a lady pushing a trolley arrived to see if we wanted anything. It was called the tea trolley but I don't recall there being tea. The trolley had cakes, sandwiches and crusty rolls in paper and cellophane bags. Brian didn't use the trolley; he brought his own lunch in a blue Tupperware box that contained sandwiches in a Sunblest bread wrapper and an apple. The thought crossed my mind that one day I would have to make my own sandwiches for work like other old people.

One day I would also have to think about savings, mortgages and pensions, though Brian said I would never have to worry about my pension if I worked at the council. This was just as well. I could answer every *Mastermind* question about the suffragettes but I knew nothing at all about pensions.

Knowledge is strange like that. People can be experts on the French revolution but not know how to change the fuse on a plug. Despite Brian talking to me about annuities, employer contributions and added years I remained none the wiser. He could have been talking Russian for all I understood but I nodded knowingly.

In the afternoon Errol, one of the junior staff, gave me a tour of the building. The first stop on the ground floor was the typing pool, a large room with rows of women tapping away at typewriters. The rhythmic clattering was frequently interrupted by the sounds of dinging and zipping as carriages were returned to start a new line. Occasionally a typist would stop, take a tiny brush, apply Tippex, blow on the paper and adjust its position before the clattering resumed. No senior staff typed their own letters. In 1983, your seniority was determined by your distance from a keyboard.

The typing pool was just along from the staff bar. According to Errol everyone went to the bar or a local pub on Friday lunchtimes, and didn't return until late in the afternoon. He joked that lunch on Fridays was not fish and chips but crisps, KP peanuts and pork scratchings. I was uneasy about this practice. It was probably my protestant work ethic again but Thatcher's downfall wasn't going to be achieved in the bar.

The first floor of County Hall was different from the rest of the building. It had wooden panels and ornate coving. The corridors had the hushed silence of a library. Errol told me this was where the elected members lived and was called the principal floor. He said administrative staff like us were strictly forbidden from being on the floor unless we had business there. Checking no one was around Errol pushed open a large wooden door. Hesitantly we entered the members dining room which had red leather chairs and a balcony that looked out over the river towards Parliament and Whitehall.

Back in the corridor Errol stopped outside the men's toilet.

"You won't believe this," he said, and tentatively opened the door. After ensuring the room was empty he beckoned me inside. I admit I hadn't expected to get such a detailed tour of the facilities. He swung back the door of one of the stalls and pointed at the toilet roll holder on the wall. "They have soft paper tissue." In the rest of the building the toilets had hard, shiny, non-absorbent toilet paper. It was a cross between tracing paper and greaseproof paper. It didn't so much clean, as slide things around. At home, like most people, we had soft toilet tissue. But at County Hall the GLC supplies department still provided staff with hard paper. The hierarchical nature of the organisation even extended to toilet paper. Errol explained that if I ever needed to do a number two I should always go to the principal floor. I thanked him for the heads up, though I trained my bowels to go either before or after work.

With caution and some effort Errol opened the heavy door to the council chamber. We stepped stealthily inside, like we were entering forbidden territory. It resembled an Old Bailey courtroom and smelt of the polish that my mum liberally sprayed onto the wooden surfaces at home. I walked between the curved empty benches that were shaped like a horseshoe. Errol stepped up onto the platform and sat in the high-backed, red and orange leather chair that faced the benches.

"I hereby sentence you to ten years hard labour," he said. "For the crime of stealing soft toilet paper."

In the basement the corridors were lined with large pipes. Errol helpfully pointed out that there was a single unisex toilet on this floor, so that if I did need privacy, he winked knowingly, I should use that one. On *Mastermind* his specialist subject would be the toilets of County Hall.

The post room in the basement was a busy central hub and handled all of the memos and letters which were the council's main forms of communication. There was the constant sound of trollies banging doors as they were wheeled in and out. The room had a semi-circular window just above head height, where you could see the ankles of those passing by outside. Our next stop was the Supplies Office. Outside its green door Errol said, "I will now introduce you to the most important man in the building."

~

When we stepped inside the room I saw three black men sat around a desk piled high with papers. There was a sudden and portentous silence as the men looked up. From behind the desk an old West Indian guy pushed back his chair and stood up. Following his lead, the other two men also straightened and moved towards us. The older guy broke into a beaming smile. "Errol, what's up man?" He clasped Errol's raised hand and pulled him into his chest.

"Ron, this is Steve our new Admin A," said Errol. "I was just telling him, if he needs anything you are the man to speak to."

Ron looked me up and down, inspecting me as if I was a private on parade.

"So you are one of the special ones?"

I looked quizzically at Ron and then at Errol.

Ron smiled.

"Don't look so worried son, we will look after you," he said and put a large arm around my shoulder.

On the wall behind him there was a large 'GLC Against Racism' poster. Catching me looking at it, Ron said, "The councillors say they are against racism but how many black faces do you see up there?"

I looked at him blankly; I wasn't sure if he meant how many of us management trainees were black.

"There are five hundred and fifty managers in the council," said Ron. "Do you know how many are black?"

I hadn't come across any.

"Fifteen, just fifteen, and none of the top managers are black."

Ron had got the figures from the first equalities monitoring report prepared for Ken Livingstone. Less than 10 percent of GLC workers were from ethnic minority groups and they were concentrated in the supplies, cleaning and catering departments. It was uncomfortably like a form of mini-apartheid.

"You white-collar folk are special," said Ron. "You don't have to clock in each morning like we do. They don't trust us manual workers to arrive on time. It's a different world for you upstairs. We work forty hours a week not thirty-seven and a half hours like you people. We also get a lower London allowance and less paid holidays."

"That doesn't seem right," I said. "We should get the Staff Association to press for equal treatment."

Ron roared with laughter and was joined by his colleagues. I flushed with embarrassment and winced as I tried to fathom out why my suggestion merited such mirth.

Finally, Ron put his hand on my shoulder to explain. "Son, it was the Staff Association that objected to us getting the same London allowance," he said. "They insisted on maintaining their differentials. They even objected to us taking part in the inter-departmental sports day."

"That's because we would win everything," said one of his colleagues and slapped me on the back.

I didn't need Ron to tell me that managers in the council were overwhelmingly white and male. It was partly a result of only advertising vacancies internally, which meant the managers were people who had been recruited twenty or thirty years earlier. Ken Livingstone though was determined to change things and proposed advertising vacancies externally to enable the council to recruit more people from black and minority ethnic communities, and more women.

The first equalities monitoring report found that only 16 percent of council employees were women in 1981, and only thirty-five of the top five hundred and fifty managers were women. This partly reflected the misogyny of the men in the organisation. But there was also a long history of women having their careers restricted by stupid rules.

Irene in my team was working on an employment strategy for women. She peered through her thick glasses and told me that employers used to insist that women resigned if they got married.

"Men believed a woman's place was in the home and that women were no longer 'fair game' once they got married," she said. "In 1922, the Rhondda Education Authority in Wales sacked sixty-three women teachers simply because they got married. The teachers took the case to court but of course the judges sided with the misogynists."

I couldn't quite believe what she was saying; it didn't make any sense.

"The marriage bar for teachers was removed by the 1944 Education Act," she continued, "but it remained in other organisations. In the Civil Service, the BBC and here in the GLC, women still had to resign in the nineteen-seventies if they got married."

The Staff Association was appalled at Livingstone's external recruitment proposals and actively fought to protect the status quo. It wasn't what I expected. I assumed all trade unions would support the council's equal opportunity policies. They were particularly upset when Livingstone introduced a code of conduct that made sexual harassment a disciplinary offence. Male managers who regularly commented on a woman's sexual attractiveness, patted the bottoms of passing female staff, and who used their authority to demand kisses at Christmas parties, said it was completely unnecessary, as sexual harassment didn't exist in their departments.

～

In my lunch hours I explored the local area around County Hall. On York Road was the Midland Bank which stood out with its black and yellow branding. The bank was one of the first to introduce ATMs, which stood for automated teller machines, and allowed you to withdraw cash. It was a great innovation; you no longer had to queue inside the bank and write out a cheque to cash. Luckily old people were suspicious of the new machines and continued to queue inside, leaving the ATMs free for us young people. Why were old people so nervous of change and technology?

Next to the bank there was an Italian deli which had a huge silver coffee machine behind the counter. In the 1980s takeaway coffee was a health hazard. In British Rail stations they mixed coffee granules with scalding hot water in unstable paper cups which would tear the skin from the roof of your mouth. Still the coffee was better than their stale sandwiches where the edges curled upwards in an attempt to escape the plastic domes under which they were kept. In the deli, older Italian men shouted and gesticulated to each other while they constructed sandwiches like works of art. You didn't simply get ham or cheese. There was a bewildering array of extras including tomatoes, peppers and olives. No one from Swindon to my knowledge had eaten or even seen a pepper. The sandwiches were wrapped in a waxy paper and passed to beautiful young Italian women who rang up the till and handed over your order. The air was filled with the aromas of meat, cheese and coffee.

On Friday afternoon at the end of my first week Brian gave

me a '*Keep* GLC Working for London' badge, which I pinned to my coat. On the tube home I opened my copy of the *Evening Standard* and saw a headline that read, '54% of Londoners oppose abolition'. Thatcher may have won the last round but I was confident we would stop her abolishing the GLC.

30

FAST TRACK BABY BOOMERS

The first thing I noticed about Angela was her Filofax. In our Admin A training sessions she wrote notes in the leather-bound folder where she also kept contact numbers, committee dates and a 'to do' list. We regularly attended training sessions together at the Copperfield Street development centre in Southwark. In our first session we were informed that all letters had to be responded to within ten working days; it was called the GLC's gold standard. These days if someone doesn't reply to an email or message for two weeks you assume they have died.

Angela was small with straight dark hair and a gap in her teeth. She had studied history at York and also worked in the Industry and Employment Branch. After coveting her Filofax for a few weeks, I purchased my own in Covent Garden, complete with a fold out A-Z of central London and plastic inserts for my cards. Angela and I were both conscientious, ambitious and took our jobs seriously. I think we recognised that in each other and was why we became friends.

The third Admin A in our branch was Simon. He was tall and his hair was already receding despite being in his early twenties. He had studied English literature in Norwich at UEA. The three of us would meet regularly for lunch and share our experiences. Angela loved the cultural side of being in London. She would talk about the plays she had seen at the Royal Court and the concerts she had attended. She became our cultural guide. Simon and I joined her at lunchtimes listening to classical music concerts in Festival Hall and Smith Square.

One evening the three of us, plus Fiona, a friend of Angela's from university, went to see a play at the Lyric Theatre in Shaftesbury Avenue. It was called *Pack of Lies* and starred Judi Dench. It was the first proper play that I had seen. I wasn't sure what you wore to see a play. I knew what to wear to the football or to a demo but I didn't know what you wore to the theatre in the West End. I worried that I would be found out in some way, that someone would say, "What is that guy from Swindon doing here?" In the end I went directly from the office in my suit. I hoped my neutral office uniform would lessen the likelihood of making a sartorial faux pas. I relaxed once I saw Simon was also in his suit.

Angela said we had seats in the gods, which sounded much grander than it was. We were high above the stage. When I walked between the narrow seats I almost had vertigo. There were two tiers below us. I spent ages just admiring the theatre with its gilt patterned balconies. There was something thrilling about watching people perform live. I was struck by the echo of their footsteps across the wooden stage. Weeks later I couldn't recall much about the play itself but I remembered in detail the experience of being at the theatre.

Simon and Angela would often talk about literature and books by contemporary writers, such as Iris Murdoch and Malcolm Bradbury. One lunchtime, on a walk back from the Tate Britain,

Angela and Simon talked about a book called *The Sea, The Sea* which had won something called the Booker Prize. I had to draw heavily on my ability to nod knowingly. I was again having to play catch-up. The books I had read at university had mainly been older classics but I put them to good use by dropping them into the conversation. I began to pay greater attention to the cultural pages of the *Guardian*. I started to read book, theatre and film reviews, and make notes about them in my Filofax.

On Angela's recommendation we bought cheap tickets in the gods at the Coliseum to see *Don Giovanni*. I had never seen or heard opera music, other than on TV ads. Angela said the latest ice cream advert was based on a famous Italian opera song *O Sole Mio* and the original lyrics were not 'Just One Cornetto'. As preparation for our night at the opera I purchased a cassette tape of *Don Giovanni* arias, which as far as I could tell was a posh word for songs. I played them on my portable cassette player, which was like the Sony 'Walkman' but cheaper. The songs were sung in Italian and I had no idea what they were about. It was a revelation when they were sung in English at the Coliseum. It never occurred to me that the Don would be singing about his sexual conquests. I might have sung about them too, had I seduced one thousand Spanish women like the Don.

After the opera we wandered around Covent Garden. The former fruit and vegetable market had relocated to Nine Elms in 1980, and the covered market had been rebranded and opened as a retail centre. Shopping was increasingly becoming a leisure activity. Developers were building huge edge-of-town shopping malls surrounded by car parks. The week after our trip to the opera I watched a report about the opening of The Ridings shopping centre in Wakefield which had a glazed roof, glass lifts, a food court and a cinema.

Around Covent Garden new shops were opening almost

every week. I was particularly excited by the opening of a Tintin shop in Floral Street. I bought myself a small plastic Tintin figure in a brown suit with plus four style trousers and a gun slung over his shoulder which still sits on my desk. Next door was a men's clothing shop called Paul Smith, which had opened four years earlier in 1979. I couldn't afford Paul Smith but I went to Next which promised affordable versions of designer clothes. There I bought some high-waisted trousers which tapered at the ankles. The first time I wore them Simon asked if I was auditioning to be in Duran Duran.

In the evenings Angela, Simon and I explored the Archduke wine bar under Waterloo arches. The new wine bars were softer and more feminine than pubs, with their yucca plants and jazz soundtracks. They were populated by women in shoulder pads. A style driven by a combination of Thatcher, and the popularity of TV shows like *Dallas* and *Dynasty*. Their tailored jackets came to define female power dressing.

Angela said she preferred wine bars as they were not full of smoke like the pubs. "It's great that people are giving up smoking," she said one evening. "The *Guardian* says the number of people smoking has fallen from over fifty percent to thirty-seven percent." The paper had supported the British Medical Association's demand for a ban on tobacco advertising a year earlier. Of course it was attacked by Thatcherites as yet another example of the nanny state. If people wanted to get lung cancer, surely that was their right.

Saatchi and Saatchi were commissioned to create adverts that would bypass restrictive legislation on promoting cigarettes. They produced a series of striking adverts for a brand of cigarettes called 'Silk Cut' featuring purple silk that was slashed or cut. They were pasted on the walls of every tube station. The advertising worked, as Silk Cut became the best-selling cigarette brand in the UK. "How could you work for a company that promotes the Tories and lung cancer?" asked Simon.

~

On Tuesday evenings Simon and I played five-a-side football with our fellow Admin A trainees at the Queen Mother Sports Centre near Victoria. It was organised by Ges, who worked in the Equal Opportunities department. His enthusiasm was infectious and he became known affectionately as 'El Presidente'. He was also fast, racing past me to win the two hundred metres at the council's sports day at Crystal Palace.

The sports centre was full of women in leg warmers and headbands, attending aerobic classes inspired by the film *Flashdance*. The changing rooms were full of gossip about office sexual relationships. It appeared everyone was having sex. There were stories of relationships between trainees, managers, Labour Party councillors, secretaries and even librarians. I was clearly missing out.

Simon and I were members of a growing group of men who sought to avoid sexist behaviour but wanted to sleep with women as much as our colleague Jake, who spent his evenings asking every woman he met if they wanted to fuck. Bizarrely Jake's approach worked; he always found someone who said yes. Maybe it really was a numbers game. We were much more careful in trying to communicate our sexual desire without treating women as sexual objects. We worked hard to demonstrate that we were sensitive and also sexually attractive. I generally failed at the latter.

I turned to *Cosmopolitan* magazine in the hope it might help me plot a way through my dating dilemmas and ensure I was aware of a woman's needs. The magazine suggested women wanted orgasms but also plenty of cuddling and foreplay. It also stressed that the average period of foreplay was fifteen minutes and this was way too short. I took note of this particular advice and was caught on occasions surreptitiously looking at my watch to make sure I passed the fifteen-minute mark, which can be way longer than you think it is.

The magazine placed a lot of emphasis on sensual massage and suggested that tying up and blindfolding a woman heightened her experience by enhancing her anticipation and her senses of touch, sound, smell and taste. I wasn't sure about this advice. When I had complimented Irene in the office on her hair, she had shot dangerous Dalek lasers at me from her eyes. I wasn't going to propose tying her to a bed.

Angela invited Simon and me to her flat to meet some of her university friends for dinner and cooked us a three course meal. It was quite different to the evenings Simon and I spent together eating bowls of cereal on the sofa while we watched TV. Angela was a civilising influence on both of us. She had a pine Habitat dining table and trailing spider plants, and served food in orange dishes which she referred to as Le Creuset. It probably meant orange in French or something like that.

Angela's friends were interested in politics. Her friend Fiona had recently joined the Labour Party but seemed more excited by London house prices than socialism. With her feathered bob hairstyle and large collars Fiona looked a little like Princess Diana but that was where the similarities ended. She was ferociously bright, had studied with Angela at York and was now on the Civil Service Fast Track programme. She seemed to take charge of everything like a bossy head girl. Fiona talked about the up-and-coming areas to buy a flat. It seemed our generation had missed Islington but Brixton, Clapham and other areas were looking attractive.

"Did you see that Barbara Cartland is now the best-selling

author ever?" said Simon. "I despair at the literary choices of the nation."

"Millions of readers can't be wrong," said Angela, enjoying Simon's upset.

"Romantic bloody fiction," said Simon, grimacing. "Where heroes carry their lovers to the peak of Olympus and they become no longer human but at one with the gods."

He paused and shook his head.

"What utter bollocks."

"You have got to admit she is incredibly prolific," said Fiona. "She has already published ten new books this year."

"That says everything," snarled Simon, curling his lip upwards like Elvis.

Cartland would go on to publish seventeen books in 1984, and over seven hundred books in her lifetime. I was amazed that anyone was able to write a book every month even if it was romantic fiction. Simon was convinced that any book written in less than a month was "total crap". But amazingly each book sold over a million copies on average. Some estimates put her total book sales at over two billion.

"There are so many great books but they stuff our libraries with romantic rubbish," said Simon. "They should read *Heartburn* by Nora Ephron, now that is a funny book about relationships."

"I really enjoyed *The Queen's Gambit*," said Angela. "You would love it, Steve. It is about this girl who becomes the US chess champion."

"Thanks, I'll get a copy," I said.

"No need, you can have mine," and she jumped up to the pine bookshelf and pulled out a hard copy which she handed to me. It had a girl in a red dress on the cover who was pondering over a chess board while being watched by a white cat.

"I read the review," said Simon. "It is all about genius and addiction."

"I suppose they sometimes go together," I said. "Bobby Fisher was a genius but totally addicted to chess. He was just fourteen when he won the US chess championship."

I wanted to talk about how he always played pawn to king four but I was conscious that wasn't the expected conversational direction.

Angela made a cafetiere and placed it in the centre of the table. Over coffee we discussed how we had made it from our respective communities to London. It was something we all shared. We had escaped the geographical confines of our families and upbringing. Our backgrounds were different but we had a lot in common. We valued education and hard work. Fiona said we represented the modern meritocracy. The reality is we were the lucky ones, a small privileged group. Most people in Swindon or Stoke, or even Hampshire, didn't go to university, move to London, attend lunchtime concerts and watch opera at the Coliseum.

We had got lucky, we lived at a time of full student grants and had made the grades to get into red brick universities. We had also secured places on management schemes and would be promoted quickly. We were on the baby boomer fast track.

At Christmas the TV Times had a loving front page illustration of Charles and Diana with their son William decorating a Christmas tree. They were the epitome of a loving nuclear family even if the truth was quite different. At home in Swindon I watched *Top of the Pops* with my sister and continued to marvel at the varied tastes of the British public. Culture Club and Tears for Fears were followed by Terry and Arthur from *Minder* singing *What Are We Going To*

Get 'er Indoors. The Christmas number one was a surprise to everyone. It was *Only You* by a cappella group called the Flying Pickets. Bizarrely it was said to be Margaret Thatcher's favourite record; maybe she never knew the name of the group. It is possible; I know lots of songs but have no idea who sang them.

"So how's life in London?" Bob asked me in the club.

Tony intervened before I could respond. "I went there once. Didn't like the place, far too busy. I am happy here. As I told the missus we don't want for anything in Swindon. Not sure why you'd want to go anywhere else."

London was a faraway and magical land to the men in the club. To prove the point Tony added, "They are all a bit strange in London", without any regard for the fact I was sitting next to him.

"My daughter says they are all polyamorous," said Bob.

"What's that when it's at home?" asked Tony.

"Means they have sex with parrots," said Dad, causing much laughter around the table.

"I wouldn't put it past them," added Tony.

I might have been Cliffy's boy but to the men I was also the son with the strange views. They would explain away my views to other members of the club by saying, "He's from London" and this would be accepted with a knowing nod of the head. They no longer viewed me as a Swindon lad.

I made my annual trip to the newsagents at the crossroads and begrudgingly bought a copy of *The Times*. To be fair to me, it was that, the *Daily Mail* or the *Sun*. According to the paper's economics section it had been a good year for investors. The FTSE All-Share Index had risen by 23 percent and the US Dow Jones index by over 40 percent. It had not been so good if you were seeking work. The unemployment rate had increased to over 11 percent and three million people were still out of work.

The Times argued Thatcher was successfully reshaping the political agenda and forcing the Labour Party to accept many of her policies. What utter rubbish. We would never accept her policies on privatisation, selling council houses, cutting taxes or being a base for Reagan's missiles.

31

DON

In January 1984, Don joined our admin team. He was in his late thirties, tall and angular, with dark hair parted on one side and thick, bottle bottomed NHS spectacles. I quickly became aware that he was a radical gay rights activist. On his first afternoon Adele, a young Nigerian woman, came to our office and admired the view of the Houses of Parliament. She asked Don if he had ever been up Big Ben? He replied quick as a flash that he didn't even know the guy.

Don had no respect for authority which I loved, though of course it also meant he had no respect for my authority as his manager. He would constantly criticise the academics in our unit for being middle-class radicals with smiley badges. "Socialism is just a fucking lifestyle choice for you lot, like choosing to be vegetarian. Working-class people don't have a choice. They have to fight for higher wages and better working conditions."

Don would shout good-humoured abuse at the Communist Party members as they came in each day with their copies of the *Morning Star*. He called them 'tankies'. I thought it was because a surprising number of them wore tank tops, but later discovered it was because they had supported the crushing of the 1956 Hungarian revolution and the 1968 Prague Spring by Soviet tanks. They accepted his abuse with good grace. I think he got away with it because he was amusing, like a Trotskyist Basil Fawlty. Most of them couldn't help but smile as he abused them.

Don was a fellow traveller of the Revolutionary Communist Party. I didn't think he was a member as I was sure he would, like Groucho Marx, despise any club that would accept him as a member. Don regularly arrived at work with the RCP's paper, *The Next Step*. On his first day he laid a copy out on the desk. In bright yellow lettering the headline read, 'Who needs the Labour Party now?' Don told everyone that would listen that Labour only offered the prospect of a better capitalism when what was needed was a new working-class party not one wedded to the existing system. I started to think that maybe he was right.

My Labour Party meetings in London were attended by well-educated people concerned about fair trade, the environment, Greenham Common and gay rights. Issues which I rarely heard discussed in the club. I became frustrated when we spent more time discussing jumble sales than political theory. I was increasingly drawn to the RCP pamphlets that Don bought into the office. I didn't agree with their politics but I enjoyed their intellectual, almost academic, perspectives on politics and the openness to radical ideas.

At the end of January 1984, I went on strike for the first time to oppose the abolition of the GLC and the metropolitan councils. I joined Don on the picket line. He was standing on the top of the steps outside County Hall and hurling abuse at the scabs who were going into work. I was disappointed to see so many people going into work as I thought everyone accepted that you should never cross a picket line.

In February, the papers were full of articles about Granada Television's *The Jewel in the Crown*. It was a fourteen-episode series that traced the decline of the Raj. I didn't watch it but Angela loved the programme. She told me it was not nostalgic but a critical view of the arrogance and corruption of British imperialism. The critics also loved it. Reviews said it was complex and beautifully shot. One called it a tour de force that would never stop sparkling in our hearts and memories. Another called it the pinnacle of British drama and the series was nominated for ten BAFTAS. Don of course hated it.

"Another example of fucking empire nostalgia," he said while sat at his desk. Looking across the river he added, "Those buildings over there are monuments to the evils of colonialism and racism."

I tried unsuccessfully to put across Angela's view but was steamrollered by Don's constant stream of invective.

"Why don't they make programmes showing the massacres the British committed or the thirty-five million that died in unnecessary famines. Churchill was a fucking bastard, he said it was their own fault for 'breeding like rabbits'. They should make TV programmes about that, not people having tea and cucumber sandwiches on verandas. Fucking bastards."

The public didn't share Don's views; the programme achieved record viewing figures and won five BAFTAs.

Don was particularly exercised when the BBC banned a song called *Relax* by Frankie Goes to Hollywood because the DJ Mike Read was upset by its sexually explicit lyrics. In the office he held up a full page newspaper advert for everyone to see. It was published to promote *Relax* and had a picture of a band member in a sailor's hat saying, 'All the nice boys love sea men'. Don shouted across the office to no one in particular, "Fuck the BBC. The homophobic bastards."

The ban created massive publicity. People turned to other channels and radio stations to listen to the record. Channel 4 played the song on *The Tube*, where there was still no sign of Paul, and it rapidly became a gay anthem. The record's video, which MTV refused to show, resembled a gay S&M club with band members surrounded by muscular men in leather. According to Don it was incredibly popular in Heaven, a gay night club at Charing Cross. The record shot to the top of charts and stayed there for five weeks.

The next Frankie single, *Two Tribes*, was avowedly political. It was a protest against nuclear war and went straight to number one. The video mocked up a wrestling match between Reagan and the Russian leader Chernenko. I was sure the song's success was an indication that our unilateral nuclear-disarmament policy was finally cutting through. I was to learn later that the people who buy records are not the same people that vote in elections.

The success of Frankie Goes to Hollywood was visible on people's chests. Suddenly in the spring everyone was wearing white T-shirts with huge lettering saying 'Relax' and other slogans. Someone said that the idea came from Katharine Hamnett who met Margaret Thatcher at London Fashion Week wearing a T-shirt saying '58% don't want Pershing', the latest American ballistic missile.

The protest T-shirt was enthusiastically embraced by capitalist entrepreneurs to compensate for the falling sales of Che Guevara posters. The slogans were generally meaningless such as 'Choose Life' or 'Choose Love'. I hated them. No, don't start comparing them to badges. Badges were different. Badges were, well I am not sure, but I know they were different. It is obvious that a 'Choose Love' T-shirt is not the same as a 'Tories Out' badge. The shopping malls were suddenly full of people buying burgers in McDonald's wearing T-shirts saying 'Choose Life'. Tell that to the cows.

Frankie Goes to Hollywood was managed by ZTT, the Saatchi and Saatchi entrepreneurs of the pop industry, who set up in 1983. One of the company's founders was Trevor Horn, who previously as a member of Buggles co-wrote and sang *Video Killed the Radio Star*. ZTT embraced music videos and merchandising. The provocative marketing for Frankie was led by Paul Morley, who previously wrote for the *NME*. He understood that the ban on *Relax* was good for business. Controversy shifted records and merchandise. ZTT produced their own range of protest T-shirts with slogans such as 'Frankie Say Arm the Unemployed'. On the radio a BBC DJ argued Frankie Goes To Hollywood was successful because, "rather like the Militant Tendency - you ban it and it gets more popular".

I was optimistic when Tony Benn was selected as the Labour candidate for the upcoming Chesterfield by-election. Those who thought he had lost his Bristol seat because he was too left wing were wrong. His seat had been reconfigured as a result of boundary changes making it difficult to win. When I expressed my support for Benn in the office I received a tirade from Don.

"Benn was a member of the cabinet that supported a dirty war in Ireland. He supported sending the troops in. He supported the Prevention of Terrorism Act. He drove down wages and working conditions in Britain. He defended Britain's links to apartheid in South Africa. He signed the deal with Rio Tinto. Don't fucking talk to me about Viscount Stansgate being on the side of the working class."

Don missed no opportunity to educate me about the horrors of Benn and the Labour governments of the 1960s and 1970s. This was a new experience. I had never come across anyone who thought Benn was too right wing. I was now being castigated for being on the side of the establishment.

On the morning of 2 March 1984, I woke to the news Benn had won the by-election convincingly. "Good news" I said to Don when I arrived in the office and handed him my copy of the *Guardian* with its headline, 'Benn bounces back'. Don fumed as he sat opposite me and aggressively stapled papers together. "There is no democratic route to socialism," he said. "Those bastards won't give up their power so easily."

Later that day Ian MacGregor, the head of the National Coal Board, announced the closure of five pits, including the Cortonwood colliery just ten or so miles north of Benn's new constituency. It was part of Thatcher's plan to crush the power of Britain's trade unions by defeating the miners. She had stockpiled tonnes of coal and tasked MacGregor with provoking a strike in the spring. A strike she could win.

"The bastards are trying to provoke a strike over pit closures, rather than wages or conditions," said Don. "They know it is an issue that will divide the union. It's also bleeding obvious they are trying to engineer a strike now as demand for coal will be at its lowest over the summer months."

Thatcher and MacGregor must have been disappointed when the announcement did not result in a strike by the NUM. They raised the stakes by saying Cortonwood would be the first of twenty pits to be closed and the first five would be closed within days. It had the desired effect. The six thousand miners threatened with closure went on strike.

Arthur Scargill, the miners' leader, claimed MacGregor was actually planning to close seventy mines with a loss of sixty-five thousand jobs. Don chided me that seventy mines was still less than Tony Benn had closed when he was energy minister.

Scargill called on NUM members in other areas to support the strike but decided not to hold a national ballot of all miners. He had already called and lost three previous national ballots for strike action. Miners in South Wales, Yorkshire, Scotland, North East England and Kent agreed to support the strike but there was less support in the Midlands and in North Wales. In Nottinghamshire miners continued to work and argued for a national ballot on strike action.

I fully supported the miners but there was something about the strike that bothered me, and not just the fact the strike was starting in the spring. The NUM appeared to be looking backwards not forwards. It was portrayed as a fight for the people that had built the union and defeated Ted Heath. I couldn't really remember Heath. All I could recall was that he had an odd laugh, sailed and played the piano. The unions represented the strike as a fight to continue a way of life rather than for investment in new jobs.

Scargill's language, "Comrades, I salute you in this crucial battle", belonged to the seventies not the eighties. He also argued pits should be kept open even if they were uneconomic. He demanded that such mines be subsidised by the government and only close when there was no coal left, which seemed unrealistic.

If mines were closed it was clear investment would be needed to create new jobs locally, to retrain miners and provide a future for the mining communities. Thatcher though had no plans to support such communities. She was vicious, vindictive and appeared to thrive on conflict. She branded the miners "the enemy within", calling up memories of the Falklands War. She was almost as extreme as the FCS, whose members at Warwick University produced a songbook called 'Fuck the Trots' and called for the public execution of Arthur Scargill, as well as the hanging of Nelson Mandela.

Defeating the miners was a key part of Thatcher's plan to

change Britain. A Britain that was already being reshaped by her taxation policies. In the spring Nigel Lawson unveiled his first budget and plans to reduce corporation tax from 52 percent to 35 percent. A 17 percent reduction. It was going to be another good year for shareholders. I despised the Tories and their immoral tax cuts.

32

OLIVE MORRIS

During the summer of 1984 I moved to a flat in Brixton. This worried my mother given the riots a few years earlier, but I told her it was being gentrified. Developers had spotted the area's potential. Victorian terraced houses with bay windows were being bought up and converted into flats. Walls were being covered in woodchip paper to hide the lumps and bumps, and painted white to look light, clean and fresh. Rooms were fitted with cheap, foam-backed oatmeal carpets ready for Habitat furniture. Young white professionals like me were attracted by the vibrant community, the Ritzy cinema, The Fridge nightclub, the Brixton Academy, the Victoria line and the potential for house prices to increase.

The great thing about Brixton was the range of radical papers on sale. It wasn't just the usual socialist papers, you could buy the *Black Flag* from the anarchists and *Freedom News* from the local Black Panthers group. In 1984, the summer streets were drenched in sunshine and the air was full of heavy bass reggae music. Through open windows also came the sounds of *Free Nelson Mandela* by the Special AKA and occasionally the haunting, hypnotic voice of Jimmy Somerville singing *Smalltown Boy*.

My flat was behind Olive Morris House, a large red brick council building on Brixton Hill. Olive had co-founded the Brixton Black Women's Group and was part of the British Black Panther Movement. She died in 1979, at the age of just twenty-seven from cancer. She was a passionate activist who fought against racism and police brutality in the seventies. This was a time when the police actively framed and beat up young black men for crimes they didn't commit. She was also part of the Brixton squatters movement.

I never knew Olive but I went to a talk about her in one of the Brixton black bookshops led by an older activist. He said Olive had been very critical of the British left. She argued that trade unions didn't support black workers the way they supported white workers. She particularly disliked white middle-class people shouting, "Black and white unite and fight" at Anti-Nazi League rallies. He read out a quote from Olive, where she said, "Not a single problem associated with racialism, unemployment, police violence and homelessness can be settled by 'rocking' against the fascists, the police or the army."

Olive questioned the value of public festivals and carnivals as political events. She particularly castigated the 'Rock against Racism' carnivals organised in the late seventies including the one I had read about in the *NME*. It was held in Victoria Park in Hackney, and a hundred thousand people turned up to listen to The Clash, the Tom Robinson band and X-Ray Spex. Olive said the event made people feel good, like they had contributed to something worthwhile, but in reality it changed nothing. She said that the really important day-to-day struggles, such as local strikes, housing petitions, health campaigns and protests about police brutality go largely unnoticed by the general population.

I shifted uncomfortably in my seat and looked at the floor. Maybe I was going to such events to salve my liberal left conscience. I didn't experience the daily racism suffered by black people but I sensed the anger and despair of those in the room that did.

I thought about Olive every time I passed the building named after her. I wondered how many of those walking by remembered her? We need more buildings named after people like Olive. In 2020, the building was demolished to make way for luxury flats. I still mourn the loss and hope one day that Lambeth Council will name another building after her.

Many of the people recruited into the GLC's Industry and Employment Branch by Livingstone's administration disagreed with Olive. They were veterans of the 'Rock against Racism' concerts. The Popular Planning Unit commissioned a one-day festival to be held on the South Bank in June to promote what the GLC was doing to create and defend jobs. It was called the 'Jobs for a Change' festival.

To promote the event the Flying Pickets produced a song called *Give us Jobs, Jobs, Jobs for a Change* with Ken Livingstone as one of the vocalists. It was distributed as a CD inside *Time Out* magazine. Thousands of colourful badges were also minted and given away. They protested against racism, health cuts and the Police Bill, which proposed allowing the police to hold people for ninety-six hours without charge. The aims of the festival were laudable but after the Olive Morris talk I was sceptical.

The festival took place on Sunday, 10 June 1984. The main council chamber featured a rolling programme of political speeches, including talks by miners wives. Young people wearing badges wandered the wood-panelled corridors. There were also events in Festival Hall and the Queen Elizabeth Hall on the South Bank. In the evening there was a free concert by musicians including Billy Bragg and the Smiths. Jubilee Gardens was packed as tens of thousands of people, who hadn't been enticed by the day's talks in the council chamber, turned up for the concert.

I am not sure how but I was lucky enough to be standing with Don just a few rows back from the stage when Morrissey came on. I didn't really know who he was and wouldn't have known it was him apart from the crescendo of noise that rolled over us as he walked on stage with a rose hanging out of his back pocket. As he performed he took the rose and traced it up and down his chest, which was exposed through a baggy white shirt. Don absolutely loved it and was screaming in my ear.

The next morning all the talk was of the festival and Morrissey. The event was seen as a great success. The view was that thousands of people had attended, particularly the free evening concert, they had enjoyed themselves and they would look upon the GLC more favourably. I didn't want to be a curmudgeon but the aim had been to raise awareness of our employment policies. I wasn't convinced we had raised awareness about our economic strategy for the Royal Docks, despite me giving out hundreds of 'Docklands for the People' badges. I stayed quiet. I didn't want to dampen the mood. Almost immediately work started on an even bigger festival to be held the following year.

33

KEEP GLC WORKING FOR LONDON

"Council bans baa-baa black sheep."

A ccording to the press loony-left councils had banned the nursery rhyme because it reinforced a derogatory and subservient use of the word 'black' among children in their formative years. Of course it was nonsense, one of a barrage of fake stories designed to vilify councils like the GLC. Other stories included councils banning black coffee because it was racist, staff being forbidden from putting rubbish in black bin liners, only gay people being allocated council housing, and funding pornography on the rates.

Despite the fake stories, people continued to support the GLC's anti-abolition campaign because we had the Smash Martians and the Sugar Puffs Honey Monster on our side. Well not them exactly, but we had John Webster who had created the iconic adverts. Whatever you thought about Livingstone you couldn't deny his communication skills. He understood the media and the power of advertising, and engaged Webster and the advertising agency BMP. They created a series of black and white posters as part of the anti-abolition campaign which covered the walls of tube stations and became familiar to all Londoners. One said, 'When the GLC goes Whitehall moves in', with a snail in a bowler hat crawling in from the right.

The campaign highlighted the proposed cancellation of GLC elections. Webster developed the slogan, 'Say no to no say'. It was a simple narrative: the government is taking away your right to vote. On four hundred sites across London there were huge posters on billboards stating, 'From now on you have no say in who runs London'. It was also true and cut through with the public. Nationally the Tories were ahead in the polls but not in London where Labour led by 10 percent. Bernard Ingham, Thatcher's press adviser, wrote to her concerned that the GLC was winning the battle for public opinion. He grudgingly admired the council's advertising campaign, saying, "The devil has all the best tunes."

The success of the GLC public relations campaign contrasted sharply with the miners' dispute. Scargill insisted on being the NUM's official spokesperson. Unlike Livingstone he didn't employ advertising professionals or delegate responsibility. His aggressive shouting might have been effective at mass meetings but on TV he increasingly alienated people.

Kinnock and the new Labour hierarchy were lukewarm about the GLC anti-abolition campaign and had little time for Livingstone. They blamed him for losing the party votes in the 1983 election, despite a smaller swing to the Tories in London than in the rest of the country. The right-wing trade union leader Eric Hammond denounced the "terrorists, lesbians and other queer people in the GLC Labour Party".[1] Kinnock seemed as keen as Thatcher to close the GLC and shut down Livingstone.

I was surprised to find the Liberals were actually more supportive of our anti-abolition campaign than the Labour Party. The Liberals were strong believers in local democracy and at their autumn conference they voted to oppose the GLC's abolition. The same couldn't be said of the traitorous SDP who supported abolishing the council. It was just typical of the bastards. They hated the Labour left and Livingstone in particular.

Stuart Hall argued that Thatcher understood the innovative character of Livingstone's municipal socialism and its positive impact on the public. It was why she was determined to abolish the GLC. Her campaign was spearheaded by Lady Porter, the wicked witch of Westminster Council. On the radio Porter claimed the abolition of the GLC and metropolitan councils was not political; the fact that all seven councils were Labour controlled was just coincidence. Maybe politicians have always lied but it seemed they no longer cared that you knew they were lying.

~

When I visited Swindon I expected the men in the club to be depressed about the Town finishing seventeenth in Division Four but they were optimistic things could only get better under the new manager, Lou Macari.

"What do you think about Macari then?" asked Dad, as he put his pint down on the table.

"Good appointment, I reckon," said Bob.

"He has got to be better than the last one," said Tony, which was accompanied by nods of agreement.

"You going to sign up to this here cable TV?" asked Bob. Swindon was to be the first place in the country to get cable TV. Another innovative first for the town.

"I need to persuade her indoors but they say there will be hundreds of TV channels on it," said Tony.

"What do you need hundreds of channels for? I don't watch

the four we've got now," said Dad. This was true. My parents rarely switched to Channel 4.

"The *Advertiser* says they're digging up thirty miles of road for the cables," said Bob.

"Causing a bloody mess. I know that," said Tony.

"It will be worth it mate," said Bob. "Especially when we get them foreign late night channels." He smiled before taking a sip of his beer.

The men all laughed. I was slightly confused. I thought it was odd they were going to watch subtitled European films. The penny only dropped when Bob nudged my dad. "You won't be needing to buy as many of those magazines then, eh Cliffy?"

The conversation turned to holidays. Bob was flying to Spain on a package holiday to Benidorm.

"Bet you can't wait to get away?" said Tony.

"The missus is still anxious about flying," said Bob. "but after four gins at Gatwick she'll be fine."

"We was thinking of going to America next year," said Tony.

"America?" Bob was surprised.

"Yeah, we was watching the news about that new airline Virgin Atlantic," said Tony. "Thought we might try somewhere different."

"I am not sure I'd like to go on one of them jumbos," said Bob. "They weigh over three hundred tons. Amazed how they get into the air."

A Boeing 747 in red Virgin livery had left Gatwick Airport and flown to New York a few weeks earlier. Richard Branson had been on TV in a pilot's uniform giving champagne to people who had paid £99 for their flights. He was even better than Livingstone at getting publicity. He promised to shake up the market with fares that were less than half what the major airlines charged.

"Bloody sad about Eric Morecambe dying," said Dad.

The men nodded in agreement.

"Don't make 'em like that anymore," said Bob.

"Proper comedian he was, not like this new lot," said Tony. He wasn't a fan of *The Young Ones*.

Unlike Eric Morecambe and Tommy Cooper, who had also died a few months earlier, the new alternative comedians were overtly political. The new *Spitting Image* show ridiculed politicians. Norman Tebbit was portrayed as a violent skinhead who closely resembled the Militant caricatures I had fly-pasted on the walls in Bath. Reagan was shown as a bumbling idiot in a series of sketches called 'The President's brain is missing'. David Steel became a tiny, squeaky voiced man in David Owen's breast pocket. Kinnock was portrayed as a Welsh windbag. On balance the show probably helped the Tories as it reinforced the narrative of Thatcher as strong and powerful and Labour as weak and indecisive.

"Did you see those new drinking guidelines?" said Bob.

The Health Education Council's latest guidance recommended that men should drink no more than nine pints of beer a week, a sharp reduction from their advice three years earlier that men could drink twenty-eight pints a week. The *Daily Mail* was outraged by the new guidance; it was yet another example of the nanny state. If people wanted to die of alcohol abuse that was their right.

"I saw it in the *Mirror*," said Dad. "They reckon we shouldn't drink more than nine pints a week."

"A week?" said Tony. "Nine pints is just a good night out." He smiled and downed the rest of his pint as if to prove the point.

"There's nothing wrong with three or four pints a night," said Dad. "Hasn't done us any harm has it?" He smiled and also drained what was left of his pint.

"They don't know what they're on about," said Tony. "Can't make their bloody minds up."

"It's not as if the beer is getting stronger," said Bob. He lifted his pint to examine it. "I reckon Maureen has been watering it down."

"Drink up, I'll get the next round in," said Dad.

In the summer Don and I joined a march to support the miners. It started at Tower Hill and marched along Fleet Street, in protest against the hostile reporting of the press. It finished at Jubilee Gardens. It was a beautiful sunny day. GLC staff came out of the building to clap the arrival of the miners, who were seen as working-class heroes, the shock troops in the war against Thatcherism.

The rally was an uneasy coalition of working-class miners and middle-class London liberals. Many were uncomfortable when the miners whistled at women and asked them to get their tits out for the lads. It reminded me of the sexist banter at football matches. There might have been a shared opposition to Thatcher but there was a huge cultural gap between the liberal left and the miners. Not all the women were offended. A number offered to house miners in their homes in what was frequently referred to as the 'shag a miner' scheme.

At the rally Arthur Scargill took to the same stage in Jubilee Gardens where Morrissey had danced with his rose at the Jobs for a Change Festival. He said confidently that the miners would not lose but would roll back the years of Thatcherism. The crowd sang his name, 'Arthur Scargill, Arthur Scargill, we'll support you ever more'.

I should have been enthused by the rally but despite the clapping and cheering I was a little empty inside. I turned and walked back to my office. I was not sure the miners would win. I wondered why no one on the left, other than the RCP, was asking the difficult questions and pushing for a national ballot. It was rumoured Kinnock was trying unsuccessfully to persuade Scargill to drop his insistence that no pit could close on economic grounds. I wasn't keen on Kinnock but it seemed sensible to me.

By the end of the summer it became clear that the NUM needed the Nottingham miners to stop working to win the dispute. The production of coal from the working pits, and the stockpiled coal at power stations, meant that, unlike in the 1970s, there would be no power cuts. In order to win, Scargill had to gain backing for a national strike but he continued to refuse to hold a ballot. Instead the Nottingham miners held their own ballot and voted three to one to carry on working. The issue of a ballot was the subject of heated discussions in the pub. Mark told me he was furious with the Revolutionary Communist Party for calling for a national ballot.

"The miners should have the Labour movement's unconditional support," he said.

"Absolutely. The RCP are siding with Thatcher and Kinnock," said a guy from the Socialist Workers Party who was sat with us.

I decided not to mention the RCP pamphlet Don had given me. It was called 'The Miners' Next Step' and argued a national ballot was required to give the strike legitimacy. It made sense to me but I nodded knowingly when Mark said Scargill should refuse to yield on a national ballot and "send more flying pickets to force the scab pits to close". The guy from the SWP agreed saying there should definitely not be a ballot, "as there might be a vote against the strike".

It didn't seem like a great argument, opposing a vote because you might lose.

～

By the autumn of 1984, Labour were still polling behind the Tories nationally. However, in London we were now 28 percent ahead. I was convinced this was due to the anti-abolition campaign and Livingstone's leadership. The right-wing press were infuriated that despite everything they had thrown at him, Livingstone's campaign was gaining ground and his personal popularity was rising. The GLC had become a genuine symbol of radical government. We were setting the benchmark for equalities policies on women, on race and on gay rights. Policies that were increasingly supported and adopted by other organisations.

Thatcher may have had a huge majority in the House of Commons but in the Lords there was increasing opposition to the abolition of the GLC. I was playing an important role in briefing sympathetic members of the Lords. Okay, I didn't actually write any briefings but I was the person that carried them over the bridge and delivered the documents.

It was my first experience of being inside the Houses of Parliament. I had to go to the Lords entrance where I passed through security to an area that resembled a school cloakroom from the 1960s with bags hanging from metal pegs. The staff from the Labour peers office would walk down the stone steps and through the old medieval hall to meet me. Occasionally if I had a heavy load of papers I would help carry them through a labyrinth of corridors to their offices. In some areas I was told I couldn't walk on the red carpet as that was only for Lords. We lived in a world where you couldn't even walk on a bit of carpet if you were a pleb.

Our anti-abolition campaign was slick and effective. People loved Livingstone and we were building a cross-party coalition. Thanks to our lobbying campaign the abolition of the GLC was opposed not only by the Labour Party but by Tory Lords and councillors, *The Times*, the *Financial Times*, the London Chamber of Commerce, and the Royal Town Planning Institute. I was confident that for the first time I was going to defeat Thatcher.

34

YUPPIES

Angela and I applied successfully to undertake a two-year part-time Diploma in Management Studies at the South Bank Polytechnic and were granted day release by the council. We spent each Thursday filling our Filofaxes with quotes from the latest management gurus. I wrote down their advice about the danger of acting with yesterday's logic and that the essence of strategy is choosing what not to do.

Our tutor recommended a book called, *What They Don't Teach You at Harvard Business School* by Mark McCormack. Obediently, I purchased a copy from a shop in Charing Cross. The book was simply written with short sections and full of practical advice which I carefully typed out on grey lined notepaper and clipped inside my Filofax. Each morning I would prepare for the day ahead by reading my notes. They were like a mantra that I repeated to myself. 'Talk less', 'mean what you say', 'know the facts', 'act not react', 'observe aggressively'.

Observe aggressively? What did it mean? I know I had written it down but I didn't always understand the things I wrote down. Writing is a good starting point; people who don't write things down achieve little in my view, but it is not the same as understanding. McCormack said people were always communicating. I started paying attention to people's clothing, the way they walked, the expressions on their faces, their gestures and their tone of voice.

I began to understand that what they said was not always what they meant and certainly not what they felt. This particularly applied to the older male managers. When they said things were "under consideration", it simply meant we have received your request but have no intention of doing anything about it. If they said, "We must not reinvent the wheel", they meant we don't like change and prefer to keep things as they are. If they said, "We will get back to you in due course", they meant you will never hear from us again.

The male managers in the GLC thought it was a source of weakness to say, "I don't know", "I need help" or "I was wrong". But according to McCormack the opposite was true. Using these hard-to-say phrases reflected a level of maturity and confidence that allowed you to adapt, change and improve.

McCormack advised managers to dress conservatively and look as if they meant business. I was way ahead of him in my grey suit, white shirt, tie and black shoes. I wore the uniform of the deferential, designed to blend in, not to call attention to itself.

One of the secretaries told me, "You can tell a lot about a man from his shoes." After that I spent weeks observing footwear. Most middle managers wore comfortable brown or grey shoes, like the ones worn by geography teachers but they didn't look professional. I made sure to always polish my shoes. I prided myself on looking professional. I reasoned that a white shirt was the most neutral. No one objected to a white shirt. I avoided colours, stripes or God forbid, those blue shirts with white collars that the Liberal leader David Steel wore.

McCormack said that making the right impression started with preparation. "Fail to prepare, prepare to fail." It all seemed common sense to me – read papers in advance of meetings, be punctual, mean what you say and do what you say you will. But many people did not read the papers in advance, turned up late for meetings and did not do what they promised. In one meeting a balding guy with his polyester shirt stretched over a rice pudding belly, tried to wheedle out of his failure to do what he had promised by questioning my minutes of the previous meeting. I made sure to record his negligence and meticulously noted every action he was supposed to take in future.

McCormack stressed that creating the right impression at work was also about attitude and impact. In my eagerness to be seen as positive and energetic I volunteered for everything, including tasks that were well outside my remit. When our first Wang word processors arrived, I offered to help manage the network of machines with their large floppy disks, similar in size to a record album. Soon every office had a bank of black and green screens, and desks were repositioned to be near power sockets.

The older managers made it clear they were not going to use the new machines; they were not going to be typists. Unlike the old people I was enthusiastic about the new technology but the Staff Association wouldn't let any staff, including me, use the word processors unless the council agreed to an additional technology allowance. I had to wait until everyone had gone home in the evenings to learn how to use the new machines.

After a few weeks the council agreed to pay a technology allowance and we were given consent to use the machines. It was a bit bizarre to get paid more for using machines that made your job easier but I didn't make the rules. I gratefully accepted my additional allowance for helping to manage the network in our office. My skills came in particularly handy when Charlie typed 'bollocks' into the computer screen and panicked when he couldn't work out how to remove the word.

When the Labour administration abolished the practice of only recruiting internally they also set aside the rule that prevented staff from applying for jobs more than a grade above them. I decided to take advantage of the change. Despite only having been on the graduate scheme for a little over six months I applied for a new Admin C job that had been created to support my team. I was different from my dad. He was a shop floor worker and to my knowledge he had never applied for a promotion. He was paid the same as his mates and they fought for higher wages collectively. I fought for my promotions as an individual, often in competition with my colleagues.

I didn't expect to get the job but I wanted to show that I was ambitious. To my surprise the panel recommended appointing me. This caused pandemonium in the personnel department who intervened to prevent this perceived atrocity. One of the outraged senior managers wrote to our director, Robin Murray, saying I should never have been allowed to apply for the Admin C role. Despite having never met me, he insisted that if I was able to do the job it must be incorrectly graded.

At Angela's flat in Islington a group of us dipped crusty bread and vegetables into a red Habitat fondue pot suspended over a tea light. As we swirled our bread in the cheese sauce, and listened to Miles Davies on the record player, we denounced the yuppies in the city of London.

"They're paid ridiculous sums they don't deserve," said Fiona.

"The *Guardian* says they're pouring into the Docklands and

driving up property prices," said Simon. "One of them paid £200,000 for a flat in Wapping. It's just mad."

"According to the *New York Times*, they're part of the post-war boomer generation who are shaping politics and driving consumer trends," said Angela, holding her long fork in the air as if about to conduct an orchestra.

"You mean they all vote for Reagan and Thatcher," said Simon.

We drank Nicaraguan coffee, which Angela had bought in support of the revolutionary Sandinistas, while she shared her latest learning from our course. She took down a book from her bookshelf, called *In Search of Excellence* and laid it on the table.

"Fiona, you should read this. It highlights eight attributes of successful organisations," said Angela. "There's a lot we could apply in the public sector, such as treating our service users as customers and reducing the layers of hierarchy."

"God, there is so much bureaucracy and inefficiency in the Civil Service," said Fiona shaking her head and rolling her eyes at the same time. "I am beginning to think it does need Thatcher to shake things up."

I gave her my best death stare.

As we made our way through a box of After Eight mints the discussion turned to our relative success in the world. I say relative as we were not high earners but we were aspiring managers, civil servants, accountants and lawyers. The people our mothers and fathers respected. Simon said our generation valued education and expertise. We had studied hard, achieved our places at university and made sacrifices, such as moving away from our families to London. We deserved our success. We hadn't been born with a silver spoon in our mouths; we were not like the yuppies - we were making our way in the world based on our own efforts. It wasn't quite Norman Tebbit's 'on yer bike' speech but it wasn't far off.

"My financial adviser advised us to get an endowment

mortgage," said Fiona, who had been the first of the group to buy a flat.

"The prices are rising so fast," said Angela. "Two-bed flats on Upper Street are going for over £30,000."

"You need to get on the housing ladder now," said Fiona. "Or you may never be able to afford a place."

The Halifax Building Society had helpfully launched a house price index earlier in the year which tracked property price increases. Nationally prices had risen by over 15 percent since the start of 1983, but in London prices had increased over 30 percent in less than two years.

We viewed ourselves as a generation of risk takers, prepared to buy in areas that others had ignored, albeit after much evaluation and tracking of prices. According to Fiona we should be looking at Clapham and Wandsworth. When I mentioned Brixton, where I lived, it was clear Fiona thought that was a step too far.

"You are very adventurous Steve," she said, in a voice that sounded like Thatcher slowly explaining Right to Buy to stupid people on the TV.

Fiona was one of those people who always dressed up her patronising superiority as praise. It annoyed the hell out of me and I spent many evenings lying awake working out how best to respond. The strategy I adopted was to accept it with humour.

"You should see me in the bedroom," I replied.

As I searched for remaining mints – what sort of person puts empty wrappers back in the box – I was surprised to hear Fiona discuss Kinnock.

"He is doing a good job," she said. "He will kick out Militant and make the party electable again."

"You mean he is moving the party to the right," I said.

"We can't stay stuck in the seventies," said Fiona. "The party will never get elected promising higher taxes and nationalisation. Also privatisation is not such a bad idea for organisations like British Airways."

It seemed to me that Fiona thought Labour would be fine once it dropped its socialist policies.

"You are just a Tory", I wanted to say, but what I actually said was, "If you support privatisation, why not just vote Tory?"

Fiona stared at me.

"Because we need an alternative to Thatcher's Victorian social values," she replied.

"Ugh, too right," said Angela. "We have to get away from all this marriage, church and nuclear family stuff. I am proud of the GLC supporting gay rights and alternative lifestyles."

"When I go back home to Stoke it is a different world," said Fiona. "My old school friends are so reactionary. So many people there are homophobic, misogynistic and racist."

"At least they vote Labour," I said. The previous week Jack Ashley, a Stoke MP, had introduced a private members' bill to outlaw discrimination on grounds of disability. Of course the Tories voted it down.

Angela swapped Miles Davies for Bruce Springsteen on the record player. As we sat listening to *Hometown* I reflected that we were like a working-class diaspora settled far from our original homes. Our graduation certificates were like passports that had given us permission to travel. We all had a fondness for our home towns but we also had a sense of displacement. Each of us in our own ways had a feeling of being at odds with where we came from.

35

BT PRIVATISATION

"**M**ake someone happy every day," said Buzby, a cartoon bird used to promote British Telecom on TV. The voice was unmistakably that of Bernard Cribbins, who also narrated *The Wombles*.

After years of planning the government launched a mass marketing campaign to promote the privatisation of BT. Millions of people, including Bob in the club, were swayed by the advertising and registered their interest in buying the shares. BT was being sold at a knockdown price and every Del Boy was applying to purchase stock. Millions of greedy bastards didn't want to miss out on a guaranteed quick profit. I bought an anti-privatisation badge from a Socialist Workers Party stall outside Elephant and Castle. It was bright blue with a picture of Buzby saying, 'Privatisation, No Thanks'.

The Labour Party reaffirmed its opposition to the privatisation of British Telecom at their conference in Blackpool in October. It was purely symbolic. It would be no more effective at stopping privatisation than my badge but it was principled. I unconsciously placed my hand on my heart on hearing the news.

From what I could see on TV it was a fractious conference. There was one hell of a palaver when Derek Hatton, a Liverpool Militant councillor, moved a motion to support councils that broke the law and didn't comply with government imposed rate-capping. Despite vigorous opposition from the party leadership, the motion was passed on a show of hands. It was a humiliating defeat for Kinnock, and one he wouldn't forget.

There was more pandemonium on the conference floor when Arthur Scargill was served with a writ threatening to seize the union's assets. The High Court had unsurprisingly declared the miners' strike illegal because of the lack of a national ballot. Tony Benn responded by saying the party was fully behind the miners despite the strike being unlawful. The next morning the *Daily Mirror* said the conference decisions were pure lunacy and, "The party might as well have jumped off Blackpool Pier."[1]

A few days later the Conservative lead in the polls increased from 4 percent to 9 percent. This wasn't how party conferences were supposed to work. The Tories were now polling at 44 percent despite the highest unemployment since the thirties. Thatcher's support was even higher than it had been in the previous year's election and it was growing. She was going to be unbearable at the upcoming Tory Party Conference in Brighton.

On 12 October 1984, I woke to the news that someone had tried to assassinate Thatcher. I switched on the TV. There was a gaping hole in the front of Brighton's Grand Hotel. Norman Tebbit was being carried out of the rubble, clearly in pain. An MP, Sir Anthony Berry, and four other people were killed. Thatcher escaped unharmed. The newsreader said she had

been lucky, and only escaped because she was still up working on her speech when the bomb exploded.

People in the office that morning condemned the bombing but there was little sympathy for Thatcher herself. Morrissey summed up the thoughts of many when he said, "The sorrow of the Brighton bombing is that Thatcher escaped unscathed."[2] Later in the day the IRA put out a statement claiming responsibility. My eighteen-year-old self would probably have been happy to see Thatcher assassinated but I no longer believed you won by killing your opponents. I wasn't a pacifist but you had to win the political argument.

My views were not shared in the office or by Mark, who told me how happy he was at seeing the battered body of Norman Tebbit being dragged from the building. I grimaced inside. I lowered my head and tried to avoid eye contact. I knew my face would betray my disappointment with him. I made my excuses and left the pub early. I was increasingly disillusioned and disenchanted with those who called themselves socialists.

At least Militant and the Socialist Workers Party both recognised the bombings were counterproductive and condemned the IRA's actions. The RCP as always took a different line. They refused to condemn the bombing. In the November edition of the *Next Step* they said, "We support unconditionally the right of the Irish people to carry out their struggle of national liberation in whatever way they choose." The reality was the bomb repelled most of the population and reinforced Thatcher's image as a tough and capable leader. After the bombing her personal ratings were almost as high as they had been during the Falklands War.

Despite the assassination attempt Thatcher didn't slow down or take time off. She met Gorbachev at Chequers, flew to Beijing to sign the Hong Kong handover agreement and then flew directly to Washington for a Camp David meeting. Her busy schedule goes some way to explaining her one hundred and eighteen hair appointments that year. At Camp David she congratulated Reagan on being elected for a second term with an even bigger majority. This time only two states voted against Reagan. The great moving right show was steamrollering ahead in both the UK and the US.

At the end of November British Telecom was privatised. It was the biggest share issue ever. Two million members of the public, about 5 percent of the adult population, bought shares. Overnight it almost doubled the number of share owners in Britain. The staff themselves bought just under 4 percent of the shares. Almost all BT employees, including Bob in the club, bought shares. They were priced at £1.30 and were three times oversubscribed.

On 3 December 1984, the shares were floated on the stock market and traded at £1.73 at the end of the day. A 30 percent profit at no risk for investors. Share dealers immediately sought to buy up stock from individual investors and over half a million people had sold their shares within six months. The BT employees that bought shares were happy with their cash gains but it came at a cost. The new managers slimmed down the privatised company to increase profits and within twenty years over one hundred thousand jobs, around half the workforce, would be gone.

I removed the 'Privatisation, No Thanks' badge from my jacket and added it to the growing pile of lost causes in my desk drawer. My old badges were becoming like cultural artefacts through which you could trace my defeats and disappointments. It felt like a significant stage in the great moving right show, the culmination of a series of victories for Thatcher. Journalists called it a landmark moment for neoliberalism. The sale of BT became the model for the next twenty years of government privatisations.

In the club at Christmas Bob sought my advice on what shares he should buy next. When I said I didn't invest in shares he looked surprised. "You're missing out," said Bob. "The missus and I have made a killing on our British Telecom shares."

"You are not very bright for someone who has been to university," said Tony, looking at me across the top of his pint of three Bs. "Even I bought the shares, despite knowing they employed Bob."

At home Boy George and Bob Geldof were on the TV singing *Do they know it's Christmas?* It was the best-selling record of the year. I agreed with Morrissey, it was good to have concern for the people of Ethiopia but it was another thing entirely to inflict daily torture on the people of England. I remained conflicted about charitable giving as it was not a solution to global inequality and poverty. We needed a collectivist, government response. It was probably better than doing nothing but I was uneasy that Band Aid was in many ways a Thatcherite response. My views were again at odds with the public sentiment.

The start of 1985 was marked by the first mobile phone call made in the UK. Ernie Wise led the PR campaign. Mobile phones seemed to me like skiing holidays. They were exotic and exciting but they were not for the likes of us. There was no real point thinking about them as it seemed unlikely I would ever own one.

As January drew to a close the winter was over and the ongoing miners' strike had not forced the government's hand. Many miners were drifting back to work and it was difficult to blame them. As the evenings became lighter it was clear that, unlike in 1972 and 1974, there would be no power cuts, no three-day weeks. Thatcher had successfully seen out the peak demands for heating and electricity. Power stations continued to operate normally and the numbers on picket lines dwindled.

By February, the miners' strike had ground on for almost a year. Miners' families were struggling to survive despite the food parcels and regular collections. On 3 March 1984, the miners agreed to return to work. It was Terry Thomas, the NUM vice-president in South Wales, that proposed to end the strike.

He later said, "The men returned to work not because they had stopped believing in what they were fighting for ... Houses were being repossessed, marriages were breaking up, the kids were going without, and there was no end in sight. We had no right to demand that they continue with the strike."[3]

When the miners returned to work the atmosphere was funereal. In Grimethorpe the men walked to work behind a brass band like the mourners that follow a coffin. There was pride and sadness. Those that looked on clapped with tears in their eyes. A year of extreme hardship had achieved nothing. Forty-seven injunctions had been granted against the NUM and 10,372 criminal charges had been brought against the miners and their supporters. Following the strike forty pits were closed within two years. Thirty-five more were closed by 1990. A total of seventy-five pits as Scargill had predicted.

I agreed with Terry Thomas when he said it was a defeat for the whole working-class. Scargill disagreed; he called the strike a tremendous achievement. He argued the actions demonstrated to the working class that if they make a stand they can win improvements. It was nonsense. The *Daily Mirror* also pretended that somehow Thatcher hadn't won. It said there were no winners and that people now realised that Thatcherism was 'unacceptable'. On the same day the latest poll had the Conservatives polling at 42 percent, six points ahead of Labour. I added my 'Coal not Dole' badge to the desk drawer.

Labour's pollster Philip Gould found that the things people associated with the Tories, such as champagne, swimming pools, large houses, and fast cars were actually the things they wanted for themselves. He found that the working class aspired to be middle class. They were buying their council houses, filling them with new consumer goods and investing in privatised shares. Gould concluded that working people admired Thatcher, "even if they loathed her."[4] It was partly why they also opposed tax increases on the rich. They had aspirations, they might not become rich but they hoped their children and grandchildren would.

The one piece of good news from Gould's survey was the majority of people were still in favour of public ownership. The bad news was they thought it meant privatisation.

36

SPRING 1985

There is a golden rule when it comes to badges. They should contain a succinct slogan that is easy to read and repeat. In March 1985, the badges being given out on the steps of Lambeth Town Hall read, 'Lambeth Council says No to government's rate-capping cuts. Local people know best.' There was far too much text. Old people would need to stand on your toes with their reading glasses to work out what you were protesting about. The badge was clearly not designed by Saatchi and Saatchi.

I was tempted to give those handing out the badges my advice on badge design but felt it would probably not be appreciated. Instead I pinned one to my jacket and applauded the council leader, Ted Knight, who made a speech against rate-capping and held his hands aloft in victory after the council refused to set a rate. I bought a copy of Mark's *Labour Herald* in which Knight predicted the campaign by local councils would, "blow the government out of office".

I didn't wear the badge at my interview for the post of Policy Assistant to Pamela, the Assistant-Director General responsible for Fire and Civil Defence. She was tall and incredibly striking, with ginger hair piled up into a beehive on the top of her head. The job description said the role would require attendance at the Director-General's board.

"So," said Angela, when I told her I was applying for the post, "what is it that attracts you to being at the centre of power?"

It was a good question. I wasn't sure where my ambition came from but an article about entrepreneurs, recommended by our course tutor, resonated with me. The *Harvard Business Review* said they had high levels of energy, challenged prevailing orthodoxies and embraced new ways of working. I wanted to be like the entrepreneurs. I wanted to make things happen and drive through changes that the old people resisted.

My diligence and determination, plus the lack of badges on my suit, clearly impressed the interview panel and I was appointed to the job.

~

In April 1985, I moved up three floors to start my new job with Pamela. I was based with the Fire and Civil Defence committee team which was headed by Sarah, an older woman with silvery-grey hair and round glasses.

The team included two camp men, called Anders and Tim. They were not much older than me, and referred to themselves as the queens of civil defence. On my first morning Tim described how in New York he had met Madonna, who the week before I had watched on *Top of the Pops* in a long pink wig singing *Like a Virgin*. Jeff, a rather pudgy young man in an ill-fitting suit, was impressed by Tim's story.

"So what's she like?" asked Jeff.

"She's a complete tart, she'll sleep with anyone," said Tim. "She'd even sleep with you Jeff. Seriously, she definitely would."

Jeff's neck reddened a little as he thought about the prospect.

"I just love her though," Tim added. "She's so raunchy." He did a little twirl and smiled over his shoulder at me in my M&S suit and tie.

In Pamela's office, she closed the door, put a large pile of papers on her desk and asked me to pull up a chair to go through them with her. As she leafed through the day's post she passed me various items to handle and used words which were unfamiliar to me.

"This is not our locus," she said, handing me a piece of paper without looking up. "Can you send it on to Peter Brayshaw." She constantly passed pieces of paper to me with associated tasks.

"Can you liaise with the section head on this one and draft a response for me?"

"We need to do a short report on this, do you think you can prepare one?"

I nodded each time, wrote a note in my Filofax and took the papers. As we continued to work through the papers she placed her hand on my thigh. Her fingers pressed against the inside of my leg; I felt their warmth spreading. After a short while she patted my leg reassuringly. "Good, now let's get to work. If you need anything just ask Jane."

When I attended the Director-General's board with Pamela for the first time, I sat upright and directly behind her with a lever arch file of relevant papers and information. The meeting was chaired by Maurice Stonefrost, the Director-General. Much to my disappointment the meeting was full of routine administration like any other meeting. It was not the masterclass in strategic planning I had anticipated.

Working for Pamela was how I imagined it might be working for Thatcher. She was driven and hard-working. I stayed long into the evenings making sure she always had the responses and reports she needed. There was also a side to her that was quite motherly. Maybe it was the same with Thatcher. She took care to make sure I was alright. Each morning after going through the papers, she would ask if I needed anything, squeeze my thigh and say, "Good, let's get to work."

I would return to my desk with a pile of papers and work out who I needed to call. I was helped by Sarah, who would come and sit next to me. She would tell me who to contact to answer enquiries and brief me on people, like Duncan Campbell, who was working on a civil defence paper. She was an invaluable support during those first few months.

One evening Sarah and I went to a new wine bar under Waterloo arches. It had large green plants in the windows by the door. She talked to me about the guys in the office and asked how I was enjoying the job. We walked back along the South Bank. It was still light and the April air was warm. We passed people sitting on the slatted wooden benches that look out across the river.

As we walked she moved closer and held my hand with both of hers, almost falling into me as she did so. Smiling up at me she said, "This is one of my favourite things." I was about to say walking on the South Bank was also one of my favourite things, when she added, "Walking in public with no panties on".

I wasn't quite sure how to respond. My eyes were drawn ineluctably downwards. She was wearing a rather dull, conventional dark blue skirt whose hem came below the knees. She snuggled into my arm and said, "It feels nice, like skinny dipping."

I had missed the Admin A training where they taught you how to respond when your older colleague informs you they have no panties on. A breeze gently lifted strands of Sarah's hair, causing it to float from her shoulders.

An hour later we were in her flat in Upper Norwood, which

was somewhere in South London near Crystal Palace. I wasn't entirely sure how I would get back home. To me places that were not on the tube map were a bit like those places on the edges of old maps marked 'here be dragons'. Her flat was the ground floor of a two-storey house with a large bay window.

In the lounge she had a cabinet with brightly coloured, almost gaudy crockery. Sarah saw me looking. "Clarice Cliff," she said. "I collect it." She told me how she explored jumble sales looking for pieces as it was undervalued. I wasn't sure why she was talking to me about crockery. I reasoned it was her age. Sarah must have been in her mid-forties, a similar age to my mum, which I then tried to put from my mind.

Afterwards as I lay in bed holding her, my mind was trying to work out how I would get home and wondering when I could leave without seeming rude. I hadn't read any Cosmo guidance on the minimum period required for holding and hugging after sex. Advice which many men, not just Nora Ephron's Harry and myself, would find useful.

I sneaked a glance at my watch; it was past midnight and I figured it was okay to go. As I tried to get up Sarah held on to me, she was keen for me to spend the night. I made an excuse about needing to get home. Reluctantly she gave me instructions on how to find the night bus. Upper Norwood at night was like darkest Peru. I was relieved and slightly surprised to find the bus stop. I was even more relieved when a number two night bus approached after twenty minutes.

On Easter Sunday Andy, Dad and I went over to the club at lunchtime. We joined Tony and Bob at a table under the stairs by the skittle alley. Tony was animated about the change in the CIU rules that allowed women to join the club as associate members for an annual fee of fifty pence. It was a discount on the two pounds paid by the men but it wasn't a particularly generous deal. Women were not allowed to vote in committee elections, did not get the six free drinks that men were allocated on public holidays and were still only allowed into the bar if they were accompanied by a man.

It would be a further twenty years until the National Executive of the Clubs and Institute Union would vote to give women equal access and the right to attend without an escort.

"It won't be the same with women in the bar," said Tony, who had led the resistance to female associate members.

"You'll have to mind your Ps and Qs now," said Dad. He smiled across the top of his pint at Tony.

"It ain't right," said Tony. "This has always been a men's bar, since the day it was built. I don't know why they have to go and change things."

The men's worries were extensively discussed by the committee which agreed to address their concerns. To placate the men they passed a new rule that people were not allowed to hold hands in the bar. As Tony explained this was a working men's club; they didn't want any of that nonsense.

"Next thing, we will have a bloody women's committee like the GLC," said Tony, looking at me.

I thought it was reasonable that women should be able to join the club but I didn't say anything. At university, or at work, I would have argued the case for women's rights but I remained quiet in the club. I am not sure why, maybe I was conscious of my dad's presence. Maybe I knew I was never going to change Tony's mind. Instead I offered to get the next round in.

"Cheers, Steve," said Tony, as I carried back the last of the round to the table.

"I see that new Volkswagen car is selling well," said Bob.

The Volkswagen Golf had been launched in the UK the previous year and *What Car?* magazine had called it the car of the year 1985.

"It ain't as good as the Austin Montego," said Tony. "It looks bloody fantastic in Moonraker Blue."

The new British Leyland car had been launched at the same time as the Golf. The Metro was still the best-selling small car in the UK; the patriotic white cliffs and landing craft adverts had worked wonders, but the company needed a medium-sized car. Unfortunately the early Montegos had quality issues and were losing sales to the Golf and the Vauxhall Cavalier.

"Sales of them foreign cars have been growing ever since we joined the Common Market," said Dad.

"I don't understand it," said Tony. "Letting the Germans and the French import cars tariff-free. Why can't we protect our own car industry?"

"We need another of them Buy British campaigns," said Bob.

From the corner of the room there was a cascade of coins which Dave scooped from the slot below the one-armed bandit.

"Did I tell you what happened last week?" said Tony.

He looked around the table at us before he continued.

"This old lady came up to me at the garage and asked me to help her, as she couldn't get her car started."

He paused, straightening the beer mat under his pint with his fingers

"I said to her 'Is that your Citroen?' She had one of them big ugly CX cars that looks like a frog. She told me it was, so I told her straight I did. Said I would love to help you but that's a French car so you had better go and find a Frenchman."

Bob couldn't stifle his laughter. It was infectious, my dad started laughing and I found myself laughing as well.

"You're a mean bugger," said my dad.

"No, those bastards buy foreign cars and put us out of work. Fuck 'em," said Tony, and picked up his pint.

37

JOBS FOR A CHANGE

The second 'Jobs for a Change' festival was held in Battersea Park on the 7 July 1985. It was huge; encouraged by the sunshine over half a million people attended. The face painting stalls were doing brisk business as I made my way to our tent, where we were running a workshop on the London Industrial Strategy. I don't think The Communards or Billy Bragg were that worried by the competition.

After our workshop we wandered from stage to stage listening to various bands. The event was consciously multi-cultural with Ravi Shankar, Aswad and Thomas Mapfumo. As the sun sank over West London we sat on the grass and listened to Billy Bragg on the main stage. Over by the second stage a large crowd were going mad watching a raucous band called The Pogues.

As I watched the Battersea sunset I could hear Olive Morris in my ears. She was probably right that festivals were not the best way to raise political awareness but people did associate the event with Livingstone and the GLC. Maybe that was enough. Too often left-wing politics was driven by a puritanical seriousness.

We had to wear a sackcloth and ashes as well as our badges. We could only watch serious films approved by the socialist film police such as *My Beautiful Laundrette*. Billy Bragg said the Battersea festival showed people that socialism could also be enjoyable. Maybe simply associating socialism with having fun was justification enough; it didn't matter if no one went home enthused by the London Industrial Strategy.

The following Saturday I spent the day with Mark. I had passed the first year of my Management Studies course at the Polytechnic and it was good to have a weekend free of studying and writing essays. We wandered Brixton in the morning. Mark introduced me to a tall guy from Fly Press who told me their aim was to promote opposition to Thatcher through posters.

We spent the rest of the day watching the Live Aid concert on TV. We made toast for lunch while Status Quo opened the event at Wembley. Cooking a meal, even a simple one, was too much effort. Besides what was wrong with toast? We never made a donation despite being berated by Bob Geldof; our excuse was we never had a phone though I was also still conflicted by charitable giving.

The GLC had become genuinely popular among Londoners during the anti-abolition campaign which was remarkable in the circumstances. Opposition to abolition was running at 74 percent according to one poll. Livingstone seized on the findings. On every tube platform there were black posters with huge white letters declaring, '74% say No'. Maybe the Fly Press guy was right about the power of posters. We had won the battle of public opinion.

I was convinced our cross-party coalition in the House of Lords was going to defeat Thatcher and put aside my concerns about an unelected second chamber. However, on the night of the critical vote, the Tories wheeled out, quite literally in some cases, the old hereditary peers who held a seat because their ancestor was a baron in the fifteenth century. One hundred and seventy-eight of the unelected, hereditary Lords voted to abolish the GLC. We lost by twenty votes.

The GLC was going to come to an end at midnight on 31 March 1986. Maurice Stonefrost resigned and Pamela became the acting Director-General, which meant I became the policy assistant to the most powerful officer in the council but not for long. Not content with taking away my milk monitor role, Thatcher was going to abolish my dream job.

In her office Pamela squeezed my thigh and suggested I start applying for posts in the successor bodies. I nodded in acknowledgement but couldn't raise my eyes from the floor. My body felt heavy and I couldn't face going back to my desk. There was a pain in my heart, something was tearing each auricle and ventricle apart.

~

September was not a good month for Swindon; the town lost three games in a row to Peterborough, Crewe and Hartlepool. But there was worse news to come. British Rail announced that after 150 years the Swindon Railway Works would close in March 1986. The Guardian said the job losses had become a weekly ritual for a depressed Britain. The National Union of Railwaymen branch secretary said the management should be castrated. Over two thousand workers, including my dad, were given notice of redundancy. Dad and I would both lose our jobs at the same time.

Dad was slumped in his chair when I arrived home at the end of the month. He said nothing about the closure and when I raised it he was prickly, quickly changing the subject. There was an unfamiliar tension in the air. I think Mum and I were both relieved when Tony picked him up to play darts. Neither Mum nor Dad asked about my job. If they knew the GLC was being abolished they didn't mention it. I decided not to say anything. Once I had something sorted out I would let them know. Maybe it was some form of pride, but it wasn't the done thing to talk about your difficulties, the worries that kept you awake at night. The outward image my family projected to the world masked our real emotions and deepest fears.

I spent the evening chatting with Mum, or rather nodding as she talked non-stop about the plans for my brother's upcoming wedding in January. We were watching the TV when the BBC newsreader Jan Leeming popped up with a special news report.

"Fires are still burning in Brixton in South London after an evening of rioting," she said.

My eyes widened as the report talked of petrol bombs, burning cars and widespread looting. There was footage of a four-storey building on Coldharbour Lane engulfed in flames. As the camera crew was filming the building collapsed to the audible sound of people cheering. Mum became distracted from the wedding plans and looked at me. She had always been a bit reluctant to believe my reassurances that Brixton was a nice place to live.

The next day's papers said the riots were a reaction to the police shooting a black woman called Cherry Groce earlier in the day. They were looking for her son when they inexplicably shot the unarmed woman in front of her three children. She was hit in the shoulder, leaving her paralysed from the chest down. One person died in the riot, fifty more were injured and over two hundred were arrested. The Sunday newspapers were full of pictures of burning cars. I struggled to reconcile the images in the papers with the Brixton I knew.

I was lucky, I didn't suffer the constant harassment and racism; the police didn't raid my flat and point guns at us. I suspected Brixton might be quietly removed from the Evening Standard's list of the ten most up-and-coming property hot spots.

I joined Dad and Andy in the club at lunchtime, and was surprised to find the men in good humour despite the news about the railway works closure. Over pints of three Bs the men shared stories of their time in the railways. Dad said in the old days the foremen wore bowler hats and had the power to fire a worker on the spot if they crossed them. He also talked of the tricks played on new apprentices. "Young Pete fell for everything," said Dad. "He actually went looking for a left-handed screwdriver."

The men laughed and spluttered over their beers.

"In our place," said Bob, "we always told them to go the stores and ask for a long stand. One young un came back and said the storeman asked 'How long did we want the stand to be?' We said thirty minutes should do and he was halfway back to the stores before he cottoned on."

Maybe humour was the mask they used to hide their fears and insecurities. They didn't talk about how the guys who did the riveting inside the boilers went deaf from the noise. Or how the boilers were lined with asbestos and how many of the men died from mesothelioma. Memory is a selective thing. Maybe life is easier if you focus on the positives; as Dad often said there is no point crying over spilt milk.

"I worry about what's going to happen to the young uns," said Bob. "There ain't any apprenticeships around here. Not like there used to be."

"It's because we don't make stuff anymore. We buy everything from Germany and China," said Dad.

"Don't forget the Japs," said Tony. "We will be making their cars soon. Did you see they are opening that big new plant in Sunderland? On the telly they said over twenty-five thousand people have applied to work there."

"At least it's jobs I suppose," said Bob.

The men were pensive and looked at each other for a while. Tony broke the silence. "It's a bloody shame what's happening to our country."

The Swindon engineering works had once employed over 14,000 people. No more. The last 2,000 workers would leave the works for the last time in six months. The *Guardian* reported that 950 of the men were aged over forty-five, and added, "They may have no prospect of working again." My dad was forty-six.

38

BAYONETTING THE WOUNDED

"I am telling you," said Don. "They are going to turn this bloody place into a luxury hotel."

I smiled at him.

"Don't you fucking smile at me like that," he snapped. His eyes sparkled behind his lenses, laughing at me. "You will be one of the first to stay in the executive suites."

He paused and looked at me seriously; his eyes stopped smiling.

"And you shouldn't be fucking co-operating in the abolition process."

Don was furious with me for working with Pamela on the handover of services to the GLC's successor bodies.

"We need to provide information so there is a smooth transition," I said. "It's not going to hurt the Tories if it is a mess. It is service users that will suffer. It might even mean more jobs are lost."

"Don't give me that bollocks," said Don. "By co-operating you are helping them to make workers redundant. You are as bad as Livingstone, he backed down as soon as the going got tough."

He was referring to the campaign against rate-capping and how Labour councils said they would refuse to set a rate in protest at Thatcher's new laws.

The GLC was the first council to back down after Thatcher threatened to use the full force of the law against rebel councillors. One by one, like a collapsing row of dominoes, the Labour councils caved in. Only Lambeth refused to set a rate. In the pub Mark expressed support for the local councillors. Evidently all the other three hundred councils, those not led by the WRP, were just cowards and traitors. I was reminded of that saying, if you can keep your head when everyone else is losing theirs, then maybe you have misunderstood the situation.

"We've raised £3,000 for the fighting fund," said Mark, rattling a red collection tin at me. I took the hint and folded a one pound note, which I pushed with difficulty into the small slot at the top of the tin.

The initial fine levied on the Lambeth councillors was £120,000. It was obvious that no matter how many jumble sales the local party organised, or how many supporters toured the pubs with their collection tins, it would be impossible to cover the mounting costs. I was not sure if the rebels were brave and principled, or simply deluding themselves.

What were they expecting to happen? The revolutionary overthrow of Thatcher seemed a tad unlikely despite the huge sales of protest T-shirts. The latter having become particularly popular after Wham! sang *Wake Me Up Before You Go-Go* on *Top of the Pops* wearing 'Choose Life' T-shirts. I hadn't been in Russia in 1917, but it didn't feel like the start of a revolution.

When a mass uprising failed to materialise, the councillors, including Ted Knight, finally gave way in the face of personal bankruptcy. They acquiesced to Thatcher, cut the council's services and passed a legal budget. They were surcharged and banned from holding public office for five years. Outside the court Knight said it was an historic day, and claimed the councillors had shown the Tory government could not trample on local democracy. Mark's *Labour Herald* said the councillors were 'the heroes and heroines of their time'. The left it seemed were becoming experts on claiming defeats as historic victories.

An even bigger historic victory awaited Militant in Liverpool. To force Thatcher to give the council more money they adopted the bizarre tactic of making the entire council workforce, all thirty thousand people, redundant. It was a modern-day Charge of the Light Brigade and just as futile. The debacle gave Kinnock the opportunity he had been waiting for.

On 1 October 1985, he took to the stage in Bournemouth and savaged Militant. Mark and I watched *Newsnight* as Kinnock talked about the grotesque chaos of a Labour council hiring taxis to scuttle around handing out redundancy notices to its own workers.

"He is just trying to emulate Thatcher," said Mark. "He wants his macho moment."

I looked up and offered him a digestive. He took the biscuit and held it in his hand.

"You know, like Thatcher defeating Galtieri and Scargill," he said. "Except in this case Militant have already been defeated by the Tories. He is just walking onto the battlefield to bayonet the wounded."

On the TV Kinnock was busy bayoneting: "I'll tell you and you'll listen", stab. "You can't play politics with people's jobs", stab. "Implausible promises don't win victories", stab.

I dunked a biscuit in my tea and watched as Eric Heffer walked off the conference stage in disgust and Hatton shouted, "Liar!" Just days later Hatton was expelled and the Liverpool district Labour Party was suspended. Militant fared no better in the High Court. The prospect of judges finding in favour of revolutionary Trotskyists always seemed to be somewhat remote. The councillors were found guilty of 'political perversity', fined and banned from office.

The fallout from the rate-capping campaign was bitter and rancorous. At Labour's HQ in Walworth Road, disgruntled rebels tried to feed rat poison to their comrades. It wasn't that bad in Lambeth but anyone who hadn't supported the rebel councillors was branded a traitor. Those that questioned the wisdom of being the only council in the country to adopt a no-rate strategy were silenced with threats of comradely violence. I decided to give meetings a miss for a while.

In County Hall, staff were resigned to abolition and began a guerrilla operation which involved moving office equipment out to community groups, or their own homes, rather than leaving it to the Residuary Body. Computers were wheeled out on trolleys along with fax machines and photocopiers. Stationery cupboards were raided and bags were stuffed with staplers, pens and Tippex. Staff swapped their slim bags and briefcases for large sports holdalls which they struggled to carry home at the end of the day. Some decided that, as their posts were being abolished in less than six months, there was little point working at all. Fewer and fewer staff turned up for work and those that did often arrived late and took long lunches in the bar.

Despite Don's admonitions I carried on working long hours for Pamela to get as much completed as we could before abolition. One of my tasks was to secure planning permission to erect a statue dedicated to members of the International Brigade in Jubilee Gardens before the council was abolished. I managed to get the planning permission expedited with some help from Lambeth Labour Party councillors. It is definitely not what you know when it comes to getting decisions from local councils.

I was never sure about public art as a kid. The first statue I recall seeing was the one of Isambard Kingdom Brunel in the Swindon shopping centre. Statues all seemed to be of long dead men. My favourite statue was called 'The Watchers' in Toothill, West Swindon. The artist, Carleton Attwood, had been inspired by a family he observed watching football at the County Ground. A father was holding his raincoat around his wife to shield her; she in turn held her raincoat around a child, who in turn was sheltering a dog. There can't be many statues inspired by Swindon Town football fans.

As I watched the unveiling of the International Brigade memorial statue by Michael Foot, I realised that public art could be radical and political. There were four bronze figures supporting a fallen soldier; one arm was raised to protect their comrade while another arm was raised in a clenched fist, a symbol of political solidarity and revolution.

My feelings were reinforced in October when Angela and I watched Oliver Tambo, the President of the ANC, unveil a bust of Nelson Mandela outside Festival Hall. The GLC had commissioned it to celebrate anti-racism year in 1984, as a symbol of hope and strength for oppressed people.

Thatcher of course still considered Mandela a terrorist. Her close ally, MP Teddy Taylor, said Mandela should be shot and the Federation of Conservative Students produced a new edition of their 'Hang Nelson Mandela' poster. Even the Tory Party were embarrassed by the FCS extremists and John Selwyn Gummer withdrew their Conservative Party grant. A year later Norman Tebbit, Thatcher's skinhead, would finally ban the organisation when he was chairman of the party. Imagine being too right wing for Norman Tebbit.

A week after the Mandela bust was unveiled the GLC councillor, Tony Banks, formally opened the Hackney Peace Mural. It had been commissioned by the GLC as one of six murals on the theme of 'Peace through Nuclear Disarmament'. The muralist Ray Walker, inspired by local festivals, created the mural at Dalston Junction, which immediately became iconic with its vibrant colours, energy and positive spirit. I loved the brass players; to me it resembled a Cuban jazz festival.

Thatcher might abolish the council but at least we were going to leave behind a permanent body of public art that would send a message about our values. It seemed more productive than engaging in futile fights where the odds were stacked against you.

~

In December 1985, the consumer economy was booming and streets were packed with Christmas shoppers. Stores were full of young women with grungy hairstyles wearing gloves, mesh tops, black lace, bangles and large crosses, as they copied the street urchin style of Madonna in the film *Desperately Seeking Susan*. They paraded their unwavering support for the latest fashion trends down Regent Street as Bob Geldof switched on the Christmas lights.

On Christmas Day the BBC broadcast a feature-length edition of *Only Fools and Horses*. It was my dad's ideal evening viewing. "Lovely jubbly," he said as he made himself comfortable. Dad wasn't alone in admiring the dodgy dealers and wannabe businessmen. Del Boy was on the front cover of the *Radio Times* smoking a cigar, while on the front of the TV Times was Arthur Daley, the socially ambitious, second-hand car dealer from *Minder*. Daley summed up the country's optimistic entrepreneurial spirit with his catchphrase, 'The world is your lobster.'

39

ABOLISHED

On 26 March 1986, the railway works closed in Swindon. Five days later the GLC was abolished, along with the metropolitan county councils. I attended the goodbye party at County Hall to mark the final hours of London-wide local government. I wore my 'GLC: We'll Meet Again' badge more in hope than any realistic expectation.

The council staged the largest pyrotechnic display ever seen in London. A quarter of a million pounds of fireworks exploded in the night sky. It was a brief moment of noise and excitement which died all too quickly, leaving sulphurous smoke drifting down the Thames. In the silence that followed I walked along the Embankment towards Westminster Bridge and could hear someone playing Elgar's *Nimrod* on the members terrace.

Halfway across the bridge I stopped and looked back at the solemn grandeur of County Hall. The building, opened by King George V and Queen Mary in 1922, had sat proudly on the south bank of the Thames as the home of London government for sixty years. But no longer. The sign that used to proclaim the unemployment numbers above the sweeping curve of the Edwardian baroque pillars was already being dismantled.

The *Daily Mirror* said the greatest tribute to Ken Livingstone was that Thatcher had to abolish the GLC to get rid of him. The paper claimed he had achieved the impossible: 'He was both far left and popular.' The paper acknowledged his administration had made positive changes in the capital city. It had cut tube and bus fares to reduce road traffic, banned heavy lorries at night, expanded parks, helped orchestras, assisted charities and community groups, improved the Fire Brigade and created jobs through the Greater London Enterprise Board. The paper's article finished with the words, 'We suspect that like Eros, he will be back.'

Kinnock didn't want him back. He viewed Livingstone and the GLC as an electoral liability. He felt the high profile anti-racist and anti-homophobic stance cost the party votes. I disagreed. If that was the case the Tories wouldn't need to abolish the GLC; they could defeat him at the ballot box. Opinion polls revealed that 'Red Ken' remained popular, a fact reinforced fourteen years later in the first London mayoral election. Livingstone stood as an independent after Tony Blair rigged the selection to stop him standing as a Labour candidate. In the vote, despite both Labour and the Tories campaigning against him, he secured three times as many votes as the official Labour candidate and won the election. The people of London chose Livingstone.

It was a short-lived experiment in municipal socialism. The historian Dominic Sandbrook argues that Livingstone's radicalism was limited to a series of eye-catching gestures, which seriously underestimates the council's achievements. Yes, Livingstone understood how to get attention and how to use advertising, but his commitment to a political solution in Ireland, to gay rights, to women and to ethnic minorities helped to change attitudes in the UK.

The GLC celebrated diversity and difference. It emphasised the rights of minorities and supported these groups in organising and representing their views directly. Livingstone believed in inclusive politics and was responsible for reshaping the social agenda. The policies the GLC initiated, such as equalities monitoring, became common practice across organisations.

Sir Tag Taylor, the man appointed by Thatcher to oversee the break-up and disposal of the GLC's assets, was explicitly told to sell County Hall so it could not be brought back into municipal use by a Labour government. It was Thatcher's equivalent of shooting the children of a royal family; she wanted to eradicate all traces of the GLC.

On my last day as a GLC employee I took a single crested teacup and saucer from the member's restaurant as a memento. I put it on my desk, above the drawer that held my growing collection of lost cause badges. Later I wished I had taken more crockery but at the time something held me back. Sir Tag had no such compunction. He acquired and kept for himself a complete set of the crested crockery. On the sale of County Hall he celebrated by serving Thatcher tea in the GLC's porcelain tea cups. They were like hunters smiling over the bodies of the animals they had shot.

40

THE WORLD IS MY LOBSTER

In the summer of 1986 unemployment increased again but things were different in Swindon. As the south's economy expanded a new generation of warehousing was being driven by retailers, particularly DIY retailers that benefited from the property boom. With the introduction of forklift trucks, wooden pallets and larger lorries, more and more freight was being shipped by road. The new distribution centres were looking for low cost space on the edge of towns near a motorway. Swindon was ideally located with its two M4 junctions. New warehouses and distribution centres were popping up like large Lego blocks.

In Swindon the new jobs in warehousing, offices and retail centres were rapidly outstripping those lost in factories. Unemployment was less than half the national average and we remained the fastest growing town in Europe. The new warehouses did not require skilled craftsmen or toolmakers but they needed reliable, hard-working and fit men. It meant there were plenty of opportunities for those being made redundant from the railways. Dad secured a job in the Early Learning warehouse. The new job was not what he had dreamt of; his happiest days were in the railways, but it was work, and he could pay the mortgage.

I also secured a new job, thanks to a glowing reference from Pamela. I was to be the head of administration for the new Legal Services department in the Inner London Education Authority (ILEA). I would be based in County Hall, at least until the building was disposed of by Tag Taylor.

Angela and Simon had secured new jobs outside of local government. Angela became a management consultant and Simon worked at the Arts Council. When we met for lunch at Festival Hall, they were both animated, their eyes sparkling as they talked about their new roles. When they asked about my new job I struggled to muster as much enthusiasm. Angela, perceptive as always, said I could use the experience as a stepping stone to something else. As I walked back to the office I realised that she was right. As soon as I finished my management course I would start looking at new opportunities.

In April I moved to a rented flat just off Shoot Up Hill in Kilburn, which the residents referred to as West Hampstead. My mum was upset I had split up with my latest girlfriend. She was hoping I would 'settle down' like my brother. The prospect of me providing her with grandchildren had receded but she was happy I would no longer be living in Brixton. When talking to her friends she always said I lived in London; if pushed she might say South London, never Brixton. Now she could say I lived in West Hampstead.

My new room was in a large thirties mansion flat that I shared with two women in their mid-twenties, Stella and Annika. Stella showed me to the large West facing bedroom. She said I would be paying a larger share of the rent, which she explained was only fair as I had the largest room. I didn't mind as it meant I had space for my desk. Every time I moved the first thing I set up, was my small habitat desk. Virginia Woolf was right about having space to write or study.

After I finished setting up my new Amstrad computer, I sat and looked out across North London. The abolition of the GLC, splitting with my girlfriend and the move to the flat gave me a sense of release. I felt liberated, almost weightless. I was enthused with a euphoric feeling of freedom. My mind raced; I wanted to get on with things. Arthur Daley was right, the world *was* my lobster.

～

Annika was classically Swedish with her blonde hair and blue eyes. She worked for Habitat, which was great for getting discounts. The flat was littered with items from the store, from lamps to cereal bowls. I say that Annika worked for Habitat but most of her income came from 'hostessing' in the evenings. She worked for an agency which arranged dinners with businessmen who wanted a dinner companion to talk to about art and stuff. But someone who they could also bed at the end of the evening. As I understood it, the agency kept their fee for arranging the dinner and the hostess kept any fee agreed for post-dinner activities. I am not sure there was always dinner, as some evenings Annika would get a call at eleven which seemed a bit late for dinner. Maybe they were Spanish and ate late.

Stella had a shiny bob of black hair and smoked continuously which stained the ceiling of her room a dirty mustard colour. She was a media buyer and spent her days negotiating prices. One Saturday we had a guy come to fix the washing machine. After he had installed the new parts and put the machine back together Stella refused to pay the bill. She insisted that he either halve his bill or remove the parts he had installed and leave. He walked up to her, eyes bulging and fist clenched. She stood her ground. "Take it or leave it," she said, holding out a wad of notes. In the end he took it and slammed the door loudly on the way out. My heart was pounding but

Stella nonchalantly lit a cigarette and went back to browsing the *NME*.

∽

A few weeks after I moved in with Stella and Annika, Labour won a by-election in Fulham. The Tory vote fell 12 percent. It had taken a long time but people were finally realising the truth about Thatcher. The following morning I relayed the good news to Stella who was already smoking and making tea in the kitchen. She stopped flicking through a magazine on the counter and stared at me. She removed the cigarette from her mouth and blew smoke up towards the ceiling.

"Fucking idiots," she said. "Labour will just wreck everything again. Surely you can't support that moron Kinnock."

She turned off the boiling kettle and glared at me. I decided it was probably not the time to argue about politics.

"I don't like Kinnock," I said. "But the new MP Nick Raynsford seems like a good guy."

She raised a cynical eyebrow as she poured hot water into her 'Tears for Fears' mug.

"Labour are all fucking nutters," she said. "They want to reverse all the good things Thatcher has done."

Stella picked up the mug and made her way out of the kitchen. She pushed her copy of *Time Out* into my chest as she passed me and said, "Take a look. This is not the seventies anymore."

I put the magazine down and took a carton of skimmed milk out of the fridge for my Alpen. Stella and Annika were health conscious, other than their smoking and drinking. They talked about low-fat diets and often ate grapefruit which they said helped them lose weight. They bought fat-free milk in cartons. In Swindon milk still came in bottles, including the extra creamy Gold Top. I took my bowl and the copy of *Time Out* into my bedroom to eat at my desk. David Bowie stared out from the front cover. He was in a sharp suit holding a cigarette between his two fingers, just like Stella.

There was an article about the Metrocentre in Gateshead, Europe's largest indoor shopping centre and how Thatcher was relaxing planning controls to encourage the construction of more large American style out-of-town shopping malls. The magazine had a pullout section called, 'The Gay Guide to Paris'. There was also an advert for Perrier mineral water headed 'Picasseau'. A lunch in London was no longer complete unless it was accompanied by a bottle of Perrier. The green bottle was a badge; it said something about you. It should have said, 'Look how stupid we are paying for water.' But what people believed it said was, 'Look at us, we are chic, sophisticated and continental, we are the trend-setters.'

Capitalism was amazing. We had free drinking water flowing from the taps but the advertisers persuaded the public to spend millions buying bottled water. Perrier marketed water as a luxury good, almost like champagne with slogans like 'eau-la-la'. Their TV advert had a model stepping out of a sunny swimming pool to pick up her Perrier saying, "It's refreshing, it's natural and it doesn't have one single calorie." The marketing worked. The company sold over a billion bottles a year. It was so profitable, Perrier water became known by investors as liquid gold.

On TV there was a Listerine dragon pushing the benefits of mouthwash. Did I have bad breath? I had never thought about it; maybe that was the point of advertising to create needs that didn't previously exist.

In the lounge one evening Stella and I were sat facing each other at opposite ends of the large sofa. She was browsing the latest edition of *Time Out* while I was reading the day's *Guardian*. The front cover of her magazine had a picture of

Jamie Lee Curtis in a leotard and leg warmers posing on a chair Christine Keeler-style under the heading, 'The perfect body and how to get it'. The headline on my newspaper was 'Russians confirm nuclear disaster'. According to reports, a surge of power during a systems test at Chernobyl had released huge amounts of radioactive material into the air.

"This radiation leak looks serious," I said.

Stella looked up from her magazine.

"I'm glad we don't have a communist government," she said. "You can't believe anything they say. Lying bastards."

"I'm not sure you can believe any government, when it comes to nuclear accidents," I said. "Our government covered up the extent of the incident at Windscale for years."

"You can't seriously compare us to the Russians," said Stella. "That's ridiculous."

"I'm just saying governments cover this stuff up."

"At least we have a free press. In Russia you can't say anything against the government."

"There are some positive signs that things are changing under Gorbachev," I said. "Even Thatcher seems to think things may improve now he is the leader."

Stella grunted at me and pulled on her sweater.

"Thank God we have Thatcher to stand up to the communists," she said, getting up and walking out to indicate our discussion was over.

The weather forecasters said the radioactivity from Chernobyl was being carried to the UK by high winds. That weekend we had a heavy rainstorm that sent rivers of water cascading down Shoot Up Hill. As I splashed through puddles I wondered if it was radioactive rain from Ukraine.

41

METAMORPHOSIS

Angela took me to see *Room with a View*, an adaptation of E. M. Forster's novel. I had low expectations. It didn't sound like my sort of film. I was sure Merchant and Ivory's latest release would not be on the Trotskyist approved viewing list. I squirmed in my seat to get comfortable, it was going to be a long two hours. At seventeen I would have hated the film. All that nostalgic stuff about aristocrats on the Grand Tour and soft-focus scenes in cornfields, like adverts for Cadbury's Flake. But I was captivated; it was romantic escapism and I absolutely loved it.

I was enchanted by the visually sumptuous images of Florence bathed in golden sunshine and the lazy English summer scenes, which reminded me of Somerset fetes and morris dancing. I loved the character of George. There was something about his intensity, his passion and his free spirit that resonated with me. I was also a little jealous of his relationship with Helena Bonham-Carter, for whom I set aside my dislike of posh people with double-barrelled names.

Most of all I was completely hypnotised by Puccini's aria, *O Mio Babbino Caro*. Angela told me it was about a woman who threatens to go to Ponte Vecchio in Florence and throw herself into the river Arno if her love is in vain. A day later in the foyer of the Royal Festival Hall I purchased a cassette tape of Puccini arias. For weeks I played it constantly on my cassette player as I walked up and down the South Bank.

∼

I met Mark in Brixton. He asked what the Labour Party was like in Kilburn. I avoided looking at him directly, suddenly finding an interest in a stall selling flowery retro shirts with huge pointed collars.

"I am not sure," I said hesitantly, lifting out a hideous orange shirt from the rack. "I have been so busy with my dissertation that I haven't had a chance to attend the local ward meetings yet."

I didn't mention I had time to watch *Room with a View* or that I had spent a morning at the Tate gallery. I had recently discovered exhibitions and found they inspired me. It didn't seem to matter what the subject was. I loved the space between the exhibits, the shapes cast on the floor by the sunlight, and the hushed silence of the cavernous galleries. I also didn't mention to Mark that I had also spent a whole Sunday afternoon reading the May edition of a business magazine called *Inc*, that one of Stella's boyfriend's had left in the flat. I was surprisingly energised by the stories of entrepreneurs in America and hastily wrote notes in my Filofax before I forgot the key points.

I felt a tinge of guilt about not attending Labour Party meetings but mainly I felt happy and excited. On sunny mornings I felt like someone had given me an adrenaline shot; I would almost run to the tube station. After the GLC's abolition I had a sense of rejuvenation, opportunity and an overwhelming feeling of not wanting to waste time. As they said in *Inc* magazine, you had to keep moving or you would be run down by the competition. At work I became highly talkative as I shared my notes about how we could use computers to improve our productivity.

My mood was helped by Swindon Town's results. Thanks to Lou Macari we had won the Fourth Division. Okay, it was only the Fourth Division but we had smashed it. The team amassed 102 points, the most ever in the football league. We finished eighteen points ahead of second placed Chester City. At one point the team went almost nine hours without conceding a goal. We should have been promoted two divisions for such a performance. In the Town End the chant was now, "Lou Macari's Red and White Army".

In Swindon my friends and family didn't go to exhibitions, listen to Puccini or do the Grand Tour, though an increasing number were making it to Majorca thanks to new, low cost airlines. In 1985, Ryanair had started flying small Bandeirante aircraft from Luton Airport, which despite being some thirty miles outside the city they called London Luton. The airport had been made famous by Lorraine Chase in 1979, in an advert for Campari. When asked if she had been wafted to an exotic location from paradise, Chase replied in a South London accent, "Nah, Luton Airport." In May 1986, Ryanair extended their flight offering to Dublin at less than half the price of the lowest British Airways fares. It kicked off the first airline price war in Europe.

There was also growing competition on transatlantic routes. In June 1986, Virgin Atlantic added a second 747 to their fleet and opened a new route from London to Miami. Stella was one of the first passengers. For weeks afterwards all she talked about was Miami and how much better everything was in America and having her eggs 'sunny side up'.

The most exciting part of her trip was meeting Nick Kamen in a bar. Kamen was a model from *The Face*, and the star of a Levi's advert that had been playing on our TVs continually since Christmas. It was set in a 1950s launderette, to the sound of Marvin Gaye's version of *I Heard It Through The Grapevine*. Watched by girls in bobby socks, Kamen slipped his T-shirt over his head and removed his 501 jeans. Wearing just a pair of white boxer shorts he casually placed his clothes in the washer and sat down to read his magazine. He was the epitome of cool.

The advert was a huge success. Levi's reported an 800 percent increase in sales following its release. Stella was ecstatic when her holiday photos were developed. There were three photos of her with Kamen. A day later one appeared in a black frame on the lounge windowsill.

Stella told me pointedly that only sad people stayed in on Saturdays. Her Saturday nights frequently stretched into Sunday mornings. At 4 or 5 a.m., I would be woken by the sounds of *Absolute Beginners* through the wall and Stella singing. Sometimes it was a duet and other sounds kept me awake.

During my first week in the flat Stella had lectured Annika and I about orgasms. She told us firmly that people were responsible for their own orgasms. She was like a strict high school teacher talking to misbehaving students. I am not sure what prompted the conversation, or why she was staring at me. Stella had a straightforward, almost functional perspective on sex. "If you fail to come then it is your fault; you have not given them the right instructions." From the sounds next door she was good at giving directions.

On Sunday afternoons Stella would lie on the sofa in her pyjamas and silk dressing gown, recounting tales of the night before. At least the parts she remembered. Annika was different. On Saturday nights, if she hadn't been booked, she would stay in and hope for a late night call. We would often watch *Saturday Live* together on Channel 4 while she waited. The programme was fronted by an energetic Ben Elton, who made continual jokes about Thatcher, which would not have pleased Stella.

When Julian Clary appeared in heavy eyeshadow and a studded dog collar, Annika told me she had something similar that she wore with her maid's outfit. I never saw the maid's outfit but she would occasionally walk into the lounge in her new lingerie to see what Stella and I thought. My thoughts were generally that I wished I had a girlfriend who wore stockings and suspenders. One that gave instructions would also be helpful.

On *Saturday Live*, Harry Enfield created a character known as 'Loadsamoney'. He was a London plasterer, who went down the dole, not to sign on but to wave wads of money at the unemployed. It was a satire on greed that uncomfortably reflected life under Thatcher. Life imitated art when Tottenham Hotspur fans started waving twenty pounds notes and shouting, 'Loadsamoney' at visiting fans from northern clubs.

As the months went by I was surprised to find I warmed to Stella, despite her being a Thatcherite. She gave me a glimpse of a different London. While I would talk to Mark about the significance of Kinnock's latest poll ratings, Stella and her friends dressed to the nines, drank heavily, took drugs and danced until the early hours. I enjoyed being part of her world, if only vicariously.

One Saturday afternoon Stella sauntered into my bedroom and announced she was taking me out with her. "Come on, you can't be a boring bastard all your life." Without any invitation she began inspecting my clothes, holding up various items from the wardrobe with anguished looks. She picked out a white T-shirt and instructed me to put it on. Inspired by *Miami Vice*, she dressed me in my blue jacket from Next and rolled the sleeves up my arms with some difficulty. She stood back to assess her work. "Okay, put your lenses in and I will do your hair," she said. It seemed I had passed some form of Stella test.

She made me sit at her dressing table and picked up a can of L'Oréal hair mousse. I was obviously worth it. She sprayed the expanding foam into her hand and then worked her fingers through my hair. I closed my eyes taking in the heavy, almost musty aroma of long dead cigarettes in her room. She stood behind me stroking and massaging my head. After a short while, far too short, Stella moved around in front of me. I sensed I was being assessed on some form of Nick Kamen scale.

"Hmm, not bad," she said. I figured I had scored at least five out of ten. "Just a little more at the front." As she pushed her hands through my hair and reached the back of my head, I was conscious of her breasts brushing against my face.

I felt like Don Johnson when Stella and I entered Tangerine Twisters. We were greeted by bubbly people with sparkling eyes and bare midriffs. As we pushed our way through smiling faces to the bar I recognised the synthesised marimba beat of *Africa* by Toto. Stella ordered us Blue Hawaiians and became encircled in a crowd of bodies rippling with laughter. The barman placed the drinks on the bar in front of me. The glasses were huge and shaped like an hour glass. A blue sculpted Marilyn Monroe of a drink topped with an umbrella and a chunk of pineapple. The barman put large red and white striped straws into the glasses. I was definitely not in Swindon anymore.

Stella introduced me to Ines, Ava and a myriad of other names that were lost in the sea of music and floated out of my head as soon as they were mentioned. Despite trying to stay close to Stella I lost her multiple times during the evening. The last time I saw her she shouted to me above the music that they were going on to a club and I should join them. I promptly lost her again and found myself stood at the edge of a group discussing the differences between cocaine and a new drug called ecstasy. I nodded knowingly as they spoke but had nothing to add. All I knew about drugs was that Nancy Reagan said "Just say no," and it seemed an inappropriate time to share this knowledge. After failing to find Stella, I slipped away to get the tube home, sure that no one would notice my absence.

In the flat I began to browse Stella's magazines as frequently as my copies of the *New Statesman* and *Marxism Today*. I also bought my own copy of *Inc* magazine and another American magazine called *Entrepreneur*. I was enticed by the name and the front page which promised to let me into the secrets of America's hottest businesses. Inside, an article titled 'The road to success' encouraged readers to have the courage to set up their own business. According to the author it wasn't enough to dream, you had to act.

The magazines reminded me in a strange way of the Militant pamphlets I had read as a teenager. They portrayed entrepreneurs as innovative modern rebels, challenging the old guard and reinventing business practices. They were going to change the world. I wanted to be like the entrepreneurs and shake up the old ways of thinking. One of the magazine articles argued the best innovative ideas came from young people. I found myself nodding in agreement as I thought of the grey-haired bureaucrats who argued I was too young to be promoted. They were so backwards they didn't even know how to create a word processing document or use a fax machine.

There was so much we could do to improve our productivity if only the old people would remove their blinkers. We had to embrace change as Rosabeth Moss Kanter said in my new favourite book, *Change Masters – Innovation and Entrepreneurship in the American Corporation*. She argued that while job security used to come from being employed it now came from being employable. She was so right; we all had to keep our skills, knowledge and experience up to date in a fast changing world.

The skills Dad learnt on his apprenticeship might have seen him through most of his working life but things were different for my generation. The introduction of computers and spreadsheets meant we had to keep learning constantly. I didn't understand the old men in ill-fitting suits who wouldn't do any training unless the council paid for it. They would soon be obsolete.

The magazines were full of adverts for menswear fashion designers. Names such as Hugo Boss, Ralph Lauren, Giorgio Armani and Calvin Klein were emblazoned in large lettering alongside square-jawed men, with Rupert Everett cheek-bones. I don't recall a single item of clothing worn by my father that had a logo on it. Now designer logos were visible everywhere. Watches were no longer for telling the time, they were fashion accessories. Swatch watches came in every colour emblazoned with Tintin and Coca-Cola logos.

I also became aware of male beauty products. I considered myself sophisticated because I had upgraded to Paco Rabanne, thanks to Alison, and no longer liberally applied Brut and Old Spice aftershaves but now I was learning there was a whole new world of moisturisers, scrubs and oils.

One Monday lunchtime, on Annika's recommendation, I

visited The Body Shop at Oxford Circus. The store smelt like the jelly sweets we used to buy in paper bags at the ABC Saturday morning cinema. I bought myself a cocoa butter moisturiser which came in a small plastic bottle with a dark green label and black screw cap. A few weeks later I replaced the Vosene shampoo, that my mum had sworn by, for a banana shampoo. I also treated myself to a tea tree and mint body wash, which fizzed on my skin in the shower. In the mornings the bathroom smelt like an After Eight factory, with a hint of mellow banana.

Stella and Annika made me acutely conscious of fashion and clothing. I started to pay attention to the attire of the private lawyers and QCs that came to our meetings from across the river. Their suits were not like the ones worn by council officers. The lawyers' suits were made from the finest wool and were tailored to broaden their shoulders and to create long, lean lines. They didn't sag or hang loose; they seemed moulded to their bodies. The hems of their trousers just touched their black leather shoes, which were polished to within an inch of their life. Their shoes also had leather soles rather than black rubber ones like mine. Their shoes said look at me, these are the most luxurious shoes you can buy.

It was the same with their shirts. Power and confidence oozed from shirts made with Egyptian cotton and decorated with mother-of-pearl buttons. Their double cuffs, extended precisely half an inch beyond their suit sleeves and were held together by expensive cufflinks. These shirts came from a different planet to my M&S shirts with their single cuffs and plastic buttons.

As I sat in the meetings I became increasingly conscious of Mark McCormack saying we were always communicating. My clothes were saying 'This is a working-class boy from Swindon. No, we have no idea what he is doing here either'. I was from a different tribe. It was not just apparent in my clothing. While I took notes with my Bic biro, they removed wine red fountain pens with golden trims from their inner pockets. They also pulled out large luxurious Filofaxes, and buff folders tied with pink ribbons, from their leather briefcases. I became embarrassed by my plastic briefcase, with its two pop-up locks, that Mum had given me.

The lawyers also spoke differently. They enunciated their words deeply and deliberately. When I was speaking my words often tumbled over each other as my brain raced ahead of my voice. "Stop mumbling," my mum would say. In contrast the lawyers' voices were slow and sonorous.

People say be yourself, or if you can't be yourself be Batman. But it is hard to be yourself, we are social animals, and most of us are constantly adapting and adjusting to our social groups. Do we even know who we are, really, deep down? Is the real me the one that that wants to give up everything, move to Madrid and learn Spanish, or the one that is anxious about having savings for a rainy day? As a teenager I envied the likes of Bowie, he was brave enough not to conform, to be himself. But was he really? Ziggy Stardust and Aladdin Sane were characters behind which Bowie could hide his real self.

Maybe it was the chameleon in me, possibly in all of us, but I wanted to fit in and be like the rich lawyers. I no longer wanted my clothes to communicate I was from Swindon. Maybe it was just me being shallow or insecure. The radical academics in the Industry and Employment Branch, didn't envy the clothes of the lawyers. They were comfortable in their jeans and jumpers. Their clothes made a different statement, a counter statement that they didn't need expensive clothes to argue robustly with lawyers and QCs about the council's powers to fund community groups. I am not sure where their confidence came from, maybe their middle-class backgrounds, their private schools and their Oxbridge degrees. They were another tribe.

When I sought Stella's advice on clothing she enthusiastically took me under her wing and made me her project. First, she sent me to her hairdresser in Covent Garden to sort out my hair. I emerged with an expensively crafted hairstyle which the stylist said was a variation of the Caesar cut designed to make my head look square and strong. The back and sides were cut short with clippers, while the hair on top was longer and brushed back. I admired myself in shop windows as I walked back to the tube station.

To complement my hair Stella took me shopping for new clothes. She picked out a dark grey, single-breasted suit by Yves St Laurent. Double breasted suits were in fashion but she said they didn't really suit my body shape. To be fair I was still super skinny; I may have touched ten and half stone on a good day. Double-breasted suits were more useful for men whose shirts stretched over their stomachs and hid a multitude of sins. It was only when she picked out a thin tie from TM Lewin that I realised Stella was dressing me like David Bowie in *Absolute Beginners*.

On Jermyn Street we browsed shirts at a store called Thomas Pink. The black sign and gold lettering made it look old but it had only opened the year before. I purchased two white cotton shirts with double cuffs. To fasten them Stella bought me a set of silver cufflinks from Liberty that had an inset of paisley material. At my next meeting one of the external lawyers commented on the cufflinks and asked where I got them. I walked back to my office ten feet tall, and with a smile that could not be contained, though I did resist the urge to punch the air.

My final two purchases were expensive. I bought a pair of Barker shoes with leather soles. Initially the shoes were so stiff they cut into my ankles. However, it was worth it for the opportunity to reveal my tan soles to the world. I only discovered later, when I was sitting on my backside in the rain, that the smooth leather soles had little grip on wet pavements. I also discovered that leather soles are not as hard wearing as rubber soles and need replacing within a year. Finally, after coveting it for two weeks through the shop window in Fleet Street, I bought a satchel-style leather briefcase. It fastened with two brass buckle straps and was exorbitantly priced.

In my new clothes I felt like a million dollars, which was a good return on my investment. I didn't just change my clothing. In the office I consciously moderated my voice and mimicked the slow deliberate tone of the lawyers. I carefully considered and articulated each word as I spoke. By the autumn of 1986, my metamorphosis was complete. I wasn't Batman but I no longer looked or sounded like a boy from Swindon.

My transformation was about more than clothes. Part of me was still the teenage socialist who belonged in the Town End but an increasing part of me was also a middle-class London graduate who enjoyed the opera and admired entrepreneurs. I was no longer sure who I was.

42

_____

GREED IS GOOD

Over dinner in Angela's flat Fiona told us she had invested £3,000 in a Personal Equity Plan. PEPs had been launched by the Chancellor, Nigel Lawson, on my twenty-fourth birthday. They were a tax-free shelter designed to encourage people to buy shares and grow Thatcher's share-owning democracy. According to Fiona investing in a PEP was such a no-brainer even her brother had done it. Simon agreed and said he had invested in a something called a Capital Growth Fund. I refused to support capitalism by buying shares; I couldn't see Trotsky investing in a PEP.

Fiona made it clear I was missing out. The papers agreed. The *Financial Times* said it been another great year for investors. By the end of December 1986, the Dow Jones was up 20 percent on the previous year. The new FTSE 100 Index finished the year up 19 percent. Despite my personal boycott, it seemed computerisation, and a major series of Stock Exchange reforms known as the 'Big Bang', had led to an enormous growth in share trading.

Wages were growing faster in the UK than in any other

major western country. My own salary was more than double what it had been when I had joined the GLC three years earlier. In London house prices and property values were rocketing. Fiona told us proudly that the value of her flat had increased by over 30 percent. Everyone was conscious they had to get on the property ladder before the prices became unaffordable. Even interest rates of 11 percent couldn't dampen demand for mortgages.

A new Thatcherite architecture of steel and glass was emerging in London, designed by star architects like Richard Rogers and Norman Foster. In November 1986, the new Lloyd's building was opened by the Queen. It epitomised a new age of technology and innovation. The lifts were on the outside of the building and reminded me of the escalators at the Pompidou centre in Paris. The area around Liverpool Street became a building site as they constructed the Broadgate complex. From Primrose Hill the London horizon was full of cranes, like large worker ants rebuilding and reshaping the skyline. Former derelict industrial warehouses and buildings were being redeveloped as retail units, offices and housing. London may have had an historic centre but it was not a museum it was a living city. A city that was regenerating. The population had fallen to six million at the start of the 1980s but things were changing. The city was growing again. It was palpable. The ground trembled under huge drills, the dust of building sites filled the air, and streets were lined with skips and 'Sold' signs as my generation took our first steps onto the property ladder.

Workplaces were also being revolutionised by computer technology and new working practices despite the resistance of the old people. Rupert Murdoch shifted newspaper print production from Fleet Street to a new plant in Wapping, where journalists could use terminals to input copy directly. He made the workers who did the traditional Linotype printing redundant. Mass demonstrations were held and the Labour Party called for everyone to boycott Murdoch's newspapers. I pinned a new badge to my denim jacket urging people not to buy *The Times*, the *Sun* or the *News of the World*. A badge which I sometimes had to remove in Swindon when in search of a *Guardian*.

At the end of the year British Gas was privatised. One and a half million avaricious bastards bought shares, including Fiona and Stella. I didn't buy any; I still had principles. Any fool could make money buying privatised shares. You just cut out a coupon from a newspaper, sent it off with a cheque for £1.35 a share and received in return share certificates worth 60 percent more than the price you paid. Privatisation represented a massive transfer of wealth from the public to private shareholders. The managers also did okay, a year after privatisation the salary of the chief executive of British Gas increased from £50,000 to £370,000. My body quivered with rage when I read about his pay increase; I wasn't sure about assassinating politicians but maybe CEOs of privatised utilities were fair game.

To exploit the new opportunities created by privatisation, companies like Price Waterhouse, Coopers & Lybrand, Ernst & Whinney, Arthur Young, Touche Ross and Peat Marwick were growing their public sector management consultancy practices. They started to actively recruit staff like Angela, whose new job was with Ernst & Whinney. She arranged for us to have lunch at the Institute of Directors to update me on life as a management consultant.

The IoD was a wedding cake of a building on Pall Mall. Before I entered I checked my tie, pulling it up tighter around my collar, adjusted my shirt cuffs to the requisite half an inch below my suit sleeve and stepped up to the reception desk to ask for Angela. I was directed to wait for her in a large hallway, where I sat in a low leather chair to one side of a central stone staircase that swept upwards and fanned out on two sides before a white marble statue of a Roman general. On the stairs a regal carpet was held in place by brass stair rods. The smell of polish hung in the air. It reminded me of the mornings my mum cleaned our house, liberally spraying Pledge onto the surfaces before wiping them down with a yellow duster.

Angela had booked a table in the restaurant on the ground floor. It had large windows, golden wallpaper and tall palm plants. The thick carpet and heavy patterned drapes muffled the sound of hushed conversations taking place at tables across the room. We were directed to a table by the window and sat down opposite each other in chairs that curved around us. The lunch menu was secured by its four corners inside a leather bound folder. It read like a cryptic crossword puzzle.

- Ballotine of duck liver
- Langoustines à la nage
- Gravlax and devilled eggs
- Turbot Dieppoise and kohlrabi

I was still working out two across when a waiter appeared in a white shirt and black waistcoat to enquire about our order. Angela interrupted my thoughts, "I am going to have the Gravlax, what about you?"

"I will have the same," I said.

"Wine? What about a bottle of wine, a Pouilly Fumé?"

"Sounds good. I don't have much to do this afternoon."

I closed my menu and handed it to the waiter. I hoped that I would enjoy whatever it was we had just ordered.

"Oh, and also a bottle of Perrier," added Angela, before also handing over her menu.

"So, how is life in the private sector?" I asked.

She told me it was the best move she had ever made. The salaries were higher but it was the benefits she particularly appreciated.

"When I turned up on the first morning I got to choose a car from the pool. It was amazing. I was just given a list to choose from."

I didn't own a car but I liked the idea of being given one.

"We also get free private health and life insurance, four times my salary if I die in service, not that I plan to," she said. "We also have a free restaurant on the tenth floor of Becket House which overlooks St Thomas' Hospital and the river."

The waiter filled our glasses with wine. "Cheers!" I said.

Outside the window we could see Christmas lights and people passing by with their shopping bags. Inside our wine tasted of summer afternoons

When the food arrived it turned out that gravlax was what posh people called smoked salmon and devilled eggs were just boiled eggs with some spicy mayo piped on top of them.

Over lunch Angela enthused about *The Handmaid's Tale* which had made the Booker shortlist. I hadn't read the book, despite it being on the approved Trotskyist reading list. I couldn't recall if it was in the *Socialist Worker*, *Labour Herald* or the RCP's *Next Step* but one of them had called it a bleak but compelling story of women's oppression. Instead I talked about another Booker shortlisted book, *An Artist of the Floating World* by Kazuo Ishiguro.

"It is about an old man reflecting on his life," I said. "It suggests that everyone looking back on their lives becomes an unreliable narrator. They may start out with honesty in their hearts but as they construct a narrative of past events they often deceive themselves. The book suggests you have to look for the gaps in their story, as they are often more important than the events they report. It is in the omissions that the feelings of guilt, embarrassment and grief are hidden."

Darkness was already descending when I left the IoD. There was a light winter drizzle as I made my way north up St James Street to Piccadilly Circus. Lights reflected like colourful smudges in the damp street. In Regent Street the Christmas lights were like curtain swags that had been pulled back inviting you up to Oxford Circus.

The lights had been switched on by Leslie Grantham and Anita Dobson who played Den and Angie Watts in *EastEnders*. They were the celebrities of the moment. Their faces were on every newspaper and magazine cover except the *Financial Times*, which carried a picture of Lord Hanson. He had been named the 'capitalist of the year'. It was a sign of Thatcherism that we now had such awards. To me Hanson was the worst type of capitalist. He created nothing; he wasn't a creative entrepreneur like Steve Jobs, he was simply an asset stripper.

On Christmas Day, my family were glued to the TV as Den Watts served divorce papers on Angie. To be fair to him she had feigned a terminal illness to try to stop him from leaving her. I was never sure how that was supposed to work; surely when you didn't die the game was going to be up. The programme was watched by over thirty million people and broke the record for the highest ever British television drama audience.

~

In January 1987, the Tories were just two points ahead of Labour. It was hard to fathom because the Tories were so laughably out of touch. To prove my point the Conservative Health Minister, Edwina Currie, dispensed her wisdom to the nation that good Christian people could not catch AIDS. She also opined that old people who couldn't afford to heat their homes should wear long johns and that northerners were unhealthy because they ate too many chips. In essence we had a health minister whose advice was basically wear long johns, stop having sex, made more likely if you were wearing long johns, and stop eating chips.

Consumer spending was surging at the start of 1987. The creative advertising wizards were successfully persuading people to apply for credit cards. The advertisers signed up TV stars, such as the global jet-setter, Alan Whicker, who promoted Barclaycard. They also persuaded Dudley Moore to play a punk rocker who couldn't buy the album he wanted by Bill Smelly and the Stink Bombs because he didn't have a credit card. One of Barclaycard's most successful series of adverts starred Rowan Atkinson from *Not the Nine O'Clock News*. There was something ironic about one of the giants of alternative comedy promoting the growth of financial services. The advertising worked. By 1987, a third of the UK population had a credit card and 5 percent of all consumer spending was made on a card.

My mum was appalled at the idea of credit cards. She blamed young people's desire for instant gratification. "They should learn to save." Despite her protestations the personal saving rate halved between 1979 to 1987, and borrowing surged. Ironically, Thatcher, like my mum, was committed to the values of thrift and hard work but she could not control the free enterprise capitalism she had unleashed. Easy credit was fuelling a consumer-led economic boom.

There was no shortage of things to buy with your credit card, including the music you had already purchased on vinyl and cassette. Annual sales of compact discs rose from three million in 1983 to over forty million in 1987. Annika bought home a blue Habitat CD rack to house our growing collection of CDs. The Habitat catalogue was now required reading for my friends as they furnished their newly purchased flats with colour co-ordinated washing up bowls and drying racks.

~

In February 1987, British Airways was listed on the London Stock Exchange at £1.25 a share. It had been eight years since Thatcher promised to privatise the company. Eight years of cost cutting to make the airline profitable and attractive to investors. The workforce had been reduced by 20,000 people. A TV advert declared that British Airways was now not only the world's favourite airline, but also the most profitable. The soundtrack to the advert was *Land of Hope and Glory*.

The initial share offering was oversubscribed as a million greedy bastards sought to make another quick profit from privatisation. On the first day of trading, the shares rose by 35 percent. Another public asset sold cheaply to private investors by Thatcher. I begrudged yet another capital gain being pocketed by Fiona and Stella.

While Del Trotter was dreaming of being a millionaire those in the city had bigger dreams. Bill Gates became the first self-made and youngest billionaire. It was no longer enough to be a millionaire, people wanted to be billionaires. A new generation was obsessed with making money.

In one of the year's best selling films, *Wall Street*, the lead character Gordon Gekko argued "Greed is good". Gekko was based on a real person – Ivan Boesky, an American arbitrageur. He had famously made a graduation speech at the Berkeley School of Business in 1986, where he said, "Greed is all right, by the way, greed is healthy... You can be greedy and still feel good about yourself."[1] He was later jailed for insider trading.

The printers strike at Wapping finally collapsed after fifty-four weeks of industrial action. Despite holding out longer than the miners, the dispute didn't gain the same attention or the same sympathy. On the TV there were no large marches in support of the printers and despite my badge, the boycott of the newspapers had little impact. Within a year most national newspapers followed Murdoch to the Docklands, and adopted the new printing methods. It was another defeat, one that was impossible to dress up as a victory, and worse was to come.

43

THATCHER VS PORKY THE POET

In February 1987, there was a by-election in Greenwich. The Labour candidate was Deirdre Wood, an ILEA councillor. I had met her a few times and she seemed a good choice. However, Kinnock opposed her selection saying she would be an easy target for the 'bastards' of the press. He was right. Within hours of her selection the *Sun* had nicknamed her 'dreadful Deirdre', cast aspersions about her private life and called her part of the loony left. The *News of the World* called her a feminist, anti-racist and gay rights supporter, like these were bad things.

The SDP candidate was Rosie Barnes. Her campaign was reminiscent of the campaign the Liberals had run against Peter Tatchell. It attacked Deirdre's personal life and reinforced the tabloid smears. Barnes said Wood's support for gay rights was ridiculous and the SDP campaign stoked fear about AIDS and gay people. It confirmed my view that the SDP were the lowest of the low. In the week of the by-election there were three cases of arson against the homes of gay people in London, a gay coffee shop was destroyed by fire and two gay men were beaten up in full public view during the evening rush hour.

Barnes romped home with 18,000 votes. The Labour Party had lost one of their safest seats, despite bussing in more than fifty Labour MPs during the campaign. It was the first time the SDP had won a seat from Labour, as the newspapers kept reminding us. The narrative was clear; Labour were no longer the main party of opposition. An internal Labour memo from Patricia Hewitt was leaked, *in which* she blamed the loss on the continuous ridiculing of the loony left by British newspapers. In particular, she noted, "The gays and lesbians issue is costing us dear amongst the pensioners."

The RCP's candidate, Kate Marshall, received a grand total of ninety-one votes, which of course they claimed was a major victory. They said the working class had lost confidence in Kinnock and the RCP would now attract hundreds of thousands of people away from Labour to become a mass revolutionary movement. I suppose many things were possible. It was possible, in a world of infinite parallel universes, that Debbie Harry might call me up to discuss my dissertation on performance management at the ILEA. In the world of infinite universes the RCP had chosen the one where ninety-one votes in a by-election heralded the revolutionary overthrow of capitalism.

After the by-election Labour's support collapsed, falling ten points in the national polls from 40 percent to 30 percent. A week after my twenty-fifth birthday, two opinion polls put the Alliance ahead of Labour. I took what reassurance I could from a *Sunday Times* Mori poll that at least had Labour and the SDP Alliance neck and neck. I took less comfort from the double-digit lead held by the Tories.

In April 1987, on the anniversary of Chernobyl, I joined Mark on a march from Victoria to Hyde Park organised by CND and Friends of the Earth. The posters for the march featured a cartoon of a two-headed sheep drawn by Steve Bell of the *Guardian*. As everyone was gathering I bought a badge that read 'April 25, March for a Nuclear Free Britain' with the image of Bell's two-headed sheep.

In the spring sunshine we marched past people wearing Aviator sunglasses, as they mimicked Maverick from the film *Top Gun*. There was a new confidence in London. It was visible in the way people dressed and the way they walked. Saatchi and Saatchi no longer advertised products; they promoted lifestyles. In Seattle, Howard Schultz started marketing Starbucks coffee shops as an affordable indulgence because we all deserved a little luxury. People were buying expensive handcrafted cappuccinos, bottled water and designer clothing because they were worth it.

Everyone in London wanted to get rich and the yuppies were seizing the opportunities offered by Thatcher's free market economy. Rather than being embarrassed, they flaunted their affluence. Newspapers and magazines celebrated wealth and *The Times* started compiling a list of the UK's richest people. Del Boy was right; yuppies loved to talk about money. But in Thatcher's Britain income inequality was growing faster and more dramatically than ever before. There was a growing divide between the 'haves' and the 'have nots'. The wealth of those who owned shares and property was booming but there was also a marked increase in the number of households with no wealth at all.

On 11 May 1987, the Evening Standard published an NOP poll that had the Tories eighteen points ahead. The next day Thatcher called a general election. I imagine it was a short conversation. Shall we call an election? We are eighteen points ahead, yes, why not? The task for Labour appeared impossible. The BBC *Newsnight* presenters speculated that Thatcher might become the first prime minister in the twentieth century to win

three consecutive elections and become the century's longest serving prime minister. I switched off the TV.

A group of musicians, inspired by the GLC festivals, set up Red Wedge, a campaign to engage young people in politics and encourage them to support the Labour Party. It was led by many of my heroes including Billy Bragg, Paul Weller and Jimmy Somerville. It also involved alternative comedians, such as Phil Jupitus, who performed as Porky the Poet. It was asymmetric warfare. Kinnock, Red Wedge and Porky the Poet versus Thatcher, Murdoch and MacKenzie.

On 15 May 1987, Neil Kinnock gave a moving speech to the Welsh Labour Party Conference. "Why am I the first Kinnock in a thousand generations to be able to get to university?" His soaring rhetoric moved me; I was also the first Rayson to go to university. He talked of people who couldn't find work, of young couples that couldn't find a home, of old people afraid to turn the heating up in the cold and people whose lives are turned into a crisis by the need to buy a new pair of shoes. Despite all my misgivings about Kinnock, the guy could make speeches. Maybe, just maybe, we could win the election this time or at least deprive Thatcher of a majority. I would take anything, I would even settle for a one-seat Conservative majority; at least she couldn't do much with that.

The election became a battle of the advertising agencies when Labour engaged Wolff Olins, one of Saatchi and Saatchi's competitors. To make Labour more friendly they replaced the traditional red flag logo with a red rose. Maybe it was a subliminal move away from the *Red Flag* that was sung at party conferences. I could see that the song's tales of martyred dead, cowards, traitors and gallows grim was not the look they were going for. Labour's key campaign broadcast was made by Hugh Hudson, who directed *Chariots of Fire*. The advert was about Kinnock rather than Labour, with romantic footage of Neil and his wife, Glenys, walking on clifftops. I was not convinced but Kinnock's ratings went up by a remarkable sixteen points.

The Tories retaliated with a series of Saatchi and Saatchi attack ads. One read, 'So this is the new moderate militant-free Labour Party'. It had pictures of Diane Abbott, Ken Livingstone, Jeremy Corbyn, Valerie Wise and Militant's Pat Wall. The latter was quoted saying he wanted to abolish the monarchy and the House of Lords. Quite right but I knew it would upset my mum.

The most effective Saatchi attack ad was a mock poster about Labour's defence policy; it was a picture of a soldier holding his arms up in surrender. Kelvin MacKenzie backed it up with a mock-editorial in the *Sun*, 'Why I'm Backing Kinnock, by Joseph Stalin'. Labour's policy of unilateral disarmament might win the approval of party delegates, and people like me, but it wasn't winning votes with the public. Stella thought the policy was the height of insanity. Reagan and Gorbachev didn't help. Reagan said Labour's election would threaten NATO, while Gorbachev said Thatcher was an Iron Lady, standing up for Britain.

I was frustrated when Labour decided to drop its opposition to Right to Buy but at least it did support the reinvestment of sale proceeds to build new housing stock. I was also angry at the party's refusal to commit itself to reversing the abolition of the GLC. It didn't stop me volunteering to help the local Labour Party but my contribution was limited to a few evenings leafleting nearby estates. I no longer had the enthusiasm of the seventeen-year-old me that spent hours campaigning in 1979.

The front cover of my *New Statesman* had a drawing of Kinnock in front of the door of 10 Downing Street with the headline, 'Possible'. I was encouraged by Labour's promise to start reversing the income tax cuts made by Thatcher, who had reduced the basic rate from 33 percent to 27 percent. Kinnock said he would raise income tax by 2 percent if elected, while the Tories committed themselves to a further reduction of two pence. There was now a clear choice, a 2 percent increase in income tax which would fund better public services or a 2 percent reduction and cuts in services. It was obvious to anyone, other than Stella, that Thatcher had made the wrong call.

∼

When I visited the club the men were each sitting in their usual places, a pint of Arkell's ale in a straight glass in front of each of them. Next to the one-arm bandits men and women were playing dominoes. Sat by the window guys were pegging out cribbage scores on a wooden board. A green glass ashtray was full of stubbed and squashed cigarette butts. Evidence, if it was needed, of the source of the grey-blue clouds that hung beneath the strip lighting. A guy I recognised was sitting on his own at the bar reading the *News of the World*. By the stairs two men were playing darts and chalking up their scores. The skittle alley in the back room was empty and silent. No one played skittles on a Sunday lunchtime.

"So what's going to happen in this 'ere election?" asked Bob looking at me.

The vote was less than two weeks away, I knew a discussion about politics was inevitable and that it would make Dad uncomfortable.

Tony made it clear he didn't want Kinnock to win the election. Apparently not so much because he was Labour but because he was Welsh. In March the men in the club had cheered when England's Wade Dooley, a policeman no less, broke the jaw of the Wales number eight in three places with a right hook. The match in Cardiff resembled a Saturday night brawl in the car park of the Moonrakers pub rather than rugby.

England were the main aggressors but the men in the club didn't see it that way. "It was the Taffy sheep shaggers that started it," according to Tony.

The men didn't love Thatcher but they were thankful for the ability to buy their council houses and for the profits they had made on privatised shares. Bob was sitting on a nice gain from his BT shares and had recently received an 8 percent dividend. In Swindon the economy was booming and the shops were full of consumer goods. The aspirations of people were visible, like the carriage lights Bob had installed outside his newly painted front door. The men in the club now went to Benidorm for their holidays rather than Barry Island or Bognor Regis. Life was good and to top it off Swindon had won promotion to the Second Division, having beaten Gillingham at Selhurst Park in the Third Division play-offs.

Tony was appalled at Labour's proposal to add two pence to income tax. He said it would all be wasted on bureaucracy and benefits. Around the table there was a vigorous nodding of heads in agreement.

"I wouldn't trust Labour with my money," said Tony, aggressively holding an unlit cigarette in the air like a claw hammer. "Red Ken would just give it all to black lesbians." He looked over at me and added, "No offence, Steve. But he would."

I did think of explaining that the GLC had been abolished the previous year and, even if Ken was elected as an MP, there was little chance of Kinnock promoting him but I thought better of it.

"I am glad I am not bisexual," said Bob. " I couldn't stand being rejected by men as well as women."

The men laughed. Tony lit his cigarette, took a deep draw and blew smoke to the ceiling. Dad took a swig of his pint, wiped his lips and returned his glass to the beer mat on the low Formica table.

"So Second Division next season. What do you reckon?" he said.

I noticed the subtle shift away from politics.

"If we can keep hold of Lou Macari I think we will be okay," said my brother.

Tony tugged on his earlobe and replied, "Nah, straight back down again I reckon."

"That second goal by Stevie White against Gillingham was just like the goals you used to score Cliffy," said Bob, who had watched the highlights on HTV, the local TV station.

"He's a proper west country boy, our Stevie," said Tony, rolling his Rs to emphasise his point, "born in Chipping Sodbury, he was."

"Yep, we don't need no Argies playing for us, eh, Cliffy?" added Bob.

This was a dig at my dad who was a Tottenham Hotspur supporter. The Argentinian Ossie Ardiles had helped Spurs reach the cup final a few weeks earlier. A match they had lost in extra time to Coventry.

"Yeah, shame about that cup final," Tony added with a smile and nudged my dad with his elbow.

As I headed back to London that evening I didn't understand how the men could vote Conservative. The Town's railway works had only closed a year earlier but it seemed they had already moved on. Swindon wasn't suffering the unemployment experienced in northern industrial towns. It was at the heart of the prosperous M4 corridor and families were upgrading their Metros for Montegos. Some were even eyeing up the Honda Accord, following the Japanese company's purchase of a three hundred and seventy acre site on the edge of the town. According to Tony the new Honda factory was going to be "bloody massive".

44

THATCHER 3 – BADGELAND 0

On the evening of 11 June 1987, Annika got a call at 9 p.m. Fifteen minutes later she had showered and left the flat. On the TV David Dimbleby had abandoned his pink tie in favour of a red one. He opened the election night programme by saying it was going to be a close result. The BBC poll estimated that the Tories would win a twenty-six seat-majority. However, he emphasised there was a 2 percent margin of error which might mean Thatcher would fail to win a majority.

"It's going to be close," I said to Stella, who was sat next to me. On the table on my side of the sofa were two packs of Leibniz chocolate biscuits, on Stella's was a half-empty bottle of Chardonnay and a pack of Silk Cut. She took a long drag on her cigarette. After exhaling she held it up by her ear.

"Are all you socialists deluded?" she said. "Maggie will win by a mile. I don't know anyone mad enough to vote Labour, except you and ... well, you're weird. You have to admit."

She looked at me pointedly but with the faint hint of a smile. I think I amused her. I put down my *New Statesman* guide to the election, and offered her a biscuit which she declined with a dismissive wave of her cigarette.

The first result declared was from Torbay. The young Tory candidate was called Rupert. Of course he was.

"Why do the Tories all have names like Rupert, Hugo and Jacob?" I asked Stella.

"At least they are not called Charlene, Scott, Jason or Kylie," she said. "What muppets name their children after characters in *Neighbours*? Seriously, can you imagine a Prime Minister Charlene."

The BBC's veteran political commentator Anthony King said that their election model forecast that Rupert would get 26,000 votes. He got 29,000. An 8,000 majority, much better than the model predicted. King said they may have to revise their forecast Tory majority upwards.

"See I told you," said Stella.

"It is just one result,'" I said. "You can't forecast an election after one result."

Stella really knew nothing about politics. I turned back to the TV and nibbled the chocolate from the edge of my biscuit.

More results were announced; Torbay was no outlier. The BBC revised the Tory majority upwards. After just twelve results they forecast Thatcher would have a majority of fifty-two. There was a growing heaviness in my stomach. It was like that sense of foreboding you have in the dentist's waiting room just before you are about to have a root canal.

"Well, I think that's fairly conclusive," said Stella. "I'm off to bed. You going to stay and drown your sorrows?"

I debated going to bed but it was like watching a slow motion car crash. No matter how terrible the results might be, I could not stop watching.

"I am going to stay up a bit longer," I said. "It's still early. You may be surprised when you wake up, there are still a lot of seats to be declared."

"Yeah, right," said Stella picking up her glass and pack of

cigarettes. "I am sorry but you really are dumber than I thought if you seriously expected Kinnock to be prime minister."

~

An hour later the BBC forecast was revised again. This time Peter Snow said Thatcher was on course to win a majority of ninety-four. For fuck's sake, ninety-four. Thank God, Stella was no longer around to gloat. I found I couldn't physically watch the TV; it was like there was a magnetic force repulsing me. I went to the kitchen to make coffee. As I waited for the kettle to boil the reality struck me that Thatcher was not only going to win, she was going to continue to dominate British politics.

When I returned to the lounge Anthony King said Labour's vote was stabilising at 32 percent, the worst since 1931, ignoring the disaster of the last election. As each result was announced something in me died. I was being battered like a punchbag. It was unrelenting, the Conservatives were even winning new seats. Conservatives gain Ipswich. Conservatives gain Battersea. Conservatives gain Thurrock. Conservatives gain Fulham. We couldn't even hold onto the seat we had won in the recent by-election.

In Swindon the Tories held the seat with 29,358 votes. The most they had ever won in the constituency.

Annika returned around 3 a.m.

"You still up?" she said.

"Not for much longer, looks like Thatcher has won again."

"Oh, that's good. I mean I am sorry for you, but Kinnock versus Thatcher. It wasn't much of a contest."

She was probably right.

"How was your night?" I asked.

"Long. Very long," said Annika and rolled her eyes to the ceiling. "I always like the Danes, very considerate. Which is all very well but … let's just say I had to fake it, otherwise he would still be down there."

I once made the mistake of asking a girlfriend if it was true that women faked orgasms. She reassured me that it happened all the time.

"Right, I am knackered, see you in the morning," said Annika.

My mood was lifted temporarily when the SDP's Roy Jenkins, the architect of Labour's demise, lost his seat. Good riddance you Tory bastard. At least Labour was doing better than the SDP Alliance; they were not going to become the main party of opposition. I was also cheered when the leader of the SNP lost his seat. Goodbye you Tartan Tory.

There were other isolated pockets of good news. Ken Livingstone was elected in Brent East and four ethnic minority candidates were elected, Diane Abbott, Paul Boateng, Bernie Grant and Keith Vaz. There were also forty-one women MPs elected. It was less than 10 percent of the total but a record number of women MPs. But it was scant compensation. The Militant Labour MPs Dave Nellist and Terry Fields increased their majorities and another Militant MP Pat Wall was elected in Bradford, despite wanting to abolish the monarchy. Kinnock and my mum would not be happy about that.

By the time the programme finished, at around 4 a.m., the projected Tory majority was over a hundred. So much for the experts who had predicted it might be close. I climbed into bed. I wasn't sure I was interested in politics any more.

~

People say you should sleep on things as they always look better in the morning. This is not true. The result looked much worse in the daylight. When I walked into the lounge Stella was eating cereal in front of the TV where Peter Snow was still conducting the post mortem, he must have been on cocaine or something.

"I told you," said Stella looking up at me. "One hundred and two seat majority."

More people had voted for Thatcher than in 1983. Thirteen point seven million people had cast their votes for her, seven hundred thousand more than in the last election. It was her third election victory in a row, an achievement unmatched by the great prime ministers I had been taught about at school, such as Churchill, Gladstone and Disraeli.

The more I reflected on Thatcher's success the less I was sure I knew anything. A German Field Marshal once said, "No plan survives contact with the enemy." Our beloved socialist plans, our policies of unilateral nuclear disarmament, nationalisation and increasing income tax, that had looked so good on paper, and in constituency party meetings, hadn't survived contact with the electorate.

The morning's *Guardian* headline read, 'Thatcher cruises home to easy victory'. The *Daily Mirror* headline was, 'You have another five years of her'. That was optimistic; with a hundred seat majority, she might be there forever.

The week after the election was unusually cold and wet; the temperature failed to reach 16 degrees. The test match at Lords between England and Pakistan was washed out. The pitch was flooded and only seven hours of play were possible across the whole five days. The first day of Wimbledon was also washed out as heavy showers and hailstorms punctuated the dark skies. The weather summed up the mood of those of us in Badgeland.

Labour's Bryan Gould tried to put a positive spin on the

result but I was not consoled or convinced. The *Guardian* was right when it said it was self-delusion to assume things would be better next time. Any honourable Labour leader would have resigned after the election but not Kinnock.

Kelvin MacKenzie said, "The nation simply does not rate him as a possible prime minister." Regrettably I thought MacKenzie and Stella were right. The press caricature of him as a Welsh windbag, hot-headed and emotional had cut through. The clip of him falling in the sea at Brighton had been played over and over again. A leader has to look prime ministerial and Kinnock simply didn't. He was a hundred seats behind; there was no way he was going to win the next election.

If there was a bright side to Thatcher's victory it was the poor performance of the SDP. It was like the brief joy you get as a Swindon fan when Oxford United get beaten but at least it was something. The SDP-Liberal Alliance won just twenty-two seats. But was this really democracy? Seven million deluded people voted for the Alliance, a third of those voting. They won just 3 percent of seats. Thatcher won 61 percent of seats in Parliament and a hundred seat majority with just 42 percent of the vote. If that was democracy I was a cucumber. I hated to admit it but maybe the Liberals were right when they argued for proportional representation.

I wasn't the only one questioning the system. The blatant unfairness of the result was reflected in the anger of the letters pages in the *Guardian*. A letter from Peter Scott pleaded with Labour to embrace proportional representation for the sake of the oppressed. Kinnock rejected the idea but many senior Labour figures thought that if Labour ever won power again it should change the system for the better. But when Labour was winning it also benefited from the unfairness of the system.

In 2005, Tony Blair would win 55 percent of the seats with just 35 percent of the vote. It was a travesty but Blair decided that the first past the post system was not so bad after all and defended his right to implement policies that two-thirds of the electorate had rejected. The simple truth is political parties are not interested in electoral fairness when they are winning.

$\sim$

In the summer of 1987, the tectonic political plates were shifting under me. The post-war consensus of a mixed economy, collectivism and full employment had been replaced by Thatcher's consumer individualism and 'the market knows best'. In two terms she had deregulated the Stock Exchange; privatised British Telecom, British Gas and British Airways; and transferred over one million public sector jobs to the private sector. She had defeated the miners, sold more than one million council homes, decimated manufacturing jobs, caused three million people to become unemployed and slashed tax rates for the rich. Now after the election, and with a hundred-seat majority, she was free to pursue an even more aggressive privatisation programme including British Steel, British Petroleum, Rolls Royce, water and electricity.

The young people who had supported Labour in the 1970s were now in their thirties and forties, and had voted overwhelmingly for Thatcher. Maybe Victor Hugo was right. He certainly had evidence on his side.

As we sat around Angela's Habitat dining table listening to George Michael and Bruce Springsteen, my friends said they no longer recognised the country, or rather the country they thought we were. Like me, they forgave the British people in 1983 because of the Falklands War and Michael Foot's leadership, but in 1987, there were no excuses. Everyone knew what Thatcher represented. We were let down by the British public. I was particularly frustrated with the 25 percent of people that didn't even bother to vote.

As we ground coffee beans with Angela's new espresso

machine, we agreed that Thatcher had won the war of ideology. Her narrative of renewal, free enterprise, entrepreneurialism, consumer individualism and meritocracy was now dominant. Over thirteen million people believed they would be better off under the Tories.

I no longer believed the Trotskyist gurus, whose words I had read so keenly when I was seventeen. The conclusions that the RCP, SWP and Militant drew from the defeat were as predictable as they were wrong. They argued Labour's third election defeat was due to a lack of radicalism. I wanted to believe this was the case, that if we had been more radical people would have flocked to our cause, but it was not true.

Seriously, would Labour really have done better by proposing to raise the basic rate of income tax by 6 percent rather than 2 percent? If it had said it wanted to give unions more power, and nationalise British Telecom, would that really have increased the party's vote share? It seemed unlikely that working-class communities in the south were voting Tory because what they really wanted was a more left-wing Labour Party.

The Trotskyist predictions of capitalism's imminent collapse were equally deluded. On news of Thatcher's victory the stock market rose. Over coffee Fiona told us, almost gleefully, that the market was 50 percent higher than it had been at the start of the year. "I did say you should have invested in a PEP," she said, looking at me like a child that hadn't done as he was told. The booming market was great news for those who had bought privatised shares. A new optimism sent car sales to record levels and house prices increased by a further 25 percent in 1987. There had never been a better time for those that owned property.

"I can't believe it," said Simon. "Support for the Conservatives is at almost fifty percent, higher than at any time since Thatcher became prime minister back in 1979."

After eight years, and despite all of my campaigning, she was more popular than ever. Thatcher was so well entrenched even Dad's new bingo call was "Maggie's Den ... Number Ten."

After the election the *Sun's* circulation reached new highs, just under four million copies a day, and in the summer it became the UK's best-selling newspaper. Kelvin McKenzie celebrated in his new office on the sixth floor at Fortress Wapping. In the summer Thatcher's favourite advertising agency, Saatchi and Saatchi, completed their thirty-ninth acquisition and became the undisputed leader in global advertising. Her supporters in the corporate boardrooms and the press were stronger than ever.

What was the point anymore? I was a competitive person but when do you give up? When do you have to stop banging your head against a brick wall? I was like a sprinter that couldn't break eleven seconds in the hundred metres. What was the point of turning up day after day for training, knowing you could never win a race? Had I even helped grow the Labour vote? Had I converted a single person or simply reminded them to vote Conservative?

On the TV Volkswagen ran a series of adverts with the strapline, 'If only everything in life was as reliable as a Volkswagen'. The ads were shot in the early morning light. In one, a man was leaving a casino as dawn was breaking. The voiceover said, "This is the man who put a million on black and it came up red." In another, a woman left her mews house in tears. She removed her wedding ring and posted it through the letterbox. Each advert ended with the characters getting into a Volkswagen Golf, looking out through the windscreen, breaking into a broad smile and driving away into a new dawn and a new day.

After the election of 1987, there was no car parked at the side of the road waiting to lift the spirits of those of us in Badgeland. We were not smiling. We had been comprehensively beaten. We had put our million on red and it had come up blue.

45

TROTSKYIST ENTREPRENEURS

At the end of June, the sun came out again and the pavements dried as the temperature lifted into the eighties. In Swindon boy racers drove around the town centre in their XR3i's, a souped-up sports version of the Ford Escort with alloy wheels, go faster stripes and winged spoilers. They played *Pump up the Volume* so loud from modified speakers that their cars throbbed to the music.

At Waterloo station men wore double-breasted suits with ridiculously big lapels, while the women wore shoulder pads so large they might have been playing American football. Their hair was crimped, permed, banged and sprayed, as they backcombed and sculpted it to new heights. It became so big it caused fights in cinemas. Power dressing was accompanied by swift purposeful walking. In London people walked faster than in other cities; they didn't have time to waste. They had houses to buy and shares to sell. They wanted to get rich quick.

Harry Enfield's character 'Loadsamoney' became so popular that Enfield released a record to cash in. The song *Loadsamoney (Doin' Up the House)* went to number two in the charts.

Over the summer two Labour MPs, Gordon Brown and Tony Blair, reflected on Labour's defeat in the small parliamentary office they shared. They were joined by Peter Mandelson. In the windowless room, with papers piled high on Gordon's desk, the trio agreed that improving the party's presentation would only take the party so far. They concluded the party's policies had to change and more specifically that Labour's statist, unilateralist and class-defined prospectus had to go. Basically the party had to give up on socialism. Ironically this was the summer that Rick Astley topped the charts with *Never Going To Give You Up*.

The trio argued Labour should ditch its defence policy and adopt Thatcher's core policies on tax, the economy and privatisation. They thought it wasn't possible to win elections by promising to reverse Thatcher's anti-trade union legislation or policies like Right to Buy. They argued that rather than reverse tax cuts and privatisation, Labour should promise to cut taxes further and privatise even greater numbers of state industries. They believed Labour could only win if it widened the party's electoral appeal to the aspirant middle-classes and had Murdoch, and the *Sun* in particular, on their side. Their views were shared by a new generation of Labour supporters like Fiona.

In the October 1980 issue of *Marxism Today*, Tony Benn had worried that the Labour Party might forget its working-class roots and be swamped by the middle class. He was right to be worried but many of the new Labour supporters were not born middle class. They were born in working-class communities; they were the first in their family to go to university and, like me, they were increasingly disconnected from their home towns. They were citizens of the world and embarrassed at overt displays of English patriotism. The flag of St George uncomfortably reminded them of the National Front. They preferred identity-based individualism to the old collectivist notions of class, conformity, family and social morality.

They didn't say it openly, but they increasingly looked down on working-class people. They criticised their lifestyles, their unhealthy eating, their parenting or lack of it, their drinking, their violence and their perceived bigoted attitudes.

I couldn't accept that Thatcher was right but I also knew the public were not going to vote for nationalisation, tax increases and unilateral nuclear disarmament. Maybe this was real politics. Maybe you had to adapt your policies to the public mood but, unlike Fiona, I couldn't support the direction the party was taking; I couldn't countenance cosying up to the likes of Murdoch and MacKenzie. I also didn't believe Kinnock could win the next election even if he adopted all of Thatcher's policies. You couldn't overturn a hundred-seat majority, particularly if you were not going to change the leader. If Labour wanted to adopt her core policies they could do it without me.

I resented the choices Labour was being forced to make. I was disillusioned and I wasn't the only one. Many of my former GLC colleagues left the party. The more optimistic ones formed an organisation called the Socialist Movement but others became disenchanted. Like me they no longer wanted to attend meetings listening to people who had neither answers nor access to power. Maybe the Revolutionary Workers Party was right and we should welcome aliens as our liberators; it was more likely than Labour winning.

After the election the Tories were polling at 50 percent, it was incredible, they would be in power for at least ten more years. Ten years is a long time when you are twenty-five. It was reportedly Joseph Kennedy, not Billy Ocean, who first said, "When the going gets tough, the tough get going." I wasn't tough. I remembered Benn saying we had to bloody toughen up and fight over and over again for socialism. But three election defeats in a row were enough for me.

In Swindon the men in the club didn't believe there was a yellow brick road to a socialist utopia. Instead they embraced Thatcher's popular capitalism. They were uncomfortable with inequality but they accepted it. They were happy they owned their own homes, had an Austin Montego on the drive, went to Spain for their holidays, watched *Last of the Summer Wine* on twenty-six-inch colour TVs, and saw the value of their privatised shares continue to rise. In the allotment they pined for their old jobs in the factories but all in all they decided they mustn't grumble.

In late August 1987, I met Angela for lunch at the Reform Club. It was a little further west along Pall Mall from the Institute of Directors and more exclusive. Angela explained the club had always been committed to progressive ideas and it had been one of the first gentlemen's clubs to admit women in the 1980s. As we walked up the stairs she told me that the fictional Phileas Fogg was a member of the Reform Club. He had accepted a bet from fellow members to circumnavigate the world in eighty days, beginning and ending at the club.

The central courtyard of the building had a double height atrium and glass roof, with colonnaded balconies on the first and second floors. Angela said it had been designed by Sir Charles Barry, who was inspired by the Parthenon in Athens when doing the Grand Tour. We sat at a small table in the first floor gallery.

"It is far more relaxed here than the other clubs," said Angela.

"You mean I can take off my jacket?" I smiled.

Angela returned the smile. "Of course," she said. "Jackets

can be removed at any time during the summer months of June, July and August. I also believe you can remove your jacket in the billiards room, though I haven't actually been there."

"So how did you become a member here?" I asked, admiring the paintings and golden columns.

"Some of the senior civil servants I work with are members, and they encouraged me to join."

"And they let you in?"

"Yes, there were no black balls."

I couldn't imagine why anyone would want to blackball Angela. She was cultured, intelligent and thoughtful.

After we ordered food, Angela asked me about life in ILEA and we moved on to politics. She was as depressed by the election as I was.

"I have decided I am too old for politics," I said. "And I have given up on the Labour Party."

"Really? I don't believe it," she said.

"Seriously," I said. "I have campaigned against Thatcher for eight years and achieved nothing. She now has a bigger majority than in 1979. It is only a matter of time until she abolishes ILEA. I don't want to go through that again."

"So, what now?" she asked.

"I am not sure but bizarrely I feel excited."

It was true; I had become so animated reading *Inc* and *Entrepreneur*, that I had filled my Filofax with scribbled notes and ideas on how to improve organisational performance.

"I have lots of ideas about how computers can change how we work and improve productivity. I think I will look to do something in computing or even start my own company."

"So you are going to trade Tony Benn for Steve Jobs?" Her eyes twinkled mischievously and she tapped her knife gently on the side of her glass. "Come on, admit it."

"Don't laugh. Maybe people like Jobs will change the world

far more than politicians. Maybe entrepreneurs are the new radicals."

She looked at me in studied silence. There was a delay, a hesitation as she wrinkled her nose and bit her bottom lip as she reflected on what I had said.

"You want to be an entrepreneur?" she asked incredulously, as if finally working things out in her head.

It was my turn to be silent. She reached over and playfully punched me in the arm.

"Thatcher would be proud of you."

"I just don't feel I would fit in the corporate world."

"He says, in his posh suit and tie."

"Okay, I know I am not working class. Thanks to you I listen to Opera, read Kazuo Ishiguro and watch ballet. But I really don't fit in with middle-class people, not really."

"People like me?"

"No, you know what I mean. I always feel out of place somehow, I feel like I want to change things or break things. I am not sure if that makes sense."

"So Mr Branson." Angela leaned forward. "What makes you think you will make a good entrepreneur?"

"Well," I said, taking my time. "It is an underappreciated fact that Trotskyists make the best entrepreneurs."

Angela almost spat out her soup.

"I am being serious," I said. "I think all startup founders should join a Trotskyist group as a teenager. It is far more valuable than studying for an MBA. They run weekly education sessions, they give you homework and individual mentors. They make you do presentations and coach you on the art of public speaking."

"Hmmm," said Angela. She narrowed her eyes and gave me one of her questioning smiles. She was not convinced.

"Okay, you have to moderate the hand movements and stop referring to everyone as comrade."

Angela did her impression of a Cheshire cat and grinned at me.

"But seriously," I continued. "It was Trotskyists who helped me achieve my 'A' level grades to go to university."

I put down my spoon and continued in earnest.

"Trotskyists teach you sales skills the hard way. They put you outside M&S with newspapers saying 'Smash the Capitalist System' and challenge you to sell as many copies as you can. It is the sink or swim school of sales training and is better than any selling course.

"Trotskyists also teach you the values of persistence and the importance of being relentless. They demonstrate how to build organisational capacity and communicate a consistent vision to their members. They generate revenues that are out of all proportion to their small size and are incredibly resilient. They create and publish national newspapers. They are also experts at guerrilla marketing which is a required skill for entrepreneurs."

"Okay, okay, I get it," said Angela. "So no more badges?" She looked at the empty lapels of my best suit.

"I have started to think that Mick Jagger was right, you can't always get what you want," I said. "Maybe I have to come to terms with the world as it is and not how I want it to be."

"Careful," said Angela. "You are sounding like a mature twenty-five-year-old."

"Maybe," I conceded. "I might not be able to change the world but I still can try to nudge it in the right direction."

After lunch I walked back through St James Park and stopped, as I always do, on the bridge over the lake, where I had once stood with my father twenty years earlier. It looked the same as it did in the square, white-edged photo in the bureau drawer at home. The metal railings were still painted in the light blue turquoise colour that reminded me of the sixties. It was the same colour as my nan's kitchen cupboards, police panda cars and my mum's saucepans. The sky was a brilliant blue and light bounced across the water. Groups of young people were relaxing in the dappled shade of the trees.

I breathed in deeply and lifted my chest. Those of us in Badgeland would find new ways to live, new ways to gently push the world in the right direction.

In the summer of 1987, Labour's pollster, Philip Gould, conducted a survey of young people aged twenty to twenty-five. He found they were hard-working and ambitious; that they believed in free enterprise and meritocracy; and that they valued individualism, autonomy and agency. Many of them also aspired to be entrepreneurs. He called them 'Thatcher's children'.

EPILOGUE

On Monday, 16 July 2018, the club closed. A printed notice about the closure was Blu-Tacked to the window. Arkell's Brewery planned to convert the club into residential flats. Six days before the closure my dad passed away. He had been the longest serving member, having joined fifty-six years earlier.

The club was not alone in being closed. Over two-thirds of working men's clubs had been shuttered, a consequence of deindustrialisation, smoking bans and cheap supermarket alcohol. Andy said it was good that our dad didn't live to see the closure as he would have been devastated. After a little lobbying, the brewery agreed to open the club for Dad's wake on 30 July 2018. It was the last event to be held there.

My wife and I drove to Swindon for the funeral from Brighton. We left the M4 at junction 15 and passed the new Great Western Hospital, which replaced the demolished Princess Margaret Hospital where my appendix had been removed. The Brunel Tower was standing guard in the town centre, casting a watchful eye over everything, still looking like something from the future. Many familiar buildings were also still standing but their uses had changed. The ABC Cinema had become a Wetherspoon pub.

Swindon had become home, rather incongruously, to the National Trust headquarters and the UK Space Agency. The railway village still existed; it had been listed and saved from demolition after a campaign by the poet and architecture enthusiast, Sir John Betjeman. The railway works buildings, where my dad was exposed to blue asbestos, were also listed by English Heritage. Some of the sheds had been converted into one of the largest retail designer outlets in Europe. In the food court was a 4930 Hagley Hall locomotive that had been built in the factory.

As we left the bypass for Stratton we passed the Honda factory. Its closure had been announced earlier in the year and the day we drove past, the day of my dad's funeral, the final vehicle left the production line. We continued past large blue-striped distribution centres that disappeared high into the sky.

The crematorium was in the village of Stanton Fitzwarren. It had originally been on the edge of the town but had been swallowed by Swindon's relentless expansion. The town's population had grown to almost a quarter of a million. Next to the crematorium there was a large board announcing the development of new care homes and sheltered housing.

For some time before he passed Dad had been struggling to understand the world. When we visited him in the care home, he stared at us as though searching for something. Most days though he still recognised us. I know this because once, in the final months, all three of us children arrived to see him. This was rare. He was quiet and working things out behind his eyes. He tilted his head, like a dog questioning his master and managed to whisper, "Am I dying?" I held his hand and said, "No, of course you are not dying." He didn't say anything else; he just sat in his wheelchair and looked down.

Over a hundred people came to the funeral. The club

reception buffet was as Dad would have wanted; everything was beige. The sausage rolls, sandwiches, quiche and crisps, all curated on a brown table under a nicotine-stained ceiling. I was sad there were no dominoes, cards or cribbage boards. I wished I had bought a set for each table. I regretted that every person who came was not going home with a cribbage board or a box of dominoes to remember Dad by.

I walked over to Bob and Tony, who were in the suits they wore for funerals. Suits that came out of the wardrobe more frequently these days. I wore my latest Paul Smith suit with the paisley lining. They had both been retired for about ten years. Bob left BT with a good pension and still had most of his BT shares. They had delivered a nice return, over 1,600 percent. Maybe I should have bought the shares in 1984, as he had suggested.

Bob shook my right hand while holding a pint of Arkell's three Bs in his left. It occurred to me that we had never shaken hands before.

"Your dad would be really pleased that you managed to open the club for his wake," he said. "The old bugger loved this place."

"Good to see so many people turn out," said Tony, looking around the room. "Never seen the place so full. He was a top bloke your dad."

"Thanks for coming," I said.

"We miss him at the golf," said Bob.

"Mind you, we get round a lot quicker now," said Tony, slapping me on the back as Bob grinned.

"We always had to wait for him," said Bob. "Once we couldn't work out where he had gone, until finally we found him digging up molehills. Good soil for the garden he used to say."

"The bugger was always collecting wood as well," said Tony. "Once we spent ages waiting for him and finally he came round the corner with a bloody great log on his golf trolley."

We all laughed. I had a clear picture in my mind of Dad dragging his trolley behind him.

"You still a Labour man then Steve?" asked Bob.

"I hope you are not supporting that Corbyn," said Tony. "He is another one of them vegetarians. Worse than old Tony Benn he is."

"I actually voted Green this time," I said. "We have a Green MP in Brighton, Caroline Lucas."

After 1987, I had decided to always vote for the most radical candidate, even if they stood little chance of winning.

"It's only millionaires like you that vote Labour these days," said Tony, nudging me in the side with his elbow.

Dad had proudly shared my success as an entrepreneur with everyone in the club. I was lucky. I had been convinced the old world of corporate training would be shaken up by the internet. It didn't make sense to drag staff across the country to dusty rooms with bottles of lime cordial. I had co-founded an online learning company at just at the right time and in a few years we had over a hundred staff. After selling the business I then co-founded a social media marketing company which I also sold. Like Tony Blair I would have been one of Thatcher's favourite children.

"You won't find many Labour voters here in Swindon these days," said Bob.

The town had grown so large, it now had two parliamentary constituencies. Both had been held comfortably by the Conservatives in the 2017 election.

"Your dad told us Princess Anne came to open your new offices in Brighton," said Tony.

"Yes, I was told to say 'mam' as in 'ham' when I met her," I said.

"My sister saw her once, down at Badminton," said Bob.

"So you hobnobbing with royalty these days? I remember when you said they should be put against the wall and shot," said Tony.

I grimaced.

"I am not sure that is exactly what I said," I replied.

"What about this Brexit then?" said Bob. "Do you think it is going to happen?"

"I don't think May will get her deal through, not now Johnson has resigned," I said.

"It better bloody happen," said Tony. "Be riots if it doesn't."

"I am not so sure," said Bob. "There were over a hundred thousand people on that People's Vote march last month. My granddaughter, Tracey's girl, went to London for it. Had a right go at me as well, she said us old people were taking away her future."

"That Gina woman gets on my tits," said Tony. "We had a bloody people's vote, and they lost."

The town had voted 55 percent in favour of Brexit in 2016.

"David Stoddart is very happy we are leaving," I said.

Bob raised his eyebrows and tilted his head at me in disbelief. "He still alive?"

"Yes, he still turns up in the Lords despite being ninety-two. He made a speech in favour of Brexit only last month."

"Good on the bloke," said Tony. "He was always against the European Union. I told you he was a good un."

That hadn't been my recollection but I let it pass.

"Good to see you guys," I said, and patted Tony on the back. "I better go circulate."

"Sure, good to see you again," said Tony.

"Take care mate," said Bob. "We are going to have another pint in memory of your dad."

They turned towards the bar.

As I passed from table to table, relatives and friends told me their stories of Dad. How he made up new bingo calls, how he got a group of them lost driving to Stow-on-the-Wold, how he used to escape from my mum on his Motability scooter, how he played for Highworth despite having a broken leg, how he had a strop when he lost at skittles, and how he used to fall asleep in a deckchair on holiday with a handkerchief on his head.

When we left the club Andy took down a sign that hung on the wall and carried it home. It had also been his club. It had never been mine; I had never been a member. Three months after our dad's funeral Andy left Swindon for Cornwall.

When Dad died Labour were no longer the working man's party that he had supported. In 2018, over three-quarters of the party's members were from the top three social classes, ABC1. Only a third were members of a trade union; almost as many were members of the National Trust. Fiona and many of my former colleagues enthusiastically embraced New Labour. Over the years I would see their names in the New Year's honours lists. Fiona became a baroness and took her place in the House of Lords.

Not all of my contemporaries gave up the fight for socialism. Many from the GLC's Industry and Employment Branch joined the Socialist Movement and created a newspaper called *Socialist*, which folded after a couple of years. Out of the ashes came *Red Pepper*, a quarterly magazine, founded by Hilary Wainwright. By its own admission it survives on a shoestring and the goodwill of volunteers.

Militant, true to its Trotskyist traditions, split into two factions in 1992. The majority of Militant's members rejected entryism and left the Labour Party to form the Socialist Party. Ted Grant formed Socialist Appeal, the British section of the International Marxist Tendency, and continued the tactic of entryism. He passed away in 2006, but his ideas live on through

Socialist Appeal, which runs the student Marxist Society and a newspaper called *Revolution*. In July 2021, the Labour Party's National Executive ruled that Socialist Appeal members would automatically be expelled from the party.

Paul from university became a comedian called Ian Cognito, or Cogs to his fans. In 2019, he made national news when he passed away on stage. He was known as Britain's 'most banned' comedian and once threw a television out of a hotel window when his room service was late. There are clips of him performing on YouTube. As he says in his *Song For My Sons* he was not a model of sobriety but as he also says, he didn't kill the spiders that came to visit him at night. Inside Ian Cognito was Paul, the gentle and sensitive soul I had known.

Angela returned to public service and we lost touch, something that was easy to do before the internet. According to LinkedIn she became a senior civil servant and expert bridge player. I also lost touch with Stella and Annika. Out of curiosity I did search LinkedIn but could find no trace of them. Maybe I was searching the wrong site.

Don became a radical academic. In 2022, I attended the launch of his book, along with people I recognised from the RCP forty years earlier. Don spoke about how working people have consistently dumfounded and dismayed the left, and how the working class have developed a love-hate relationship with capitalism. They love mass consumption and, despite hating inequality, they refuse to countenance alternatives to capitalism.

Don was right about County Hall. Sir Tag Taylor sold the building to a Japanese investor and it became a five-star hotel promising stunning views of Big Ben and Westminster Bridge. The hotel's website says the wood-panelled rooms have witnessed important moments in London's history. In each bedroom there is an orange armchair, a tribute to the orange and red leather seating in the former council chamber. You can book a room with a view of the Houses of Parliament from £537 a night. The ground floor office, where I planned my opposition to Thatcher, became a McDonald's.

~

Two months after Dad's funeral, I started a full-time Masters programme at the London School of Economics. Out of interest I attended the Freshers' Fair, which was held in the red brick Student Union block. As I strolled around the stalls I saw students wearing a new generation of protest badges. They read: 'Fuck Trump', 'Bollox to Brexit', 'Don't blame me, I voted remain', 'Climate change is real', and 'Black Lives Matter'.

On the table of the Labour and Co-operative Society stall were dozens of red 'Tories Out' badges and some that said 'For the many, not the few'. Next to the Labour stall was the Marxist Society, the youth wing of the IMT founded by Ted Grant. Copies of *Revolution* were neatly displayed on the table. The main headline, in white capital letters on a red background, was 'The Crisis of Capitalism'. Behind the table a male student in a blue jacket, like those worn by trendy architects, chatted to an Asian woman wearing a mustard coloured beanie hat.

I bought a copy of the newspaper. As the young man searched for change, I motioned that it was okay.

"Consider it a donation," I said.

"Thanks."

I saw him looking at my grey beard and receding hairline.

"Are you a student here?"

"Yes, I am doing a Masters in Politics," I replied. "It has been a long time since I was a student."

"Ah," he said, as if he had found something that he had been searching for. He added, "Actually, we are running a series of sessions next week, you might be interested."

He handed me a list of events. They included a 'communist

manifesto reading group' and sessions on 'what is Marxism' and 'Marxist philosophy'. I set the list down on the table and picked up a book about Rosa Luxemburg.

"You should come along," said the woman. "We are discussing how students can support the fight for socialism."

She was small and slight, but with a determination I recognised. She looked at the book I was holding.

"One of the most fundamental lessons Rosa taught us," she explained, "is that we need to build a revolutionary organisation capable of guiding the working-class to victory."

I smiled at her.

"Good luck with that," I said.

AFTERWORD

Dear Reader,

I hope you found this book enjoyable. If you lived in the 1970s and 1980s I hope it brought back many memories.

I would love your feedback and would particularly welcome a review on Amazon. It only takes a few minutes to post a couple of sentences that sum up your thoughts. I would really appreciate you taking the time.

If you would like updates about Badgeland and news about future books please sign up to my mailing list at www. steverayson.com.

Thank you.

Steve

NOTES

6. The Labour Party Young Socialists

1. Forster, E.M. (1924) A Passage to India. E Arnold & Co, Kings College Cambridge and The Society of Authors.
2. http://socialismtoday.org/archive/168/thatcher.html
3. Orwell, G. (1937) The Road to Wigan Pier. Victor Gollancz.

13. Bath University

1. Benn, T. (1979) Arguments for Socialism, Edited Chris Mullin, Penguin.

16. The Great Moving Right Show

1. Hall, S , The Great Moving Right Show, *Marxism Today,* January 1979 https://f.hypotheses.org/wp-content/blogs.dir/744/files/2012/03/Great-Moving-Right-ShowHALL.pdf

17. Christmas 1980

1. https://en.wikipedia.org/wiki/Kelvin_MacKenzie

20. Tony Benn for Deputy

1. https://uk.finance.yahoo.com/news/jack-welch-inflicted-great-damage-172844562.html

22. Kintsugi

1. https://en.wikipedia.org/wiki/Kelvin_MacKenzie

23. Ken Livingstone

1. Sunday Express, 27 October 1981.

25. Bermondsey

1. https://en.wikipedia.org/wiki/1983_Bermondsey_by-election

26. Shotguns and Knife Fights

1. https://en.wikipedia.org/wiki/Imagined_community
2. https://en.wikipedia.org/wiki/The_longest_suicide_note_in_history

28. The Greater London Council

1. Barker (1946) Labour in London: A Study in Municipal Achievement, Routledge.

33. Keep GLC Working for London

1. https://www.independent.co.uk/news/obituaries/eric-hammond-electricians-leader-who-helped-rupert-murdoch-smash-the-unions-and-move-to-wapping-1696201.html

35. BT Privatisation

1. Daily Mirror, 2 October 1984.
2. https://www.theguardian.com/film/2010/jul/29/80s-culture-a-team-karate-kid
3. https://www.newstatesman.com/long-reads/2014/06/how-miners-strike-1984-85-changed-britain-ever
4. Gould, P (2011) The Unfinished Revolution, Abacus.

42. Greed is Good

1. Hughes, J. E. (2021) Greed Gone Good: A Roadmap to Creating Social and Financial Value, Routledge.

GLOSSARY

Abigail's Party – A 1977 play for stage and television by Mike Leigh, that satirises 1970s middle-class aspirations.

Action Man – A children's action figure launched in Britain in 1966 by Palitoy.

Advertiser – Swindon's local newspaper, formerly the Swindon Evening Advertiser.

Angel Delight – A powdered dessert product launched in the United Kingdom in 1967 by Bird's. It was mixed and whisked with milk to create a mousse-like dessert.

Basil Brush – Cockney rhyming slang for Thrush.

Brains – A character in the 1960s television series Thunderbirds.

Brenda from Bristol – A 2017 viral video of Brenda from Bristol, whose reaction to the announcement of a snap general election was: "You're joking. Not another one."

Charles Atlas – An American bodybuilder who widely promoted an exercise course for scrawny weaklings.

Crimplene – A texturised continuous fibre launched in 1959.

Dennis the Menace – The titular protagonist of the long-running Beano comic strip, Dennis the Menace.

Don Rogers – A former footballer who played for Swindon Town, Crystal Palace and Queens Park rangers.

Flashing Blade – a French television serial broadcast in the UK on BBC children's television during the 1960s and 1970s.

Football Pink – The Saturday evening local football paper

published by Wiltshire Newspapers, which gave a blow by blow account of local games, including my dad's performances.

Fortress Wapping – The News Corporation building in Wapping was surrounded with razor wire and prison-like security systems and referred to as 'Fortress Wapping'.

Joe 90 – A 1960's children's TV series created by Gerry and Sylvia Anderson. It was about nine-year-old schoolboy Joe McClaine, who became a spy who could transfer expert knowledge and experience into his brain for special missions.

Labour Party Young Socialists – The LPYS was the youth section of the Labour Party in Britain from 1965 until 1991. In the 1980s over 2,000 delegates attended its national conferences.

Magic Roundabout – A children's television programme that was broadcast from 1965 to 1977.

Morris Marina – A small family car that was manufactured by British Leyland from 1971 until 1980.

Ralgex – a spray designed to soothe painful muscles and joints. It was used liberally by the men in my dad's football team.

RCP – The Revolutionary Communist Party, known as the Revolutionary Communist Tendency until 1981.

Ready Brek – An oat based cereal which was advertised as central heating for kids.

SWP – Socialist Workers Party, a revolutionary socialist party with branches across Britain.

Wolfie Smith – The main character in the 1970s TV sitcom *Citizen Smith*. Wolfie was the self-proclaimed leader of the revolutionary Tooting Popular Front

The Wombles – 1970s children's television show which used stop-motion animation.

Worzel Gummidge – A scarecrow and main character in the TV series of the same name that ran in the UK from 1979 to 1981.

Yowza, Yowza, Yowza – A phrase used in the title of the Chic song, *Dance, Dance, Dance, (Yowsah, Yowsah, Yowsah)*, and which was first popularised in the 1920s by an American band leader named Ben Bernie.

ABOUT THE AUTHOR

Steve Rayson is a researcher and author. His previous book *The Fall of the Red Wall* was an Amazon bestseller.

He completed his MSc on Political Communication at the London School of Economics and won the best dissertation prize for his work on political podcasts.

He was previously the co-founder of four successful companies: BuzzSumo, Kineo, Anders Pink and Totara. He was also a public sector consultant at KPMG and the Director of Resources at Brighton & Hove Council.

facebook.com/steven.rayson.92

twitter.com/steverayson

instagram.com/steverayson

Printed in Great Britain
by Amazon

19047973R00222